Why Sociology
Does Not Apply

Why Sociology Does Not Apply:

A Study of the Use of Sociology in Public Policy

Robert A. Scott

Department of Sociology
Princeton University

and

Arnold R. Shore

Russell Sage Foundation

Elsevier · New York

NEW YORK • OXFORD

```
Exclusive Distribution
throughout the World by
Greenwood Press, Westport,
Ct. U.S.A.
```

Elsevier North Holland, Inc.
52 Vanderbilt Avenue, New York, New York 10017

Distributors outside the United States and Canada:

Thomond Books
(A Division of Elsevier/North-Holland Scientific Publishers, Ltd.)
P.O. Box 85
Limerick, Ireland

Library of Congress Cataloging in Publication Data

Scott, Robert A   1935-
    Why sociology does not apply: a study of the use of sociology in public
    policy

    Bibliography: p.
    Includes index.
    1. Sociological research — United States. 2. United States — Social
    policy. 3. Evaluation research (Social action programs) I. Shore, Arnold,
    joint author. II. Title.
HM48.S42   301′.07′2   79-1344
ISBN 0-444-99060-7
ISBN 0-444-99063-1 pbk.

Design: *Edmée Froment*
Mechanicals/Opening Pages: *José Garcia*

Manufactured in the United States of America

To
Nancy, Michael, Billy, Jimmy and Sarah
and
Patricia and Rachel Sarah

Contents

Preface   ix

Acknowledgments   xvii

Introduction   1

1
Sociology in Policy: An Assessment   7

2
The Disciplinary Perspective in Applied Sociology   35

3
Conceptions of Policy in Applied Sociology   63

4
Origins of the Impetus to Plan   76

5
The Limits of Planning in Politics   133

6
Toward a Policy-Relevant Sociology   203

Appendix
Knowledge for Understanding and
Knowledge for Action   224

Bibliography   240

Index   259

Preface

Within the field of sociology there exists a strong commitment to the view that sociological knowledge can be used to help transform society in desirable ways. The impetus for writing this book grows out of a frustration that we have had with understanding specifically how to make this commitment a reality. For several years, both individually and jointly, we have been engaged in applied social research. The senior author, Scott, directed a study of organizations that serve blind people in America; the junior author, Shore, spent two years investigating sociological problems associated with the administrative implementation of an experimental income-maintenance program; and, together, we have worked on portions of the New Jersey—Pennsylvania Negative Income Tax Experiment. The aim of all of these studies was basically the same—to identify and do research on sociologically significant questions pertaining to important policy problems; and, in every case the result was basically the same—the production of a body of findings which, at best, helped to illuminate theoretical questions of interest to academic sociologists, but which appeared to carry policy implications that are nonexistent, trivial, ambiguous, indiscernible or impossibly utopian.

The reader who is familiar with the results of other so-called "policy-relevant" research in sociology will know that we are not alone in our frustrations, as many other sociologists who have conducted applied studies in many problem areas—poverty, welfare, social service, mental health, education, crime, drug abuse, population, law, medicine, business, international affairs and the military—have often had the same experience as ours. Time and again they have set out to do sociological research pertaining to issues and questions presumed relevant to policy, only to produce results that address theoretical issues of likely interest to their professional colleagues, but which seem to carry no discernible or practically useful implications for policy. This book represents our attempt to understand some of the reasons why this should be so.

When we first began to look for answers to this question, we did not intend to write a book about applied sociology. Our quest began modestly with a reading of the principal works that sociologists and others have written about applying disciplinary knowledge to public policy. Included in our list were a dozen or more of the better-known books on the topic, several dozen journal articles, and numerous research reports, conference proceedings and pertinent "think pieces" applicable to the topic. (Eventually we intensively reviewed a much larger body of literature dealing with applied sociology that ran to over 300 entries, some of which are detailed in the bibliography of this book.) We studied these publications in search of enlightenment about the current status of the practice of applied sociology today, especially looking for discussions that might help us to understand its characteristic forms and its record of performance. The results of this search, though certainly interesting and at times illuminating, were generally disappointing, for instead of gaining clarification we found ourselves more confused than ever.

We found that much of the literature we had read was written only from a *disciplinary perspective.* Too often the policy processes and the policy-making groups to which sociological knowledge and advice were being offered were treated almost as incidental aspects of the activity. *Context*—historical, political and social—tended to be ignored, giving one the impression that efforts by sociologists to be policy-relevant take place *in vacuo,* or in a world made-up entirely of disciplinary and scientific concerns. We believed that the explanations given for outcomes associated with efforts to apply sociology to policy tended to be *ad hoc and piecemeal.* They focused only on the field's failures, leaving entirely unexamined the reasons for its successes, and they tended to deal only with one or a few specific problems associated with a particular piece of research, with no thought given to factors associated with the activity of applying sociological knowledge and methods of research to social policy as a whole. Finally many of the recommendations for improving sociology's relevance to policy that came out of these discussions seemed to be "knee-jerk" type of reactions to specific problems, with little thought given to their ramifications for the activity as a whole. In essence, we came away from our study of this body of literature feeling that even though most authors had recognized that recent attempts to apply sociological knowledge to social policy had not often worked, no one gave a convincing explanation of why. Lacking was a *keen* analysis of applied sociology in practice. The idea of writing a book grew out of our need to have such an analysis.

We are quick to note that the analysis that is presented in this book is *not* the one that is required to explain and to understand fully the practice of applied sociology today. We believe that the topic is too poorly comprehended at the present time to make such an analysis possible, and in any event the topic is probably too complicated to present and develop effectively in a single volume. Our book attempts to focus only on certain facets of the process of using sociological knowledge and methods of research to help policy-making bodies identify and narrow the range of alternative courses of action that might be followed in dealing with particular social problems. The particular facets of the problem with which we shall deal are ones that we believe are fundamental to an understanding of the outcomes of attempts to make sociology relevant to policy. These considerations, characteristically downplayed or ignored in existing discussions about this particular facet of disciplinary activity as it is discussed in the literature of our field, do not provide a full explanation for the practice of applied sociology today. However, we believe that no explanation of this facet of disciplinary work can be considered complete without giving significant play to the issues we will discuss. It may help our reader to understand what we are about in this book if we indicate at the outset the range of things we believe would have to be considered in order to gain a full and adequate explanation for outcomes associated with attempts to apply sociology to policy at the present time.

To explain sociology's role in policy it is necessary to understand how intellectual work has its impact on practical activities, an enormously complicated problem.* To understand it would require, at a minimum, that account be taken of the following: the nature of policy-making as a practical activity and the role which ideas can ever play in arriving at policy decisions; how intellectual work is accomplished and the nature of its final product; the way in which intellectuals and scientists become involved in doing policy-relevant work in the first place—who initiates the contact, who sponsors the research, who dictates the terms of the relationship and so on; the symbolic role of the expert in American society and its significance for the weight that can be given to his or her advice; how and when the expert's product is communicated to those responsible for identifying alternative courses of action to follow and for choosing among them; the role that social and personal values and ideologies play in limiting the range of alternative courses of action that experts ever consider with respect to any given problem; the forms in which expert knowledge is packaged and the transformations it may have to undergo to

---

*For a very recent book that attempts to deal with this subject see James B. Rule's *Insight and Social Betterment* (1978).

make it useful as a guide to practical activities; the state of the expert's craft and its adequacy for studying and explaining various types of problems confronting policy-making groups; the impact which political, economic, historical, social and cultural factors have on the range of alternatives that policy-making bodies consider realistic or practical; and the role that political factors play in determining what can be done about a problem as opposed to what experts feel must be done to cope with it effectively. Constraints of all sorts impinge on applied research efforts, determining the extent, form and final nature of the impact that intellectuals and scientists have on policy. Some of these constraints pertain to factors internal to a discipline such as the state of its theory, methodologies and storehouse of knowledge, or the extent of mastery of its craft held by particular experts who are called upon to give advice. Other constraints exist outside of the discipline. Some of them are found in idea systems, some in value systems, some in the government and some in the policy process itself. To explain outcomes associated with past and present efforts to utilize sociology in connection with social policy-making, account must be taken of these factors—as well as others.

This book deals with only a few of these issues. It is best viewed as an effort to think critically about certain aspects of the process of using sociology in public affairs. It is not an attempt to present a theory about the whole process—nor does it try to deal with all of the ways in which sociology has an effect on policy. Instead we have chosen to single out a few aspects of the process, as explained in the Introduction, to deal with them intensively.

The particular issues we have chosen to deal with are not equally salient factors in all facets of the practice of applied sociology. They are more significant for certain types of policy-relevant activities than others and for this reason we have elected to limit our analysis of them to those facets of applied sociology in which the issues appear to assume particular relevance. Specifically, the book will deal primarily with the *policy-making efforts of government*, principally at the *national level*—mainly pertaining to *domestic affairs*. Although occasional reference will be made to efforts to utilize sociological knowledge and methods of research in other spheres, our analysis is not focused on these. This means that we will deal only peripherally with a substantial portion of what is usually thought of as a basic part of applied sociology—for example, the teaching of sociology in medical, law and other professional schools, or the use of sociology in industrial or in private organizations, foundations and institutions. Moreover, within the domain of government we shall not be concerned with *all* uses of sociology by governmental decision-making bodies, but primarily only those involving efforts to employ disciplinary knowledge and research methods *directly* in connection with policy efforts. That is, we will be concerned primarily with efforts that are made to utilize particular bodies of knowledge and research methods to identify alternative courses of action and to choose among them. By "use" we mean that policy-makers paid thoughtful attention to sociological research and/or employed sociological concepts and theories in trying to understand the issues before them (J. Weiss, 1976:238). We recognize that this is of course merely one facet of applied sociology and that it excludes what many people believe are perhaps the most important contributions sociology can make to policy, i.e., calling attention to problems and enlightening policy-makers by sensitizing them in a general way to the quality of human nature, society and its problems through educational experiences based upon humanistic and social science perspective. Although we recognize the importance of sociology in this respect, we have found it impossible to study effectively its impact on policy if only because it is nearly impossible to quantify it or gauge its extent. Finally, we have tried to focus our analysis around a single social science discipline—sociology. This does not mean that other social science disciplines are ignored nor that our analysis is relevant only to this discipline. The decision to deal with one field of social science rather than with the social sciences generally arises out of our concern to "contain" the discussion and to keep it within manageable bonds.

Some will find our discussion of sociology truncated, believing perhaps that we are insensitive to the range and diversity of intellectual and methodological styles comprising our field. We can only say that we recognize that there is not one single sociology in America today, but that the discipline is pluralistic. Its pluralism complicates our task greatly, so much so that to make it manageable we occasionally have had to simplify matters somewhat by pretending that sociology is more monolithic than it is. In this analysis, as in any analysis, a certain amount of simplification is necessary and inevitable, if only because, as a practical matter, it is impossible to focus upon everything at once. To look at sociology in policy, we need to simplify both things; about the best we can do is alert ourselves and our reader to the fact that we know that we are doing this.

There is another problem we confront which is even more difficult. Much of our book is about policy, yet, much to our dismay, we have discovered that no one, least of all the experts, is sure of what policy is, much less how it is made (C. Weiss, 1976b: 226; Uliassi, 1976: 241).

What do we mean by the term "policy?" Policy scientists, sociologists, political scientists and politicians have long tried to provide a meaningful definition of this term (some of the definitions of it that have been proposed are reviewed in Chapter 3), but we (and they) find the definitions are of limited value. Some are too vague or ambiguous; others seem clear enough but appear to reflect more about the definer's conception of what policy ought to be than about how policy is conducted by government. We have no wish to become embroiled in a lengthy debate about the merits and demerits of various proposed definitions of this term. To avoid this, we will offer a simple, nominal definition sufficient to get our discussion underway. As we proceed, we will discuss in detail numerous examples of policy-making in government, and from these we hope the reader will be able to gain a clearer, more complete idea of what we have in mind when we use the term. In this book the term "social policy" refers to purposive coercive measures that are adopted by individuals and groups within government who are responsible for dealing with particular social conditions in our society to achieve certain aims, and the term "policy-making" to the process of identifying alternative courses of action that might be followed and choosing among them.

Much of the analysis we will make in Chapters 3 through 6 entails an investigation of the context—political, social and historical—within which efforts to apply sociological knowledge and methods of research to policy occur. To explain the context in which sociology is used for policy we are forced to transcend the confining boundaries of our own discipline. For example, in Chapter 4 we discuss in detail the salient aspects of the social, intellectual and political history of American society during the late 19th and early 20th centuries which gave rise to the idea of utilizing social scientific experts in connection with the method of scientific planning. Portions of Chapters 3 and 5 analyze the concepts and methods of policy science to demonstrate their relevance to contemporary applied sociology. Sections of Chapter 5 draw on studies by economists of private welfare and the public good, and in other sections we present materials on policy-making ventures in different branches of the Federal government. Conducting ventures into areas with which we were previously unfamiliar is not without its hazards, and it may help our readers to evaluate our argument if we comment on some of the pitfalls we encountered and how we tried to circumvent them.

Appreciating the importance of materials drawn from other fields and disciplines for our analysis is one thing; being competent to evaluate them critically is quite another. In many cases we could see the relevance of a particular line of historical research, or of an essay on policy, or of a study of the Presidency or Congress for our argument, but possessing no mastery of the fields of history, policy science or politics, we were unable to decide on our own how valid these studies are. Therefore, we had to turn for help to those better qualified than we to clarify issues and to locate and interpret relevant research. We acknowledge the dangers inherent in relying on one or a few persons' views of a field or problem, but as a practical matter we had no real choice but to select "guides" and ask them to lead us through territory unfamiliar to us. As a result, portions of the analysis presented in this book depend heavily on the advice of various persons qualified to assess the published literature of these fields. We hasten to add that, even though we have often followed their counsel, we take full responsibility for interpretations of the materials that we will present.

Another obstacle standing in our path is the inadequacy of existing research on many of the problems that we felt needed to be raised. We quickly learned that many of the questions we wanted answered have not yet been fully researched and therefore cannot be finally answered. Here, as in our own discipline, *more* research is always necessary; one must resist the temptation to plunge in and do it oneself. Inevitably, we had to substitute conjecture and impose simplifying ideas on issues that we know to be complex. Important problems must often be glossed over; guesses must be taken about probable answers to unresolved questions; and inferences and suppositions must be applied liberally. In short, to provide an analysis of context that draw on the literature of several fields, one must inevitably resort to a certain amount of simplification and inference. This, with the help of trusted advisers, we have occasionally done.

The difficulties of confidently using material drawn from other fields of study are not the only ones we faced. Another problem is the difficulty of keeping the discussion focused and preventing it from sprawling. A main difficulty is defining the meaning of the term "context." From one point of view virtually anything happening in America today is part of the context within which applied sociology is practiced. The task is to sort out the irrelevant from the relevant—to detect shades of gray among the latter. To do this one must have a clear idea of what applied sociology entails and what it is about. Our analysis of context is confined to discussion of the main conceptions we believe are inherent in these aspects of applied sociology that deal with effects ot use sociology directly for domestic policy by the national government. We tried to discover how and why these conceptions developed; how they operate in the world of politics; who finds them attractive (politically and ideologically) and who finds them abhorrent. Such questions helped to keep our analysis within reasonable bounds. At the same time, we freely acknowledge that future research in applied sociology can profitably deal with contextual issues that we have neglected or ignored.

Here we have tried to adopt an attitude that is detached and analytical. We have consciously sought to avoid a stance of advocacy. We have merely tried to understand how sociologists conceptualize and execute applied, policy-relevant research with which we will deal, and to identify the implications these carry for those aspects of the outcomes of their efforts. Even in Chapter 6, in which we present measures that might be taken to improve substantially sociology's contribution to policy, we deliberately avoided an advocacy stance by indicating what could be done without urging sociologists to actually do it. We adopt this analytical, detached attitude because we believe that without it one cannot understand or explain the practice of applied sociology today.

Finally, although we deal primarily with efforts to apply sociological knowledge and methods to public policy, our audience of readers will not be limited just to those members of the profession who specialize in doing work for application. Sociologists, indeed social scientists generally, may find what we have to say interesting and relevant. We say this because many of the issues addressed here go to the core of their discipline's purpose. Arguments about relevance to societal affairs have always been a main basis upon which social scientists have premised their claims for legitimacy and their requests for financial support of their disciplines. Ultimately the issue to which this book is addressed concerns the validity of these claims.

This volume is the product of a **Acknowledgments**
collaborative effort of several
years duration. The basic idea
behind the book emerged from
many hours of discussion we had about the place of sociology in
public affairs. Together we drew up the basic outline of the study and
collaborated in collecting much of the information about the practice
of applied sociology that provides the basis for our analysis. Scott,
who is the senior author, took full responsibility for writing first
drafts of all chapters—and for writing the final draft of the
manuscript—to which Shore reacted.

Many people have given generously their time in helping us to
prepare various chapters of this book. Nancy Weiss and Dorothy Ross
of the History Department at Princeton University assisted us in
gathering material for Chapter 4. Karl Hempel of the Philosophy Department at Princeton helped us to think through some of the issues
raised in Appendix A, and John Light of the Sociology Department at
Princeton and Sig Lindenberg of the Sociology Department of the University of Groningen, The Netherlands, helped us compile some of
the materials that are presented in Part One of Chapter 5. Beverly
Kern, a research assistant on this project, did some of the basic research in connection with the analysis presented in Part Two of Chapter 5 and helped with literature reviews. We are deeply indebted to all
of them for the help that they have given us and to the Russell Sage
Foundation and its former President, Hugh F. Cline.

We wish to acknowledge our gratitude to various persons who
helped us to develop some of the ideas in this book. We particularly
thank the graduate students in Sociology at Princeton for permitting
us to use them as sounding boards for our ideas. We realize that some
of the ideas that we presented to them in seminars were only in a
formative stage and probably did not deserve to be discussed publicly
at the time. We want them to know that we appreciate their willingness to listen and that we admire their civility in responding to our
presentations. We are especially grateful to Kent Smith for inviting us
to present our ideas to his graduate seminar in research methods, and
to Jim Doig of the Politics Department at Princeton for allowing us to

share some of our ideas about social science in public policy with his Woodrow Wilson School students.

A number of people read and commented on earlier drafts of this manuscript, including James Banner of the Princeton History Department, Marvin Bressler, Suzanne Keller and Robert Wuthnow of the Sociology Department of Princeton, and Paul Rock of the Sociology Department of the London School of Economics. We thank them for their assistance in helping us to make the analysis more coherent and focused.

Much research for this book was made possible by persons in charge of the social science collections housed in the libraries of Princeton and Cornell Universities, the British Museum, the Library of Congress and the London School of Economics. We wish to thank these people for their cooperation and assistance in helping us to locate relevant material.

Various people have helped us in preparing this manuscript. Ann Scorgie helped edit drafts of several chapters; Nancy Scott typed versions of the first draft of the book; and Hetty de Sterke, Joan Pifer and Annette Howard typed the final manuscript. We are indebted to all of them for their assistance and diligent attention to detail.

Finally, we owe a special debt of gratitude to Barbara Bryan, a project assistant who took responsibility for overseeing various phases of this study. Without her hard work, unfailing good humor and impressive sense of proportion it is difficult to imagine how this project would have been completed.

The problem—of seeking to produce a single social ordering of alternative social choices which would correspond to individual ordering—is academic, in the best sense of the word. In the real world, the problem of social priorities, of what social utilities are to be maximized, of what communal enterprises are to be furthered, will be settled in the political arena, by 'political criteria'—i.e., the relative weight and pressures of different interest groups, balanced against some vague sense of the national need and the public interest.

Daniel Bell, The Coming of Post-Industrial Society, 1973

It is one of the tendencies of Liberalism to simplify, and this tendency is natural in view of the effort which liberalism makes to organize the elements of life in a rational way. And when we approach Liberalism in a critical spirit, we shall fail in critical completeness if we do not take into account the value and necessity of its organizational impulse. But at the same time we must understand that organization means delegation, and agencies, and bureaus, and technicians, and that the ideas that can survive delegation, that can be passed on to agencies and bureaus and technicians, incline to be ideas of a certain kind and of a certain simplicity: They give up something of their largeness and modulation and complexity in order to survive. The lively sense of contingency and possibility, and of those exceptions to the rule which may be the beginning of the end of the rule—this sense does not suit well with the impulse of organization. . . .

Lionel Trilling, The Liberal Imagination, 1950

It is difficult to conceive of a way in which the intellectual aspects of policy formation can ever be completely isolated from their social context. Policies will always be made by and for human beings who inhabit human institutions. But, to the extent that we can handle deliberately those variables that have influenced us with or without our knowledge or with which we have been able to cope only vaguely, we can with a certain amount of justification say that we have been able to bring the policy process closer to the intellectual models of "problem solving" or "decision making." We would hope, therefore, that as individuals faced with specific policy problems understand better the complexity of the events with which they are confronted , they will become less the victims and more the masters of these events.

Raymond Bauer, The Study of Policy Formation: An Introduction, 1968

**Why Sociology
Does Not Apply**

A main objective of sociology is to produce **Introduction**
knowledge about society; some believe
that a major responsibility of sociology is
to ensure that this knowledge is used to help transform society in
desirable ways. The visions of 19th century sociologists of a socially
relevant sociology have not yet been realized by the substantial
number of sociologists of the 20th century who subscribe in one way
or another to a sociology that is applied. This book presents a thesis to
explain why attempts to apply sociology to national societal needs
often do not succeed and to offer recommendations for improving the
state of this applied art.

At the outset we need to become aware that the sociologist's ability
to understand applied sociology has been hampered by the fact that
we, as sociologists, are tied to a perspective on applications that few of
us perceive. This silent but present perspective affects just about everything we say and do in the realm of applied studies, especially
those studies addressed to social policy. It dictates how we go about
applying sociology to policy; how we execute research we term
"applied"; how we present the results of our "policy-relevant" research; and the criteria we employ in determining the success of our
efforts. In fact, the perspective we bring to applied, policy-relevant
sociology "holds" us more than we, in a conscious way, hold it. And,
because this is the nature of the case, we are prevented from gaining a
clear sense of what we are about and why we are unsuccessful in
accomplishing our goals.

To break with this perspective we need first to understand it. This
requires discourse of a special kind. Most of our present ideas about
making sociology relevant to public policy revolve around our discipline and its concerns. To appreciate this we need to comprehend an
alternative position: one which begins and ends with policy, and not
discipline, concerns. The difference in perspective, which is fundamental, is basic to our analysis.[1]

Though both make reference to sociological theory and method as
they relate to policy topics, the order of considerations and the nature
of use differ. With a disciplinary perspective, one begins with sociology; with a policy perspective, one commences, naturally enough,
with policy. In a disciplinary mode research moves from theory to

method and then (possibly) to implications for policy—once the research is done. In a policy mode, research moves from a predefined policy issue to redefined policy issue(s) to method and results. Only after policy implications have been stated would one consider (from quite a different point of view) theoretical implications for sociology.

When employing the disciplinary perspective, the methods used and their order of use are the same as those employed in *any* basic, or "not-applied," study. The final product is often private in the sense that the results are brought home to the discipline. Often they remain unnoticed by policy-making bodies. When employing the policy perspective, not only is the order of activities changed but their nature is different, too, since the purpose is to adapt method to problems involving questions and variables outside the ken of the discipline. The emphasis is on adaptability of method to problem. The final products here are public, as is the policy they address. Policymakers can use them for applied purposes and sociologists can use them for theoretical purposes. In the sense that both yield products of use to sociology, both perspectives do in fact have a common (final) meeting ground.

Here we use a policy perspective to achieve multiple goals: to understand the sociologists' own perspective toward policy-relevant work; to generate hypotheses about the conditions under which an applied sociology so conceived is likely to have an impact on public affairs; to discern clues for reorganizing the conduct of applied sociology; and, ultimately, to conceive of ways of increasing sociology's contribution to policy. *Our analysis, then, is both academic and practical.* On the academic side, we will examine applied sociology for the purpose of advancing a useful thesis about it. As this analysis neither begins nor ends with a defined policy issue, it is, if anything, a contribution to the sociology of knowledge—not to policy. On the practical side we ask what, in general terms, are the variables most relevant to policy, and how could sociology make a contribution to them? Here the beginning and ending points are policy variables as they relate to real policy issues. We will devote much time to discussing the academic questions in an effort to comprehend the nature of our applied enterprises as they are currently conducted. Only then, and toward the end of the book, can we meaningfully treat applied matters in applied studies.

Illuminating current practice in applied studies for purposes of suggesting more appropriate practices can be hazardous to one's sense of how a professional world is organized, for this activity involves leaving the familiar terrain of the discipline for the unfamiliar terrain of public policy. It necessitates simplifying disciplinary issues for purposes of being able to address concerns and issues in an area about which social scientists in truth know very little. Scylla and Charybdis were never more potentially ruinous: we run the risk of appearing simplistic to colleagues and naive to policy-makers. Yet, we believe the risks are worth the end.

Our method of presentation is incremental—or gradual. We begin with the familiar and move to the unfamiliar. That is to say, we begin by examining policy-relevant sociology in terms commonly used by sociologists. From this review, we examine basic policy concerns, an activity less often discusssed in the literature. Thus, we start with an academic thesis and end with practical policy-relevant recommendations. To make our work more accessible, we present in annotated form the main points of our argument, the signposts of our book.

OUTLINE OF PRESENTATION

The book is divided into six chapters: three shorter chapters in which we introduce the problem we will analyze, followed by three lengthy chapters in which that analysis is presented. We begin with sociology. To make our task manageable, we will limit ourselves primarily to efforts to apply sociology to policy initiatives pertaining to national domestic problems during the 20th century. [2]

In Chapter 1, after a brief general introduction to the topic, we ask: How has sociology been helpful to public policy in this realm? Reviewing the writings of practitioners, we find the judgments are virtually unanimous that attempts to make use of sociology for national policy have not been entirely successful. That is to say, based on the analyses and commentaries of sociologists who have studied the uses of sociology for public policy in America today, we find that the goal of identifying and studying sociological questions pertinent to formulate workable, politically feasible policies and programs has been adjudged unsuccessful. Their analyses point to two major conclusions: (1) although many so-called applied studies have illuminated interesting sociological questions, few produce policy recommendations of any kind; and (2) in instances where recommendations have been offered, they have often been rejected by Federal policy-makers as politically unrealistic, administratively unworkable or simply impractical.

Given an apparent consensus about the state of these applied studies, we then ask: Why is this the case? As we see it, there are two obvious factors affecting the outcomes. One has to do with the starting points in sociology and the other with political factors that can be summarized as the receptivity of government to sociologically derived studies. Clearly, part of the problem lies with the weak state of theory, primitive methods of research, incomplete knowledge and inadequate programs of graduate training in sociology—a diagnosis that stresses the youth of the discipline and the need for basic research. This is a view fostered by the prevailing disciplinary orientation in sociology toward the problem of applying sociology to policy. This orientation is explained and illustrated in Chapter 2. We argue that this position, though not completely untrue, is nevertheless misleading and because it is one-sided, it does not consider the defining role of political and administrative factors in determining the utility of knowledge contributions.

To get at this issue we take a step back at this point in the argument and ask, in Chapter 3: Are there conceptions of policy and policy-making implicit in the disciplinary perspective of sociologists toward applied, policy-relevant work? While it is true that sociologists seldom take careful note of the role that political factors can play in policy-relevant work, this does not mean that the disciplinary perspective used here is devoid of notions about policy. In fact, we find that the perspective harbors a full-blown theory of government. Like the perspective from which it flows, this theory is neither stated nor recognized and is built around disciplinary concerns. The imagery it projects about policy fits a sociologist's view of the uses that can be made of disciplinary knowledge and methods—not a policy-makers. We find that sociologists have invented images of policy to suit the conventional nature of their studies.

What are these images of policy-making? To handle this question we ask a second, namely, What would a policy-making process need to be like for the things that sociologists know and do to make a contribution to it? We argue that, as constituted, sociology could best contribute to what might be termed a scientifically based system of planning. This phrase evokes images of policy-makers concerned with the collective good who are willing to listen to reason and be persuaded by facts. The commitment of the sociologist is to discover what is required in a basic way to solve problems and to express solutions in the form of comprehensive long-range plans and programs implemented in a logical, step-by-step fashion. There are connotations of exact and shared procedures. The sociologist begins by clarifying the nature of the problems and proceeds by stating the goals of social policies. These goals are then organized hierarchically. Ways of achieving the goals are identified and inventories are taken of the full range of consequences that might reasonably follow. Options are ranked by preference with accompanying estimates of costs. A procedure exists for bringing together this information to a deliberative policy body so that a reasoned decision can be made. Once a course of action has been decided, efforts will be made to evaluate programs and to feed results back into the policy process. This is the way to correct unanticipated problems and improve overall program effectiveness.

This is the ideal-typical model of a policy process that is complementary to the work and studies of an applied sociology formulated from a disciplinary perspective. It suggests several questions which we attempt to answer in succeeding chapters of the book. Specifically, in Chapter 4, we ask: Where did this model of policy come from and how did it become a part of applied sociology? In Chapter 5, we ask: Under what conditions is government likely to be receptive to this sociologically based planning approach to policy, and, when it is, how well does it work in practice? Then, in Chapter 6, we ask: For the future, how can we redefine the starting points and procedures within sociological research to ensure greater receptivity in government to sociological studies of policy questions?

Throughout we counterpoise the disciplinary and the policy perspectives, criticizing the first as a way of highlighting the second. Because so much of applied sociology today comes from a disciplinary perspective, it may appear that we are rejecting as invalid or useless nearly everything that sociologists until now have written about applying disciplinary theory and method to policy. This, we state emphatically, is untrue. It is not our intention to reject or put down what others have had to say on the subject; this would only undermine our purpose. Much of this work is too valuable for our argument to dismiss it so cavalierly. Our purpose is to retain the residue of insight contained in the work of others and to recaste it into a slightly more expansive framework. But even here we owe a great debt to the literature, for our realization of the need to do this was made possible only because of exposure to the insights of others writing on the topic. And so, we again state that our intention is not to discard completely the established views we criticize, but to use them as a foundation for developing a larger perspective within which they can be incorporated.

NOTES

1. This distinction between policy and disciplinary perspectives derives from Coleman (Coleman, 1972). However, our analysis of the differences between the two perspectives differs in many respects from his, as the reader will note as our thesis unfolds.
2. We are *not* concerned with the use of sociology to call attention to the existence of problems, but rather with attempts to utilize disciplinary knowledge, theory and methods to develop and enact policies and programs for dealing with problems already acknowledged to exist.

In July 1895, the first issue of the *American Journal of Sociology* was published by the University of Chicago Press. In the

Sociology in Policy: An Assessment

lead article of the premier volume, its founder and editor, Albion Small, expounded his views about the function of sociology in modern industrial society. He stressed two points: "That the relations of man to man are not what they should be" and "that something must be done directly, systematically, and on a large scale to right these wrongs" (Small, 1895:3). The whole point of sociology for Small, its *raison d'être*, was to conduct scientific investigations of society and to use the resulting knowledge to transform it. "The work of the discipline," he wrote, "was to increase our present intelligence about social utilities . . . [to achieve] more effective combination for the general welfare than has thus far been organized" (Small, 1895:14). Small established the *Journal*, then, as the organ for publishing results of sociological inquiries into conditions of life in society and the proposals for ameliorative programs that they implied.

Small was one of several of social scientists—among them Lester Ward, E. A. Ross, Thorstein Veblen, William James, and, somewhat later, Charles Horton Cooley—who believed strongly in the possibility and necessity for scientifically planned social change. All shared an aversion to Social Darwinism—the philosophical tradition that dominated American social science for much of the second half of the 19th century. Herbert Spencer powerfully expressed the Social Darwinist view. For him, the objective of sociology was to discover immutable laws of the universe and to derive correlative laws governing society from them. But the point of this quest was merely a further understanding about society—not an effort to change it. The most basic law of all, Spencer believed, was the law of survival of the socially fittest, the free operation of which he deemed essential for human survival. In fact, he opposed social planning because he believed that it would lead to courses of actions that might disrupt the unfettered operation of this law. He therefore counselled sociologists to leave undone things that might be done to change society lest humanity itself be damaged by these actions. William Graham

Sumner, the most vociferous American advocate of Spencerian sociology, echoed these sentiments. He too believed that social order was fixed by laws of nature precisely analogous to those of the physical order (Sumner, 1963:179), and that efforts to reform society could only disrupt nature's destiny momentarily but never change it. He therefore concluded that reform could only do harm by interfering with the free operation of natural laws by which it was governed. For this reason Sumner formulated the moral imperative that one should not even attempt to violate the natural laws of society.

Lester Ward was one of the first of a new group of sociologists to challenge the tenets of Social Darwinism. In 1883 he published a volume bearing the cumbersome title, *Dynamic Sociology, or Applied Social Science, as Based Upon Statical Sociology and the Less Complex Sciences* (Ward, 1883). Taking a cue from August Comte, Ward held that the purpose of sociology, indeed of any science, must necessarily be "to benefit mankind." "A science which fails to do this," he wrote, "is lifeless" (Ward, 1883:I, vii). In place of immutable laws of society which Spencer and Sumner had sought to discover but not violate, Ward adopted the notion of teleology, which he described as

> A special conception of man in his social capacity seeking to improve society by the exercise of an intelligent foresight in seizing upon the laws of nature and directing them to the ends which his reason combined with his acquaintance with those laws teaches him to be those certain to serve the advantage of society (Ward, 1883:I, 28).

Ward was persuaded that progress dictated by the laws of the universe would no longer do; survival in a society undergoing industrialization depended upon teleological progress. In terms that describe well a main impetus behind the development of the profession of sociology in America, Ward delineated the tasks of dynamic sociology:

> To overcome manifold hindrances to human progress, to check the enormous waste of resources, to calm the rhythmic billows of hyperaction and reaction, to secure the rational adoption of means to remote ends, to prevent the natural forces from clashing with the human feelings, to make the currents of physical phenomena flow in the channels of human advantage . . . (Ward, 1883:I, 81).

Ward's vision was amplified by other members of the new profession. Two of the most notable were E. A. Ross, especially in his book, *Social Control*, which he dedicated to Ward and Albion Small. Small's *General Sociology* illustrates well these extensions of Ward's work. Published in 1905, it sets forth guiding principles derived from dispassionate scientific analysis that Small felt provided a basis for the conduct of social life in a society. The impulse of Small's sociology is intensely practical. Its central purpose is to explain "not how the world came to be what it is, but how to make it what it should be" (Small, 1905:655). "Its desideratum," he wrote, "is to be able to say for instance: The American people are in such and such a situation; such and such are the chief issues now prevailing; the other issues fall into such and such subordinate relations; in view of these facts, the conduct of the American people should be turned in such and such directions, so as to promise such and such results" (Small, 1905:713).

This challenge to Social Darwinism greatly influenced the next generation of sociologists trained in American universities. Indeed, by the end of the first quarter of the 20th century, many of the sociologists being trained in the main centers of graduate education in America such as Chicago, Wisconsin, Michigan, Stanford, Columbia and Brown, were in the main sympathetic, if not always wholly committed, to the idea that a major reason for developing a science of society is to acquire knowledge about it that will lead to society's improvement and perfection. These pioneers could count among their disciples leading figures in several fields, including sociologists William Ogburn, Harold Odum, Louis Wirth, W. I. Thomas, Robert Park, Shelby Harrison and Edwin Sutherland; political scientists J. Allen Smith and Charles Merriam; and economists John Commons, Richard Ely, Wesley Mitchell and Simon Patten. Each of these people was influential in establishing and expanding an applied social science tradition within the main academic centers of graduate training and in key governmental agencies. Through their efforts, the use of sociology and other social science disciplines to help public officials grapple with great national, regional and local issues became firmly established as a significant aspect of disciplinary work which is known today as "applied" or "policy-relevant" sociology.*

---

*At this point it is appropriate to explain the meaning of some terms used throughout this book. This book is concerned with attempts that have been made to use sociological knowledge and methods of research to help policy-making groups develop and implement social programs and policies designed to ameliorate and improve conditions in our society. To describe these efforts we use the terms "applied sociology," "policy-relevant sociology" and, on occasion, the two in combination. This usage of the term "applied sociology" is not entirely consistent with its usual usage in our field. Applied sociology is ordinarily used to describe a subfield or specialization within programs and collegial study groups. This meaning of the term creates special problems, as it forces a decision as to who is an "applied" and who is a "pure" sociologist (if indeed these are opposite categories), what constitutes a piece of applied research and what

APPLIED SOCIOLOGY TODAY

A commitment to the view that knowledge can transform society in obvious, self-evident and desirable ways has been a dominant theme in American sociology from Ward's time to the present. Naturally, the form of this vision has undergone transformation in the hands of each succeeding generation of sociologists. Thus, the original vision held by Ward, Small and Ross was of a sociology capable of producing grand master plans of social change for all of society, a vision greatly fostered by a prevailing theoretical tradition which viewed society as a coherent unity of interrelated parts. Sociologists, of course, soon abandoned this organic conception of social order. Abandoned as well was the dream of devising grand schemes. They were soon replaced by a more modest hope—that sociological perspectives, knowledge and methods might contribute to the formulation of governmental policies to ameliorate specific social problems. This hope is expressed in the types of work for application that are done by sociologists today. Contemporary sociologists are attempting to contribute toward improving conditions of life in society in a variety of ways. They *study policy questions* and the social institutions and professions responsible for implementing them. They *teach* sociology to practitioners and policy-makers. They *advise* policy-making groups about development and implementation of social programs. They *work directly* on policy problems in applied programs sponsored by government and, less often, they *lobby* for the adoption of strategies and programs of planned social change. Thus, sociologists use disciplinary knowledge and methods for policy in a number of different ways (to be reviewed in the next chapter) and, although questions have been raised about the final yield of their efforts, few people can question the seriousness of the sociologist's commitment to apply knowledge and methods of the discipline directly toward solving the great social questions and issues which confront the nation today.

Precise data about the extent of involvement of sociologists in applied, policy-related work in government do not exist (Ranney,

---

does not, and so on. We find this task to be futile and diversionary. Our interest is in the uses that are made of sociological knowledge, regardless of who produces it or for what reasons they do so. Sociological research is undertaken for many different reasons, among them the desire to alleviate important social problems of the day. Thus, the use of sociological knowledge is an aspect of the work of many sociologists. It is this aspect of the work of our field to which we refer when we use this or other similar terms.

1968:17; House of Representatives, 1967: I, 129, 314−341); what information there is suggests that such activity is widespread in the profession. One indication of this is the number of sociologists who are involved in federally funded policy-relevant research. According to Horowitz and Katz, some 7,658 sociologists received federal support in 1970 for research and development projects of a practical or policy-relevant nature (Horowitz and Katz, 1975:171) and federal support of social science research for this same year stood at $38,487,000 (Horowitz and Katz, 1975:171). Moreover, the involvement of sociologists in federally supported policy-related activities has increased dramatically with time. From 1900 to 1930, the involvement of sociologists in applied work was limited largely to local efforts and to selected high-level advisory work for various presidential commissions and congressional committees (House of Representatives, 1967: I, 314−341; Mowry, 1958:19−40; Kirkendall, 1966:2−10; Karl, 1969:349−353). This began to change dramatically during the depression of the 1930s when a growing number of sociologists were attracted to Washington to work in New Deal programs. Albert Biderman and Elizabeth Crawford have estimated that the number of social scientists engaged in some type of Government work in a professional capacity was about 680 in 1931. During the next six years, as more New Deal programs were established, the figure swelled to 2,150 (Biderman and Crawford, 1968:41) by which time the total dollar value of federal support to all the social sciences had risen to 19 million dollars (House of Representatives, 1967: I,328). The active participation of social scientists in governmental affairs continued through World War II and has remained at a high level ever since. In the period 1957−1964, for instance, the number of professional and technical employees of the federal government in the fields of statistics and the social sciences increased by about 20 percent (Biderman and Crawford, 1968:42). The amount of federal support for social science research also increased. According to the National Science Foundation, this figure amounted to 30 million dollars in 1956; in 1961, it had reached 96 million dollars; in 1966, 266 million dollars; in 1971, 422 million dollars (National Science Foundation, 1967−1974),[1] and approximately 433 million dollars in 1974 (Shapley, 1976:30). These figures are for all social science disciplines, but data on the field of sociology indicate that the growth in involvement of sociologists in policy-relevant research paralleled that of other social science disciplines. Thus, the number of sociologists receiving federal support for research on applied policy-related problems which stood at 3,640 in 1966, had risen to 7,658 by 1970 (Horowitz and Katz, 1975:10). Federal obligations for research and development in sociology grew from $38,487,000 in 1970 to $50,000,000 in 1971, and then to $71,840,000 in 1972 (Horowitz and Katz, 1975:171).

The bulk of money that the federal government has invested in the social sciences has been for support of so-called applied research—a point emphasized by many. For example, in testimony given to the Subcommittee on Research and Technical Programs of the House of Representatives' Committee on Government and Operations, Harry Alpert, the former Head of the Sociology Section of the National Science Foundation, states, "As the definition of the proper scope of government broadened, it supported work in a wider variety of areas . . . [but] always the emphasis has been on the development and application of practical knowledge" (House of Representatives, 1967: I, 361); and Horowitz and Katz state that the data they compiled on applied sociology "add up to a steadily increasing set of federal expenditures for human resources, public welfare, environmental impact, education, and other economic and social programs" (Horowitz and Katz, 1975:21). Finally, Shapley shows that while federal support for basic social science research declined by approximately 10 per cent between 1967 and 1974 (based upon 1967 constant dollar figures), support for applied research during the same period rose by nearly 12 percent (Shapley, 1976:30).

Applied, policy-relevant work on domestic social policies in government is, then, a significant activity in American sociology today. The purpose here is an attempt to make some assessment of how effective this effort has been. That is, we shall try to ascertain the extent to which, and the ways in which, sociology is having an impact on policy, and the extent to which, and in what ways, it is failing to achieve its goals. To do this we draw on disciplinary literature on this subject, culling from it what we are able to learn about the current status of this aspect of our (sociologists') disciplinary art. In view of the fact that most of this literature is about attempts that have been made to use sociology in connection with policy pertaining to national domestic problems, most of our discussion deals with this particular policy sphere. The conclusions to which we come, on the basis of this analysis, can be summarized in two statements: (1) although many so-called applied studies have illuminated interesting sociological questions, few produce policy recommendations of any kind; and (2) in instances where recommendations have been offered, they have often been rejected by policy-makers as politically unrealistic, administratively unworkable, or simply impractical. An explanation of the justification for these conclusions follows.

THE IMPACT OF SOCIOLOGY ON FEDERAL DOMESTIC POLICY: AN ASSESSMENT

Each generation of sociologists has left behind it a record of its attempts to realize Ward's dream of an activist sociology. This record reflects changes in the mood and spirit about the prospects for an applied, policy-relevant sociology that have occurred with time. One way in which to approach the question of sociology's impact on federal domestic policy is to examine some of the shifts in mood and spirit that have been occurring within sociology from the time the discipline first began until the present day.

The commentaries of early sociology and social philosophy abound with hope and promise. Ward, Ross, Small, Dewey, James and Cooley all exude a sense of confidence in the possibility of creating a sociology relevant to the great social challenges of the day. They felt certain that this new science would be equal to the task of ameliorating social evils. Each had an impressive faith that if enough time, money and thought could be invested in sociological research, and social policies could be devised and implemented rationally, no problem, regardless of how ancient or firmly entrenched, would fail to yield. Despite occasional disclaimers, each held high hopes about the possibilities for developing a truly useful science to develop great master plans of social change for America.

If the direct experience of grappling with the complexity of social conditions did not cool the ardor of the next generation of sociologists, it certainly imbued them with a sense of humility uncommon among their mentors. During the 1920s and the New Deal years, sociologists doing research and advising the government on such problems as crime, poverty, housing and political corruption soon discovered that these conditions were more complicated and intractable than their forebears had perhaps imagined. They also learned that producing research that yields results pertinent to the formulation of ameliorative social policies was not simple, and that getting government officials and legislative bodies to listen to sociologists could be more difficult still. Yet, in spite of the growing recognition by these sociologists that their mission was to be more difficult and complicated than expected, nevertheless their basic underlying confidence in the relevance of sociology for the great domestic crises of the time survived more or less unscathed through the Depression, World War II and even the 1950s. Indeed, it is fair to say that this confidence characterized the attitudes of many sociologists who began their research and writing during the 1960s.

The 1960s were unusual years for sociology, especially in connection with attempts to use sociological knowledge for policy-related activities. By any previous standard the investment by private foundations and federal and state governments in social science and sociological research was massive. Furthermore, as we have seen, most of this money was given to sociologists and other social scientists in hopes that they would be able to aid policy-makers and practitioners to establish and carry out more intelligent, effective, enlightened policies and programs in such fields as criminal justice, medicine, mental health, urban affairs, law, business, foreign affairs, education, social work, public health, the military, agriculture and population. To a large extent, present-day commentaries about the uses of sociology in federal domestic programs reflect the experience of this decade and of the first few years of the 1970s.

Current assessments of applied aspects of sociological work are more confusing and complicated than any heretofore presented, for they are at once optimistic and despairing. (See, for example, Merton, 1973; Lyons, 1969; C. Weiss, 1976a; J. Weiss, 1976.) Examples of the impact of sociology on public policy (to be reviewed shortly) are juxtaposed with examples of disappointments and failures (also to be considered). Absent is the confident, almost strident, tone of past writings. Though continuing to believe that sociological knowledge can and should be used to improve living conditions within society, many sociologists today seem subdued by what they perceive to be the disappointingly few instances of impact and what some regard to be an alarmingly large number of failures by sociology to fulfill its promise to provide knowledge that will result in social policies better suited to deal with the social problems of today. The mood, then, is a mixture of hope and gloom. On what considerations are these contrasting moods based?

Examples of Impact

The tones of optimism which appear in discussions of the impact of sociology on federal domestic policy seem to be founded on two main considerations. First, some of the sociological research that has been done on domestic social problems in American society has been used for the *development of specific policy recommendations* for governmental programs to diminish or ameliorate these conditions. Second, in a number of instances, this research has also had a *direct impact on enacted policy*. It is beyond the scope of this book to present an inventory detailing every instance in which sociological knowledge has served as the basis for developing policy recommendations or enacting policy. Instead, we are content to present the main examples cited in the literature in order to give our reader a sense for what the mood of optimism about applied sociology is based on. We note that the examples we will discuss are primarily ones that others have cited in the context of discussions about the impact of sociology on policy. We believe that many of the cases we will cite in fact support the contention that sociology has been useful and relevant in public affairs; however, we find that some of them are exaggerated or misleading. We have therefore tried to distinguish between the two and will note any qualifications we may have about them.

Sociology's contributions to policy recommendations. Many people have pointed out instances in which sociological knowledge, perspectives, concepts, theories, and methods have been useful in connection with the development of *policy recommendations.* Among the most heralded cases of this are the various uses made of sociology in four recent presidential commissions. For this reason we will discuss them first. They are: The Commission on Law Enforcement and the Administration of Justice (1968), the Commission on the Causes and Prevention of Violence (1969), the Commission on Obcenity and Pornography (1970), and the Commission on Population Growth and the American Future (1972). Sociologists were actively involved in all four and disciplinary research and knowledge figured prominently in the final recommendations made by each body.

The role of sociology in presidential commissions was the subject of a special plenary session convened at the Annual Meetings of the American Sociological Association in 1973, the papers of which were subsequently published in 1975 in a volume on sociology and presidential commissions (Komarovsky, 1975). Discussions were presented by sociologists who had worked directly on each of the four commissions. Lloyd Ohlin, Associate Director of the Task Force on Assessment of the Crime Problem for the Commission on Law Enforcement and the Administration of Justice, describes the role he believes sociology played in the work of this Commission. Most important, in his view, were the concepts, theories, and general perspectives brought to bear on the problems of crime by sociologists and other social scientists working for the Commission. He explains:

> Existing social science theories and data were drawn upon to formulate broad general strategy in the prevention and control of crime. The staff then developed more detailed recommendations which would serve to implement these strategies through new public policies, allocation of

public resources and proposals for changes in the specific operation and organization of the criminal justice agency (Ohlin, 1975:108).

Sociologists, then, contributed to this Commission report by providing Commission members with sensitizing concepts and theories that oriented their search for solutions to the crime problem. As an example, Ohlin cites the findings of sociological studies about the detrimental effects of imprisonment on criminals, explaining that "on the basis of such knowledge . . . the Commission adopted the view that persons should be diverted from the criminal justice system into alternative systems of social control whenever possible" (Ohlin, 1975:109).

Sociologists also contributed to the work of the Commission by adding new information that served as the basis for the recommendations supplied to the Commission by expert consultants and advisors. Ohlin states:

A determined effort was made to develop factual support for policies, general strategies, and specific recommendations. Much of this came from available statistics, studies and documents available to criminal justice agencies or published in the literature. In addition, special field studies were undertaken. Examples include victimization studies, surveys of attitudes of victims and citizens to crime and criminal justice, and studies of high crime precincts in Washington, Chicago, and Boston. . . . These surveys provided new types of information never available before for gauging public concerns of fear about crime, the experience of victims of crime, attitudes toward reporting crime and measures citizens were taking to defend themselves (Ohlin, 1975:101).

Sociologists made similar contributions to the work of the National Commission on the Causes and Prevention of Violence. In this case, research done by sociologists provided the basis for specific Commission recommendations concerning the prevention of violence (Short, 1975:84). James Short, Co-director of Research for the Commission, believes that the sociologists' most visible impact was on the progress report issued half way through the Commission's deliberations. He explains:

Despite compromise, we were able to secure Commission endorsement of our neutral definition of violence and of several 'themes of challenge' including the relativity of attribution of legitimacy or illegitimacy to violence, the essentially social (as opposed to biological or psychological) nature of most violence, the fundamental notion of "relative deprivation" and the notion that responsibility for violence often lies in the unresponsiveness of social institutions (Short, 1975:85).

The role of sociology in this Commission then was to impart a perspective to the problem of violence that in turn served as a guide to the Commission in drawing up its final list of recommendations.

In the Commission on Obscenity and Pornography, sociology's contribution to the final report was even more direct. One of the Commission's final recommendations resulted directly from sociological and other social science research on the personal, psychological and social consequences of exposure to explicitly sexual materials. In its report, the Commission recommended that federal, state and local laws prohibiting the sale, exhibition or distribution of sexual materials to consenting adults be repealed (Report of the Commission on Obscenity and Pornography, 1970:57). This recommendation was based upon extensive sociological investigation by the Commission and others that provided,

> . . . no evidence that exposure to or use of explicit sexual materials plays a significant role in the causation of social or individual harm such as crime, delinquency, sexual and nonsexual deviancy or severe emotional disturbance—Empirical investigations thus support the opinion of a substantial majority of persons professionally engaged in the treatment of deviancy, delinquency and anti-social behavior, that exposure to sexually explicit material has no harmful causal role in these areas (Report of the Commission, 1970:58).

Sociological research, or rather the lack of it, played a role in another of the Commission's recommendations: that states adopt legislation prohibiting the commercial distribution or display for sale of certain sexual materials to young persons. This proposal was based in part upon the inconclusiveness of sociological and other social science research on this issue. The report noted that, "Insufficient research is presently available on the effect of the exposure of children to sexually explicit material to enable us to reach conclusions with the same degree of confidence as for adult exposure" (Report of the Commission, 1970:63). As a result, the Commission concluded that it should recommend a safe course of action and urge adoption of legislation prohibiting the distribution and sale of such material to children.

The President's Commission on Population Growth and the American Future (1972) provides some of the clearest instances of the use of sociology in developing policy recommendations. Charles Westoff, the Staff Director of the Commission, believes that the Commission research, much of it done by demographers, had an appreciable impact on the substance of the final report. He states that sociological and demographic research "penetrated and influenced some of the basic conclusions about the effects of population growth and about policy recommendations" (Westoff, 1973:498). To substantiate his conclusion, he cites examples.

A main question raised by the Commission concerned the role of population growth in the depletion of resources and in environmental deterioration. A study sponsored by the Commission showed that in the short run population growth would probably play only a minor role as compared with technological, economic and Government policy considerations, but that in the long run, population growth would become increasingly important (Westoff, 1973:498). Westoff describes the policy implications of this finding:

> . . . that resources and environmental considerations implied prudence rather than crisis; that there certainly were no benefits to be realized from continual growth but that population was an indirect and ineffectual policy lever for environmental problems (Westoff, 1973:498–499).

Another example of the influence of sociological research on the Commission recommendations comes from research on family size. The Commission was considering a recommendation to reduce the amount of immigration to help achieve zero population growth. A paper commissioned for the report showed that the goal of zero population growth could be achieved near the same population level and in about the same time if women averaged 2.0 rather than 2.1 births, even if immigration continued at its current volume. According to Westoff, this finding was extremely influential in defeating the proposed recommendation to reduce the volume of immigration (Westoff, 1973:499).

A critical concern of the Commission was the impact of urban policy on population distribution. For some time federal government officials had been contemplating adopting a so-called "national growth center strategy" by which government spending would be used in an effort to divert population away from large metropolitan areas to smaller, presumably more viable cities. According to a research report on this problem, such a policy would make only a small dent in the expected growth of large metropolitan areas over the next 30 years because the effects of such a policy would be overwhelmed by the impact of natural increases in the metropolitan areas (Westoff, 1973:499).

Perhaps the most interesting and stimulating example involved a controversy about the best method for achieving a desired rate of population growth. Demographers agree that a critical factor in a nation's population policy is whether the stabilization of population can be achieved through the prevention of unwanted fertility or whether more radical social changes are needed to alter the number of children desired. Westoff reports that estimates of the incidence of unwanted births derived from data collected in the National Fertility Studies of 1965 and 1970 showed that the elimination of unwanted fertility alone would bring about a population stabilization. Westoff states:

> It is difficult to overestimate the policy significance of this finding. It meant that instead of trying to change a social norm, through politically difficult means, the Commission could concentrate instead on trying to provide the means to satisfy couples' apparent goals through the improvement and distribution of methods of fertility control, a "solution" well within acceptable limits. . . . Such a solution had everything. It meant helping people to achieve what they want; it did not imply any radical solution to the problem of population growth; aside from abortion, it was singularly unobjectionable; it was theoretically easy to do, and it wouldn't cost very much! It was difficult to imagine a policy with more political promise (Westoff, 1973:499).

Westoff cites other examples as well. A study showing a *negative* relationship between income and unwanted births served as a rationale for government subsidization of family planning for the poor (Westoff, 1973:499−501). Analysis of the implications for the costs of education and health resulting from the age distribution and growth associated with two- versus three-child family fertility rates contributed directly to the argument in favor of a slower growth rate and an older population (Westoff, 1973:500). The discovery of gross ignorance on the part of the American people about the size of the American population provided a basis for recommending population education (Westoff, 1973:500); and, finally, an opinion poll taken by the Commission indicated that about half of the American people felt that abortion ought to be a matter decided solely between individuals and their physicians, a finding that was subsequently used to support a liberal abortion recommendation (Westoff, 1973:500). Westoff concludes that, over all, these and other research reports were critical to the direction of the argument and the policies of the Commission: "[They were] of great importance both to the nature of the diagnoses as well as the prescription" (Westoff, 1973:500).

The study of Presidential Commissions is one example of the influence that sociology has had on the development of policy recommendations by government bodies; Caplan's study of the utilization of social science by 204 upper-level officials in the executive branch of government is another (Caplan et al., 1975). Caplan describes a number of the uses made of social science, including sociology, for policy recommendations reported to him by respondents of the study. In the interviews, mention was made of the use of sociological research as a basis for planning and evaluating programs that were designed to meet special educational needs of children from minority groups and low-income families, and for community development and residential planning programs in low-income neighborhoods. Sociological attitudinal studies were mentioned by several respondents as useful for such purposes as determining what facilities and what types of approaches were necessary for a variety of governmental information programs. Also cited was research on organizational development and its influence on policies related to administrative functions such as increasing bureaucratic efficacy, personnel selection and promotion procedures. Governmental officials responsible for planning within the Department of Defense mentioned the important role that social research played in determining the feasibility of an all-volunteer Army and for proposed changes in human relations training programs. Officials responsible for rehabilitation cited the use of social science findings as a basis for planned changes in rehabilitation programs and Department of Interior officials cited studies on public use of recreational lands and park areas as influential in altering park policy. The use of sociological findings was mentioned by people involved in planning federally subsidized building programs in the context of efforts to design safer, more crime-free and more livable public housing, and sociological research was regularly cited by officials from various departments of the executive branch in connection with efforts to evaluate programs (Caplan et al., 1975:24). The study also found that sociology was being used in a variety of planning areas in government including organizational management, education, welfare, crime, health, commerce, public opinion management, military affairs, employment, civil rights and minority affairs, the environment, transportation, housing, consumer affairs and recreation (Caplan et al., 1975:58). We cite the Caplan study because in most of the examples given, the claim was that social science research and knowledge had contributed toward the formulation of proposed policies; only in a few instances did social science have an impact on the policies that were eventually adopted.

To judge fairly, the examples cited thus far of sociology's usefulness to policy, we must consider a number of qualifications to these claims. What is claimed is that sociology has made a contribution to recommendations for policy in three ways. The first is through the *use of sociological concepts* that are said *to provide new or unique perspectives on social conditions*—perspectives that are based upon more than common sense and that may in fact be inconsistent with basic notions upon which existing policies are based. This use of sociology is illustrated by the example cited from the Commission on the Causes and Prevention of Violence. Here sociological materials presented in the Staff reports led Commission members to adopt a neutral interpretation of violence and to acknowledge that some violence is a product of the unresponsiveness of society's main institutions to the needs of its citizens. Second, *prescriptions for policy are sometimes suggested by the findings of sociological research undertaken primarily to advance scientific understanding of society.* This use of sociology is illustrated by the examples from the Report of the Commission on Population Growth and the American Future in which findings from the 1965 and 1970 National Fertility Studies led to the Commission's decision to concentrate on means for achieving desired family size. The third is *the use of sociological methods and techniques of research to obtain information about specific questions central to the deliberations of the Commission.* An example cited from the Pornography Commission illustrates this use. Studies by sociologists and others of the effect of obscene materials on adults led the Commission to recommend the repeal of laws restricting the public sale and distribution of such materials to adults.

Judging from examples that are cited in the literature which we have read to support the claim that sociology is relevant to policy, it seems to us that of the three uses of sociology, the third is by far the most common. That is, many of the examples cited in the literature involve empirical research done in connection with particular policy deliberations regarding a problem of immediate urgency. But we must recognize that conducting research is not a skill possessed exclusively by sociologists. Presumably any reasonably intelligent individual trained in the methods of social research would be capable of doing the kinds of studies that are cited to illustrate the use of sociology in public affairs. In fact, in many of the examples given, someone other than the sociologist (e.g., a member of a Commission, a legislator or a policy-maker) dictated the questions to be answered by the research. The sociologist then employed skills as a researcher to obtain information to answer the questions. But there is nothing inherently sociological about some of these questions. An example: "What are the effects of pornography on adults?" To answer this, one had only to know how to do research, and it is this which constitutes the contribution of sociology to the Pornography Commission. Thus one qualification to these claims is that in many instances the *methods* of empirical research, *not* the knowledge and concepts of sociology, have been most directly instrumental in the developmental of specific policy descriptions.

A second qualification rests on a distinction that must be made between contributions that are made to policy by intelligent, thoughtful and enlightened individuals who happen to be trained as sociologists, and the contributions of sociological knowledge and perspectives per se. In a number of the examples cited in connection with presidential commissions, as well as examples to be cited in the following section dealing with the role of sociology in enacted policy (such as the use of sociology to improve education, reduce school drop-out rates and to combat delinquency), what is claimed as an instance of sociological impact on policy entails not the application of a body of disciplinary knowledge, but the use of certain intellectual and political skills and experiences by individuals who are trained in sociology. Lloyd Ohlin of the Commission on Law Enforcement and the Administration of Justice speaks directly to this problem:

> The sociologists serving as consultants to the Commission proved very reluctant to draw out the implications of their analysis in the form of action recommendations for the Commission. When they did try to do this, the recommendations were often more influenced by personal ideological conviction than by appropriately organized facts and theories or arguments (Ohlin, 1975:110).[2]

It is difficult, of course, to sort out what portion of any advice is attributable to a discipline and what portion to the personal skills and intelligence of those seeking solutions to a problem. Yet, it appears that in many of the areas in which advice is sought, the state of sociological knowledge is elementary—and much of what is known does not lend itself readily to programmatic planning. In these cases especially, the advice given is sometimes based on the sociologist's own intuitive understanding of a problem—not on sociological knowledge or the sociological perspective as such. For this reason it is misleading to credit the discipline's knowledge in all cases in which sociology has had an impact on policy.

Finally, it is important to emphasize again that we have been concerned only with sociology's impact on *policy recommendations*, as distinguished from its impact on enacted policy. A complaint commonly voiced by those who have worked on presidential commissions and other high-level task forces is that political leaders have often rejected the very policy recommendations in which sociology has played an important role. This complaint represents one of the main bases of concern within the discipline about the possibilities and prospects for applied sociology today. For this reason we will return to it in a later section in connection with discussion of sources of concern that sociologists have about what they perceive to be the shortcomings and failings of attempts to use disciplinary knowledge and methods in connection with policy.

These qualifications notwithstanding, it is fair to conclude from this brief analysis of the role of sociology in these commissions that sociological knowledge can and sometimes does have an impact on developing recommendations for courses of action that the government might follow in dealing with national social problems. For this reason, sociologists can legitimately claim that their discipline has been and is relevant to the development of policy recommendations.

Sociology's contributions to enacted policy. A second reason sociologists give for satisfaction with the discipline's role in public affairs is that in certain cases sociology is said to have had a *direct impact on enacted policy.* Examples of this are often cited in the literature. Most often mentioned is the research by Otto Klineberg and others on the psychological and intellectual consequences of segregation on black children in the 1954 Supreme Court decision outlawing segregation in public schools. Indeed, the court case is featured as the prime example of the usefulness of sociology in public affairs by the Special Commission on the Social Sciences of the National Science Board (National Science Foundation, 1969:11–15), in testimony by sociologists to the Subcommittee on Research and Technical Programs of the Committee on Government Operations of the 90th Congress (House of Representatives, 1967:I, 126), and in other reports and essays on the policy uses of sociology too numerous to mention here. We would certainly agree that Klineberg's research played an important role in public debate about this question; yet, its role in the court's decision is less clear cut. Legal scholars and others who have studied the court's decision agree that the research in question probably did not appreciably influence the final decision even though it was cited in the majority brief. They point out that the court was almost certainly already persuaded by the larger moral questions that the case raised (Horowitz and Katz, 1975:132; Zeisel, 1967:96; Cahn, 1955:150; Kluger, 1976). Some believe that the research was merely added by the court as an afterthought to lend scholarly weight to a conclusion of which the justices were already persuaded, i.e., that segregated education is unequal education (Horowitz and Katz, 1975:132). Others have raised serious questions about the research itself and have reservations about its value as evidence in a court case of this importance (Clark, 1960:224, 236; Vanden Haag, 1960:69; Gregor, 1963:621–636). In any event, a strong case has been made that the decision would almost certainly have been forthcoming even if the court had not known about the research in question, suggesting that perhaps sociologists have made more out of the study's role in the decision than it properly deserves.

Other examples which have been cited to support the view that sociology has had an impact on enacted policy include Michael Harrington's study, *The Other America*, which is credited with bringing the problem of poverty to public attention in the 1960s, ultimately leading to the War on Poverty (House of Representatives, 1967: I, 126−127; National Science Foundation, 1969: 11−15; Horowitz and Katz, 1975:133−139); the involvement of sociologists such as Cloward and Ohlin (1960) in social action programs to combat juvenile delinquency, to reduce school drop-out rates and to prevent narcotics addiction (House of Representatives, 1967: I, 126−127; National Science Foundation, 1969:11−15); studies by demographers of population growth and the migration of people in the United States—information said to have provided the basis for "long-range planning by many of the most important sectors and institutions in American society" (National Science Foundation, 1969:137); "New understanding of the magnitude of crime in the nation through the measurement of rates of criminal acts based on reports of victims of crime" (National Science Foundation, 1969:14); and sociological research on "talent loss" as a result of inadequate educational opportunities for persons of low socio-economic status, findings that led to the enactment of remedial measures such as "the expansion of state universities, the establishment of new scholarships and loan resources, the creation of federal programs like Upward Bound, Talent Search and Vista" (National Science Foundation, 1969:14−15). Others are the recent attempts by sociologists to institutionalize the collection and reporting of social indicators measuring social change in America (Horowitz and Katz, 1975:24−26, 28−31; Gross, 1967; Office of Management and Budget, 1974): the uses of sociology in various executive departments of government (Horowitz and Katz, 1975:32−33, 38−41, 71−90; Caplan et al., 1975), and in federally sponsored research projects such as the Pentagon-sponsored Project Clear (Horowitz and Katz, 1975:139−142) and the New Jersey−Pennsylvania Negative Income Tax Experiment (Horowitz and Katz, 1975:139−142). In each case the claim is that substantial numbers of sociologists contributed research and conceptual skills toward the formulation of programs and policies that were eventually enacted to ameliorate social conditions deemed harmful to the society.

Here, too, certain qualifications are necessary. In some of the examples that are cited, sociological research appears to have been implicated in final policy decisions that were made, but it is not evident from the decisions exactly what the impact was. For example, the claim of "new understanding of the magnitude of crime in the nation" brought about by recent victimology studies is not accompanied by an explanation of the precise impact that this research was thought to have had on enacted policy nor are we told how studies of population growth and migration were thought to be implicated in policy initiatives in the area of national population policy. Several reports credit sociology for its role in social action programs dealing with juvenile delinquency, school drop-outs and narcotics addiction but do not explain what this role was. This qualification, of course, raises the important issue of *how* sociology has an impact on policy. If impact means sensitizing legislators and others to the existence of a problem or educating them about its sociological aspects then the claim is probably justified. But if we mean that sociological research led directly to specific policies, then some qualification to the basic claim is required. We point this out because many of the examples that we cited were raised in the context of discussions in which the second sense of the term "impact" was intended. If this is so, it has important implications for assessing the claim that sociology has had an impact on enacted policy, even though these implications do not entirely negate the point that sociological research had led to the development of specific policies enacted by the government.

All of the examples that we have mentioned so far pertain to the role of sociology in national policy. But some of the most impressive examples of sociological impact on enacted policy involve programming efforts at the state and local levels of government and in private organizations. The law is one such area in which sociology has had an impact on policy. Zeisel describes one example involving an experiment of pretrial procedures in the court system of New Jersey. Tradition within the New Jersey system held that pretrial hearings increased rates of settlement prior to trial. As a result, this procedure had been considered a desirable means for reducing the trial load and avoiding a problem of intolerable congestion in the courts. Zeisel explains:

> Since many cases, the trial of which would have lasted two days on the average, are settled during a half-hour pretrial conference, this notion seemed well supported. But analysis of available statistics made the point doubtful; there were indications that the cases settled at pretrial could have been settled without it and that the court time spent on pretrial might be wasted (Zeisel, 1967:83).

To find out whether pretrial hearings were time-savers or time-wasters, a controlled experiment was undertaken. Sociologists developed a design calling for the random assignment of cases by clerks of the court to one of two procedures: obligatory pretrial in one group of cases and optional pretrial in the control group, where it was held only if one or both of the litigants requested it. The conclusion was that obligatory pretrial did not save court time; in fact, it wasted it (Zeisel, 1967: 84). Persuaded by the experiment, the State of New Jersey changed its rules and made pretrial hearings optional.

Zeisel also describes a study conducted in one city that had nationwide impact. A study of bail bond procedures by the Vera Institute of New York showed that the number of defendants released without bail could be quadrupled without reducing their availability at the time of trial (Zeisel, 1967:85). Zeisel describes the impact of the study:

> The results of the experiment were stunning. The City of New York took over the interviewing from the Foundation (Vera) and established it as a permanent service. The Attorney General of the United States convened a conference on the topic, and today almost all major cities and many rural areas have adopted the Vera procedure, and with it the liberalized practice of release without bail. And the Department of Justice left no doubt as to where the credit belonged: Of particular significance is the fact that these changes have flowed not out of a crisis . . . but rather from education, through special research and demonstration (Zeisel, 1967:85).

The uses of sociological knowledge in numerous other areas of practice have also been claimed. Lazarsfeld, Reitz and Pasanella cite and analyze several instances of this, including the use of sociological research findings in a company marketing trading stamps (Lazarsfeld et al., 1975:71−74); a study directed by James Coleman on the availability of equal educational opportunity (Lazarsfeld et al., 1975:71−75); the uses of sociology for achieving organizational change (Lazarsfeld et al., 1975:14−24). Discussions also exist on the uses of sociology in the fields of medicine (Hyman, 1967:136−147), education (Gross and Fishman, 1967:317−331), the military (Bowers, 1967:234−274), law enforcement (Bordua and Reiss, 1967:287−288), foreign policy (Davison, 1967:392−399), urban planning (Gans, 1967:462−465), and public health (Suchman, 1967:572−598). Each of these fields provides some additional illustrations of the relevance of sociology to enacted policy and of the roles that sociological knowledge has played in the formulation of social policy recommendations.[3] In spite of the qualifications we have made about claims that have been put forth by sociologists about the disciplines relevance to social policy, it can legitimately be said that sociology has had an important impact on the development of recommendations that have been made for policies to deal with domestic social problems in American society and, in selected instances, on policy initiatives that have been enacted. It is perfectly understandable why sociologists have expressed a certain amount of satisfaction with their disciplines relevance in public affairs.

Bases for Dissatisfaction

At the same time there are grounds for concern about the results of efforts to use sociological knowledge and methods in social policy. There are two main sources of dissatisfaction. One is that a considerable amount of sociological research initiated for purposes of policy has proven to be pragmatically irrelevant; that is, it carries no discernible policy implications of any kind. The other is that sociological theory and research have sometimes led to policy recommendations, but most of these recommendations have been ignored or rejected by national political leaders as unrealistic or implausible. We will deal briefly with the latter problem first and then discuss the former in more detail.

We have seen that some of the optimism among sociologists today about the possibilites for applied sociology stems from the fact that sociologists have been able to demonstrate a connection between some piece of research, a particular concept or a general perspective and a specific policy recommendation. Thus, for each of the Presidential commissions that we discussed, sociology was used to help structure the final recommendations that were made. In the case of each commission, its mandate was to propose an intelligent policy that the government might follow, but, as the reader may know, most of the recommendations that were made were completely ignored by the government. For example, Charles Westoff describes the reception given to the report of the Population Commission by the executive branch as a disappointment at every level. He states, "The President's response was narrowly political and greatly at variance with the concern about population that [he] had expressed less than three years earlier" (Westoff, 1975:58). And concerning the report of the Commission on Pornography and Obscenity, Otto Larsen states, "It was conceived in the Congress, born in the White House, and after twenty-seven months of life, was buried without honor by both parent institutions" (Larsen, 1975:9). The problem seems to be that many of the policy recommendations that flow from sociological research are regarded as politically impractical or unplatable by government officials, and this fact stands as a major qualification to many of the claims for relevance that sociologists have made. Later, we will attempt to discover why this should be so. The point we want to make here is that much of sociology's impact in public affairs has been on the *recommendations* developed by commissions and task forces created to propose rational courses of action that government might follow to ameliorate or solve a given domestic problem, but *not on the policies* that are eventually enacted.

A second basis for concern about the efforts made to apply sociology to social policy is that a considerable amount of research that is done for application has produced results which appear to carry no discernible policy implications of any kind. Critics have complained that much so-called policy-relevant sociological research is stimulated by a desire to resolve disciplinary questions or to advance disciplinary knowledge. The results may add to the storehouse of sociological knowledge about conditions in the society but many of them have proven to be irrelevant to the policy-makers concerns. This point has been stressed by a number of people who have reviewed sociological research on various policy-related topics. In a review of the contributions of social science to governmental programs for the disadvantaged, Walter Williams speaks of "the lack of relevance of social science to public policy" in this area (Williams, 1971:59). He summarizes a large mass of empirical knowledge about the plight and condition of disadvantaged people, showing that very little of it is at all helpful to policy-makers trying to devise programs (Williams, 1971:62–63). Harold Orlans comes to the same conclusion in his review of social science research in six domestic policy areas. He states that, "Too much of the research is either not clearly relevant to national and/or government needs or of such a nature that even if the subject is relevant, the findings are unlikely to make any difference to anyone but the investigator" (Orlans, 1968:152).

Yehezkel Dror's review of systems analysis attempts to use sociological knowledge to inform social policies, describes the policy-relevance of such efforts as "disappointing" (Dror, 1971a:11). And, "speaking" about the Commission on the Causes and Prevention of Violence, James Short complains of "a lack of adequate scientific knowledge with clear policy implications" (Short, 1975:62). Short complains that many of the sociologists who were asked to contribute to the work of this Commission thought of the academic community rather than the policy-makers and legislators as their audience. "We continue to write primarily for each other and for our students," he writes, "perhaps out of the conviction that what we have to say won't be listened to for ideological reasons, perhaps because we are ordinarily less certain of our data and interpretations than the Commission (or policy-makers) would like us to be" (Short, 1975:83).

Various reasons have been given for the irrelevance of much of the work done for policy by sociologists. One is that it tends to be too piecemeal, specialized and partial in scope to ever be applicable to policy-making. For instance, David Easton has pointed out that when sociologists and other social scientists are invited to advise policy-making bodies, they are inclined to convert policy questions into technical problems of means (Easton, 1972:91). As a result, sociological research on policy questions has often lacked the type of general, holistic, integrated perspective that is required for developing and implementing social policies and programs. This fact is noted by other critics. Orlans describes social science research as ". . . too small-scale, fragmented, inconsequential, nonadditive, and therefore un-utilizable to advance either basic knowledge or practical actions" (Orlans, 1968:152). Yehezkel Dror describes the behavioral sciences as being "of very limited relevance to the policy-making system as a whole . . . disjointed . . . preoccupied with irrationality . . . incremental . . . and narrow in its domain as a whole" (Dror, 1971b:11−13); and David Truman complains that, "The social sciences are becoming sufficiently segmental and specialized in character that the public official who turns to them will either hear little but noise or receive fractional advice to deal with whole policies" (Truman, 1968a:510).

A second reason is that the research has implications that are so far-reaching and revolutionary as to virtually assure inaction. Some sociologists, for example, have placed the blame for conditions such as crime, violence or urban decay on "existing institutional arrangements" and have therefore urged root and branch revolution as the recommended policy to deal with these conditions, leaving policy-makers with no real alternative but to ignore the advice.[4] In a similar vein, critics have noted that sociologists have often failed to appreciate the constants that operate on those who are responsible for developing and implementing policies. Failing to comprehend the fiscal and political realities confronting policy-makers, sociologists sometimes produce recommendations that are implausible, impractical and unrealistic. Williams notes that although social scientists have studied the problem of poverty extensively, they have seldom considered it from a public policy, decision-making framework that is necessary to guarantee the production of useful findings (Williams,

1971:62). Otto Larsen bemoans "the failure of the Commission on Obscenity and Pornography to penetrate the policy realm with the principle that empirical research is relevant" (Larsen, 1975:17). He states, "Sociology equipped us to do what was essentially abstracted empirical research (but) it did not equip us to shape the research and policy alternatives. Policy was something you took up after you had done the work" (Larsen, 1975:18). In his view this was a major failing of the Pornography Commission:

> We missed a rare opportunity to link social science to social policy in an effective manner. We failed because we did not turn our tools to an empirical analysis of policy options, so that the remainder of the research effort and other elements would illuminate the costs and consequences of realistic alternative courses of action. In short, we did not have a policy-research theory to guide our study (Larsen, 1975: 23).

Others have noted that some so-called policy-relevant sociological research that has been done has provided a diagnosis of the problem but one that has no significant implications for policy. This criticism, implicit in the essays previously cited by Orlans, Williams, and Dror, is also the complaint voiced by Alvin Schorr who spent many years attempting to develop programs for the Department of Health, Education and Welfare. Schorr states flatly that in his experience social science research simply failed to come up with tangible, demonstrable, practical solutions to the great domestic crises of the decade. He speaks about "the lack of fit between social science research and problems of social policy" (Schorr, 1968:6), and the failure of research "to act as critic and prod to social policies [even] though they [politicians] were clearly vulnerable" (Schorr, 1968:6). He concludes, "The social sciences devote themselves to the means to achieve whatever it might turn out that their purpose might be, doggedly evading the very questions of purpose that would give meaning to their data" (Schorr, 1968:6–7). Yezehkel Dror reports that sociological analysis has not been "really helpful in respect to the main problems facing present and emerging society . . . neither does it demonstrate any inherent capacity for growth that will make it relevant for such problems in the foreseeable future" (Dror, 1971a:110). And Lloyd Ohlin of the Commission on Law Enforcement and Administration of Justice complains about the

> many problems in developing an effective impact of social science theory, concepts and research knowledge. The relevant social science

literature was descriptive and analytical. There were relatively few experimental or controlled studies of the effectiveness of particular program or policies Explanations concerning the courses of crime and the functioning of the criminal justice system, though informative, lacked action implications (Ohlin, 1975:109–110).

Perhaps it is this which Charles Westoff, Director of the Commission on Population Growth and the American Future, had in mind when he answered "no" to the question, "Would the final report have differed if social science dominated the Commission even more than it did?" (Westoff, 1975: 57).

These and other criticisms of so-called applied research have led some to despair about this aspect of work in the discipline. Lucien Pye, for example, wistfully asks where in the work of sociologists who seek to be relevant is that "dynamic and forward-thinking quality which C. P. Snow so graphically identified as the distinctive attribute of science?" (Pye, 1968:239). Gunnar Myrdal boldly warns that instead of speaking to the great social issues of the day sociologists are

increasingly addressing only one another. Using knowledge to enlighten the people is not encouraged: young men learn that this might lower their standing and chances for advancement in the profession. They exhibit an unhealthy interest in research technique for its own sake; they avoid taking up politically controversial issues for study, which means that they avoid issues of great practical importance; they focus their studies on terminology, methods of measurement, aimless collection of data, and similar other worldly problems (Myrdal, 1968:156).

He concludes that sociologists have become expert at "disassociating research from life" (Myrdal, 1968:156).

These criticisms cannot be dismissed as merely the private views of particular individuals. They reflect a general awareness by those in academia and government that efforts to apply sociological knowledge to the great social issues of our day have often been disappointing. [5] This conclusion is reinforced by the reports of three recent study groups commissioned to investigate the relationship of social science to public policy: *The Behavioral Sciences and the Federal Government*, the report of the Advisory Committee on Government Programs in the Behavioral Sciences of the National Academy of Sciences and the National Research Council (1968); *Knowledge Into Action*, the report of the Special Commission on the Social Sciences of the National Science Board (1969); and *The Behavioral and Social Sciences: Outlook and Needs*, the report of the Behavioral and Social Sciences Survey of the National Academy of Science and the Social Science Research Council (1969).* The earliest of the three reports refers to and agrees with even earlier commission, study panels and government groups, which have criticized "the lack of vital and economic information on critical issues and the lack of methods for analyzing information and relating it to policies and operations . . ." (Advising Committee on Government Programs in the Behavioral Sciences, 1968:1). In the foreword to *Knowledge into Action,* Philip Handler, then Chairman of the National Science Board, states that our social and domestic problems appear "even more acute while, increasingly, it is evident that approaches to their solution should be undertaken only in the light of the most sophisticated social scientific understanding . . .". But Handler is not sanguine about successes in this area: "Few mechanisms for translation of social scientific understanding into societal benefit have been institutionalized so as to assure this process" (Special Commission on the Social Sciences, 1969:vii). Finally, in the letter of transmittal of the report of the Behavioral and Social Sciences Survey Committee, Harvey Brooks of the National Academy of Science and Gardner Lindzey of the Social Science Research Council summarize an attitude that applies to all three reports: "The Report's projections and recommendations show how much still needs to be done—and how a beginning can be made toward doing it . . . before the behavioral and social sciences will be able to respond adequately to the great need of a modern society to understand human behavior" (Behavioral and Social Sciences Survey, 1969:iii).

We believe that Carol Weiss has captured the general mood of sociologists today about the status of efforts to utilize sociology for national policy when she writes: ". . . the use of research in government decision-making is a complex and difficult matter. We still have much to learn about how to improve the process. Our collective interim assessment appears to lead us neither to pollyanna expectations that improvements are simple to specify and introduce nor to gloom-and-doom judgments about the hopelessness of it all. There is work to be done to clarify the ways in which social research can contribute more effectively to policy" (C. Weiss, 1976a:223).

---

*A fourth study group sponsored by the National Research Council has issued a similar report too late for us to review here. See *Knowledge and Policy: The Uncertain Connection* (1978).

CONCLUSIONS

This analysis provides us with a somewhat clearer picture of the impact that sociology has had on national domestic policy. It can be summarized in three points: First, a great deal of sociological research done for application carries *no discernible policy implications of any kind;* second, in instances where it does, sociology has served as the basis for formulating policy recommendations, less often the basis for enacted policy; and third, most of the recommendations for policy in which sociology has played a role were rejected by policy-making bodies of government as *impractical or politically unfeasible.* These conclusions pose a major challenge to sociology, as they indicate clearly that most applied, policy-relevant work that is being done in sociology today, or at least the part of it that concerns national domestic policy, has not been very effective. Clearly, something needs to be done. Yet, before we can hope to improve this situation we need to have a viable and convincing diagnosis of what the difficulty is. Our purpose is to attempt to supply one.

As we turn to this task, there is a further point our readers may wish to bear in mind as they evaluate the analysis we present. It may occur to some to ask why sociologists should care at all whether their research and writing are pertinent to the great domestic issues of our day. What difference does it make to us or anyone else if what we produce is relevant or not relevant to public policy? The question is legitimate, and how one answers it goes to the heart of questions about the discipline's reasons for being and the basis upon which society's support for it is justified. However one may be inclined to answer these questions, one point should be kept in mind, expressed well by David Truman, who writes:

> . . . an art or a science, if it is to be supported and not merely tolerated by a society, also must be, or give prospect of being, pleasing and instructive or useful. Since the social scientist brings pleasure to few beyond our own ranks and since our instructiveness is frequently limited . . . by the propensity for every man to be his own social scientist, we can scarcely afford to ignore the requirement of usefulness (Truman, 1968b:508).

NOTES

1. For additional data on this point, see House of Representatives (1967:I, 129, 328) and Biderman and Crawford (1968:41).
2. Lazarsfeld et al. make the same point in their book, *An Introduction to Applied Sociology* (1975). See especially pages 98–100.

3. For a discussion of the role that applied research institutes have played in bringing sociological knowledge to bear on social problems, see Horowitz and Katz (1975:51–87).
4. For one example of this, see Gouldner (1970:vii).
5. For example, Carol Weiss states, "The prevalent tone is that social science research is neglected by policy-makers . . .[and that] there is sometimes the suggestion that the neglect is occasioned by the stupidity or the self-servingness of decision-makers or, at the very least, their tendency to be distracted by the dailiness of their own concerns" (C. Weiss, 1976a:221). Janet Weiss writes, "In the past few years social scientists and government policy-makers have shared a common disappointment. Social science research has not contributed to social policy-making in as dramatic or effective way as they had hoped" (J. Weiss, 1976:234). See also, Alexander (1972:132–148).

2

The Disciplinary Perspective in Applied Sociology

We begin with sociology. In this book we shall make the argument that a main source of the present difficulty with applied sociology is that attempts to make sociology relevant to policy are conceived and executed with disciplinary, and not with policy concerns in mind. This chapter is a prelude to presentation of this argument. In it we will try to show that most applied, policy-relevant work in sociology today is disciplinary in its focus. The implications of this fact will then be explored later.

We find the disciplinary focus of applied sociology all-pervasive. It is reflected everywhere—in its basic assumptions about work for application, in its concepts, in the frameworks it uses, in the procedures it follows, in the way it organizes itself to do it, and so on. One can therefore turn to any aspect of applied sociology and view it. To demonstrate and exemplify the disciplinary focus inherent in *all* aspects of applied sociology would be a gigantic task requiring a book all by itself. To make our point, a more modest undertaking will suffice. We will try to establish the veracity of our claim through analysis of the ways in which sociologists have dealt with just *three* of the myriad issues encompassing the field. The *first* concerns the question of how sociologists believe that sociological theories, concepts, perspectives and methods can be used for policy. The *second* issue concerns sociologists' ideas about the procedures to be followed in realizing these proposed uses. And, the *third* concerns their ideas about why the results of so much applied, policy-relevant research have been so disappointing and what steps need to be taken to correct this situation. These issues lie squarely at the heart of applied, policy-relevant work today. By studying how sociologists have thought about them we hope to be able to see clearly the fundamental conceptualizations around which the entire activity is organized.

For information about these topics, we turn to books and essays that sociologists and others have written about actual and possible applications of sociology to policy. Though we have studied this literature extensively, no effort will be made here to review it in its entirety. Instead we will deal with it summarily and illustratively while focusing on its main themes. And, as in the previous chapter, since so much of this literature deals with the presumed applications of sociology to federal policy relating to national domestic problems, much of our discussion in this chapter deals with this particular policy sphere.

The thesis we will expound is that when sociologists think about how sociology might be used for policy, when they try to adopt these uses to particular problems and when they consider how to do a better job of it, there is a tendency to begin, not with policy, but with sociology. Turning first toward the discipline for guidance, sociologists ask: What knowledge do we sociologists have about the problems that policy-makers are addressing? Given what we know how to do, what can we realistically hope to learn about these problems through programs of research and study? Which of our theoretical perspectives and concepts, and techniques of empirical investigation might fruitfully be applied to these problems to provide new insights into them or to produce new information about them? And so on. These questions, of course, are entirely appropriate. It is important to understand, however, that in the process of doing work for application, *when* they are asked has implications that crucially effect *how* that process operates. By asking disciplinary questions first, and policy questions not at all or later, our most basic ideas about the process of doing work for application acquire a structure which then shapes our subsequent thinking and actions. And, because the discipline is the cornerstone of this structure, most of our ideas about work for application derive from and reflect it. In fact, in most cases, if concerns about policy arise at all, they do so only after research work has been completed, at which point results and insights garnered from our studies are culled for possible implications they may have for program development and enactment.

This chapter explains the basis of this thesis. It consists of three sections corresponding to the three issues we address. The first section examines sociologists' ideas about uses of sociology for policy. The second examines the notions sociologists hold about procedures in applied research; and in the third we consider what steps the field of sociology recommends to be taken to improve the effectiveness of these uses and procedures.

USES OF SOCIOLOGY FOR POLICY

Sociologists and other persons have commented extensively about ways in which sociology can be used for policy.[1] Sociological knowledge, theory and methods of empirical investigation are claimed to be useful in making and implementing policy in five ways: (1) *to enlighten* policy-making bodies about societal conditions; (2) *to contribute substantive ideas* toward deliberations about specific policy questions; (3) *to supply information* which may be.helpful to policy-makers in coming to decisions about particular problems; (4) *to evaluate* programs that have been enacted; and (5) *to advance understanding* about policy as a social process.

Using Sociology to Enlighten

Nathan Glazer has pointed out that sociologists are preoccupied with unveiling illusions that deceive no one (Glazer, 1967:76). Not all sociologists involved in trying to bring disciplinary knowledge to bear on social policy agree. Many of them have pointed out that an important role sociology can play in public affairs is to dispel myths and illusions upon which existing or contemplated policies are sometimes based. They note, for example, that through research and writing by sociologists in a host of areas of national life—education, work, law, medicine and public affairs among them—sociological research has uncovered the existence of disparities between beliefs and reality. Often cited in this connection is sociological research on inequality— its extent and its social and psychological costs—which, it is claimed, has helped to dispel the illusion that ours is a free and open society where all persons have equal access to opportunities for success.

In what way, exactly, is such research said to contribute to policy? It is claimed that one effect of enlightening people is to change attitudes and ways of thinking held by policy-makers, politicians and the general public about social conditions in our society, which structure current policy discussions. In this sense sociological knowledge is said to contribute to policy by disabusing people of erroneous ideas that they may have about societal conditions; by disclosing complexity where others may see only simplicity; by revealing irony about matters that others view in terms of simple cause and effect; by uncovering latent functions and unanticipated consequences of established practices; and, in general, by helping policy-makers to comprehend better the inner workings of society and its main institutions. In these and other ways sociologists feel that they can help to enlighten policy-makers and the groups on whose support they depend, ensuring that leaders of our society appreciate the complicated, multifaceted character of the social conditions with which they must deal. Thus, to return to the example of research on inequality, the claimed effect of dispelling illusions about equality of opportunity and informing public officials and others about the consequences of inequality, has been to create among legislators and the public generally a greater awareness of the need for programs to improve educational and other opportunities for minorities than would otherwise have existed.

Few who have written on the subject of applied sociology doubt the value of sociology in this regard, nor do many question that general enlightenment can be a significant practical use of sociology. One staunch advocate of this view is Morris Janowitz (Janowitz, 1972) who believes that the work of sociologists involved in policy-relevant research should be guided by what he terms an "enlightened model." This model, he explains, ". . . assumes the overriding importance of the social context, and focuses on developing various types of knowledge that can be utilized by policy-makers and professions. While it seeks specific answers, its emphasis is on creating the intellectual conditions for problem solving. Its goal is a contribution to institution building" (Janowitz; 1972: 5). When this model is followed, the impact of sociology on social policy is indirect, yet, Janowitz feels, it can be potentially quite pervasive. He writes: "The impact is not to be measured and judged in terms of specific assignments and specific recommendations, but in the broader intellectual climate it seeks to engender" (Janowitz, 1972: 3).

While Janowitz is very nearly alone in advancing the view that this is the *only* legitimate role sociology can play in social policy he is but one of many social scientists who regard enlightenment as one of the contributions that sociology can make to public affairs. For example, Herbert Gans, Herbert Kelman, Elizabeth Crawford, Klaus Lompe, Yehezkel Dror and Don Price, to cite just a few, have all commented extensively on this as a possible use of sociology in public affairs.[2]

Enlightenment of policy-making bodies through exposure to sociology presumably takes different forms; two in particular are regularly mentioned. The first form entails using sociology to *clarify and examine critically assumptions* upon which policy decisions are based. Lane's essay on the subject illustrates this view. He states that social science policy analysis should force "the examination and sometimes the rejection of some of our cherished assumptions" (Lane, 1972: 83). Merton and Devereux concur, claiming that "the function of social research . . . is not simply to supply information useful in remedying problems already known . . . [but] also to make the problems known" (Merton and Devereux, 1964: 21). The second form of enlightenment entails the use of disciplinary knowledge to help policy-makers *identify alternative ways for dealing with problems*. Etzioni's definition of policy research illustrates this point of view. It is an enterprise, he writes, "concerned with mapping alternative approaches and with specifying potential differences in the intent, effect and cost of various programs" (Etzioni, 1971: 8).[3]

These quotations, drawn selectively from the large literature about applied, policy-relevant sociology, impart the basic tenor of sociologists' thinking about the use of disciplinary knowledge to educate policy-makers, to heighten their awareness of complexity and alternatives, and generally to enlighten them so that they understand better the operation of aspects of national life relevant to policy concerns.

Carol Weiss effectively captures the way in which sociology can have its effect in this mode. She writes: "Through circuitous routes and over time, it enters the discourse of informed publics. It may surface in intellectual journals and magazines of opinion, in media coverage, through teaching in university departments and professional schools, in seminars sponsored by professional organizations and elite clubs. In time, as research provides new form, shape and direction to a public issue, it can have effects on the climate of opinion. The once-accepted assumptions are challenged, the once far-out conclusions become familiar. In the doing, research broadens the range of acceptable ideas" (C. Weiss, 1976b: 228).[4]

No one can dispute that sociological knowledge, properly presented, can powerfully illuminate societal conditions, and, therefore, it is not unreasonable to suppose that those exposed to it might become more enlightened. With this we have no basic quarrel. However, we wish to note that this claimed use of sociology derives entirely from what sociologists believe they know about societal conditions: it says nothing about policy. Specifically, it neglects to address the crucial problem of what enlightened people are to do with their new found wisdom; and how, indeed whether, they can use it at all in coming to decisions about policy. Our point here is not that enlightenment can never be a consequential use of sociology. Rather it is that this way of using sociology is not suggested by considerations about how policy is made so much as it is by what sociologists feel they do or do not know about the conditions of life in our society that require policy decisions. It is for this reason that we say that this use of sociology reflects disciplinary and not policy concerns. As we shall see, the same thing is true of other suggested uses of sociology as well.

Contributing Substantive Ideas

A second proposed use of sociology is more specific. It entails using ideas and insights garnered from disciplinary theories, concepts and perspectives to assist in devising specific programs of social action to help solve or ameliorate undesired social conditions. Termed "social engineering" by some,[5] it involves the use of sociology for such purposes as helping to design optimal learning environments, plan urban settings, or to devise institutional programs conducive to rehabilitation and the welfare of those living in them, or to conceive and design alternatives to existing social service programs and so on. Here the sociologist is described as drawing on specific bodies of knowledge and techniques of social research to help policy-makers resolve basic and technical problems associated with the development and implementation of social policy.

Although accurate data are not available regarding the extent to which different kinds of uses of sociology for policy are attempted, our impression is that a great deal of what is thought of as applied sociology today involves attempts by sociologists to use disciplinary knowledge in this way.[6] Certainly, most people writing about applied sociology mention it. One of them is Herbert Kelman who states the opinion that one of the most important uses of sociology is in research designed to facilitate the implementation of new policies and action programs (Kelman, 1972: 198); another is Elizabeth Crawford, who mentions the widespread use of sociology "for engaging in technical problem solving" (Crawford, 1971: 9); and a third is Herbert Gans who identifies as a main purpose of policy-oriented sociology, that of providing the policy-designer with "specific research" conducted for the purpose of providing detailed data on specific substantive policy fields" (Gans, 1971: 22). Such research, he adds, should be based on "highly specific theories and concepts which can whenever possible analyze the concrete groups, organizations and institutions with which the policy-designer must deal" (Gans, 1971: 4). A final example comes from Miller and Reissman who imply this same point of view when they write that ". . . the professionals' most significant contribution is likely to be in the application of his skills—analytic, research, conceptualization—to the problem of social change" (Miller and Reissman, 1968: 72).[7]

Not everyone agrees that sociology can be used in this way. For example, in his book, *Maximum Feasible Misunderstanding,* Daniel Moynihan argues that attempts to use sociology in this fashion are based upon what he regards as the discipline's greatest weakness. He believes that social science is "at its weakest, at its worst" when asked to provide theories of individual or social behavior "which raise the possibility, by controlling certain inputs, of bringing about mass behavioral changes" simply because "no such knowledge now exists. . . . Evidence is fragmented, contradictory, incomplete" (Moynihan,

1969: 191)* Morris Janowitz also rejects this approach as invalid, but
for a different reason. He argues that sociology is incapable of producing definitive answers on which policy practices can reasonably be
based because sociology is merely one aspect of the social sciences,
and the social sciences in turn are only one type of knowledge that is
required for making policy decisions (Janowitz, 1972: 4). He therefore
feels that it is arrogant of the sociologist to suppose that he or she
alone can have any demonstrable or decisive impact on policy.
Moreover, he feels that sociology does not possess the kind of knowledge and information that is needed to help policy-makers design
social policy and he doubts seriously that it ever will (Janowitz,
1972: 3).[8]

These views notwithstanding, a dominant position in the discipline
is that sociology has important substantive contributions to make to
policy. The precise manner in which sociological knowledge is supposed to be fed into the policy process, and, indeed, the bodies of
disciplinary knowledge that may be useful in this activity vary of
course from problem to problem, but at the core of all such endeavors
is the assumption that the policy-making process can be aided and
facilitated by incorporating sociological ideas and methods into it. On
this point, agreement is fairly widespread.

This form of use of sociology is closer to policy than the first in the
sense that it entails efforts to bring particular bodies of sociological
ideas and methods directly to bear on specific policy problems. Yet,
like the first, it too reflects concerns that are primarily disciplinary in
nature. We say this because the form of use is suggested more by
what sociologists feel they know about problems than by what
policy-makers need to know to make policies. That is, by now sociologists have studied enough about conditions in our society to be able
to claim legitimately that we know things about them that are not
widely known by others. When these conditions, therefore, become
targets of policy deliberations there is a natural tendency for the sociologist to want to bring this special knowledge to the attention of
those responsible for making policy decisions. What this amounts to
in practice is little more than offering this knowledge up to policy-
makers for their consideration, pretty much leaving it to them to
discover how, or if, it can be used for policy (or, as Carol Weiss puts

*Moynihan's view of sociology's role in public affairs is discussed elsewhere in this
chapter.

it: "Researchers generally assume that somewhere out there, there is a potential use for their studies" (C. Weiss, 1976b: 226). Our point is that the main impetus behind this use of sociology comes primarily from the realization that as a discipline we know certain things about societal conditions. It does not derive from a particularly deep appreciation for what policy is, how it is done, and what kinds of information, packaged in what ways, is potentially adaptable for policy purposes.

Supplying Information

A third use of sociology is to supply information. Because it is closely akin to the second it can be dealt with briefly. It involves the use of techniques of empirical investigation that sociologists use in disciplinary research to gather information about the problems and conditions for which policies must be made. The point of this is clear enough; it is to provide the policy-maker with basic descriptive information and data about specific conditions.

This particular use of sociology has often been cited. A main exponent of it is James Coleman, who, in an essay, "Policy Research in the Social Sciences," argues that the *main* contribution of sociology lies in the use of its methods of empirical research. He states, "The goal [of sociology in policy] is . . . to provide an information base for social actions." (Coleman, 1972: 2). Elizabeth Crawford's review of applied social science research in government indicates that this use of sociology not only is widespread today, but that providing techniques for the collection of societal data has been an important traditional role played by sociology as well (Crawford, 1971: 9). Janowitz also cites as one of the main uses of sociology advocated by proponents of social engineering: "collecting descriptive data and charting trends" (Janowitz, 1972: 4).[9]

A widely publicized example of this use of sociology in recent times is the attempt to institutionalize collection of data about various conditions in American society and to publish these annually as *Social Indicators* (Office of Management and Budget, 1974). The intention here is to provide measures of important aspects of American life such as population growth, health, public safety, education, employment, income, housing, leisure, recreation and so on (Horowitz and Katz, 1975: 32).

This use of sociology, like others we have mentioned, derives primarily from considerations about what sociology as a discipline is capable of doing. Because of our long empirical tradition, it is a fact that sociologists know better than most how to gather information accurately and efficiently, and this fact has led us to suggest it as a possible use of sociology for policy. We do not doubt this as a potentially fruitful application of sociological skills to policy. The point we are making is that in recommending it, we sociologists have betrayed an insensitivity to policy concerns by paying so little attention to the question of what policy-making bodies are to do with the information supplied to them by our research.

Our point is illustrated by Caplan's study of knowledge utilization among federal executives. He reports that nine out of ten respondents agreed that an index of social well-being (i.e., social indicators) was a good idea, and "that it represented a major opportunity for social science to contribute significantly to policy formulation" (Caplan, 1976: 231–232). Yet, when pressed to explain what use might be made of social indicators data, he found the responses so heterogeneous and obscure as to be uncodable. He writes, "Social indicators research would probably proceed more efficiently and its potential for policy use increased greatly, if the collection of data were based upon some previously agreed upon notion of what purposes were to be served by such indicators. But, instead, we witness a widespread and often desultory collection of data conducted with the implicit hope that, somehow, from this pragmatic but goalless effort, there will evolve some notions about what is the good life and how responsible government may help to achieve it." (Caplan, 1976: 232).

The Use of Sociological Method to Evaluate

A fourth proposed use of sociology in social policy is to employ methods of sociological research to evaluate social action programs and social policies. Daniel Moynihan is a strong advocate of this idea. He states, "The role of social science [in public affairs] lies not in the formation of social policy, but in the measurement of its results . . . . All that is needed [and all that social science can supply] is a rough, but hopefully constantly refined, set of understandings as to what is associated with what" (Moynihan, 1969: 193–194). Others who also support evaluation as a proper use of sociology in policy-related work include Herbert Kelman (1972), Harold Orlans (1968), Charles Glock (1961), Howard Freeman (1963), Yehezkel Dror (1971a) and Klaus Lompe (Lompe, 1968).[10]

This use of social research in policy analysis is by now so common that an entire field of specialization has developed about methods and procedures for conducting evaluation research. Books have been written on this subject (i.e., C. Weiss, 1972; Campbell, 1972); it has been the focus of an entire program area at Russell Sage Foundation, which sponsored two major projects—the evaluation of the children's television show, Sesame Street (Cook *et al.*, 1975) and the New Jersey—Pennsylvania Negative Income Tax Experiment (Rossi and Lyall, 1976). Evaluation research has become routine in a variety of areas, including education, corrections, social services, government, medicine, law, public health, law enforcement and so on.[11]

Until recently, most evaluation research has been of one type. Programmatic activities are proposed and implemented; only after they have been in effect for some time do sociologists try to assess their effectiveness in producing the desired results. Recently there has developed a growing interest in modifying this sequence to evaluate proposed courses of social action or social policy before they are adopted more widely on a national or regional basis (Campbell, 1969, 1972). This research has taken the form of social experiments. Prominent examples are the negative income tax studies in New Jersey and Pennsylvania (Watts, 1969: 463—472), in Gary, Indiana, and in Seattle, Washington (Horowitz and Katz, 1975: 139—142). Other experiments have been proposed in the fields of health care, housing and child care to estimate costs of national programs and to discover and correct problems before programs become widely implemented or formally institutionalized.

As with most other uses of sociological knowledge, here too there is disagreement about the extent to which evaluation research can generate information about social programs quickly enough and accurately enough to be useful to policy-making bodies. Yet, the aim of such research seems clear, i.e., to help improve the effectiveness of ongoing social programs by assessing the impact they have on the problems they were established to solve.

On the face of it, evaluation research would seem to be more directly tied to programmatic policy-related activities than are the other types of uses of sociology that we have reviewed, and therefore that it would be inaccurate for us to suggest that this particular application of sociology is subject to the same criticisms as the others. This impression is misleading, however, for on closer examination it appears that this use of sociology also has roots in the disciplinary perspective, albeit of a somewhat different sort. We hasten to add that its links to the discipline are not unique for they are also tied to other types of applications we have discussed; it is simply that they are more apparent in this particular instance than in others. The disciplinary source of evaluation research is this: in order for results of evaluation research to be at all useful it is essential for policy-makers to derive and execute policy programs in a particular way, i.e., according to a method that grants a role for rational evaluation to occur and to be heeded. As we will show in Chapter 3, this method of policy-making required for evaluation to be a meaningful activity comes largely from sociology, not from the real world of political decision-making. It is in this sense that evaluation research as a possible use of sociology derives from the discipline.

The Use of Sociology to Study Policy

The avowed intention of each use of sociology described so far is to help formulate, implement, evaluate and modify social policy. These are the predominant but not the only uses to which sociologists proclaim that disciplinary knowledge may be put. Many believe that sociology may be used to study social policy as a practical activity, both to understand it and to improve and perfect it. The goal here is not to bring sociological knowledge to bear on a particular substantive policy issue; rather, it is to use the methods and knowledge of sociology to understand policy-making as a social process. As such, the use is primarily disciplinary in orientation. We say this because in each approach described up to now social policy has been the independent variable and sociological knowledge and methods of research-dependent variables. In this approach, in contrast, social policy is the dependent variable (Lane, 1972: 677—715; Ranney, 1968: 14). The goal is to achieve an understanding of social policy that will permit the development of a theory of social policy. With this it is thought that policy-makers will be able to perfect processes governing the activities in which they engage, and not entirely incidentally, social scientists will perhaps be able to develop better procedures for adapting their knowledge to this process.

This use of sociology is exemplified in a work by Herbert Gans who describes a basic aim of applied sociology as the conduct of research that "deals with general issues such as the nature of social policy, the role of the policy designer in various institutional contexts, the relationship between policy and the ongoing social-political process, (and) the nature and problems of intervention in that process" (Gans, 1971: 29—30) and Coleman, who makes the same point when he stresses the need to develop "a theory of policies" in the sense of an understanding of important differences between types of policies as independent, dependent or intervening contexts (Coleman, 1972: 17).

Although other sociologists have recognized the importance of developing theories about social policy, the bulk of discussion of this topic appears in the literature of policy science. Accepted definitions of policy science stress understanding policy-making. Yehezkel Dror, for example, describes the purpose of policy science as "the improvement of policy-making" through research aimed at understanding it (Dror, 1971b: 3). In the words of Harold Lasswell, who is generally recognized as the modern-day founder of policy science, "Policy science is concerned with knowledge of and in the decision process of the public and civic order" (Lasswell, 1971: vii). Lewis Froman also offers a description of this discipline: "It is . . . an effort to find what particular things are associated with what particular policies for the purpose of developing theoretically interesting propositions about differences in public policies and variables which are related to these differences" (Froman, 1967: 95).

Thus, the aims of policy science are in harmony with the instrumental use of sociology to understand policy-making. Most policy scientists (and many sociologists) agree on a necessary starting point for the realization of these aims: the development of categorical schemes to distinguish types of policy. Lewis Froman explains:

> If we are to develop a theory of public policy which embraces more than one policy area, what is needed is a set of categories which distinguish in a meaningful way, certain policies from other policies. The major question to be answered in policy theory research is: Do different kinds of policy have associated with them different kinds of "environmental" variables in such a way that we can say something about how certain policies are related to other phenomena (Froman, 1967: 95).

Many different categorical schemes of the sort Froman calls for have been proposed to classify social policies.[12] These classification schemes are proposed on the assumption that the policy process will vary according to the type of policy involved. Whatever the usefulness of each of these categorization schemes, the goal of each is to better understand policy-making in order to perfect it. A leading policy scientist, Dror, summarizes the process of understanding and perfection, which he calls "abstract analysis":

> [It] involves deductive construction of a preferable model of the utilization of sociologists in policy-making, based on organization theory and decision sciences, on the one hand, and analysis of sociological knowledge, on the other hand; evaluation of the actual situation in policy-making agencies in terms of the preferable model; identification of the main barriers hindering approximation of preferability; and suggestions designed to overcome these barriers . . . so as to move reality toward the preferable model (Dror, 1971a: 141).

The goal is to improve on the technical aspects of the policy process itself by using the skills, the knowledge and the perspectives of sociology. The aim is not the development of substantive policies; the goal is the perfection of a science of policy-making.

A basic notion underlying the five proposed uses of sociology we have just cited is that sociologists will be responsible for providing sociological expertise and that policy-makers will be responsible for making policy; not all sociologists accept this division of labor. Some sociologists believe that attempts to apply disciplinary knowledge to substantive policy problems are doomed because policy-makers fail to understand what is added by the sociological perspective, or if understanding it, choose to ignore it. To achieve a greater impact on social policy, they have proposed that sociologists themselves move directly into policy positions to gain control of the policy-making machinery. Sociologists in decision-making positions would then combine disciplinary knowledge with responsibility for enacted programs of planned social action; such experience might also help them to better understand the problems of developing and implementing policy, and appraise more realistically the uses of sociology in policy-making.

A number of variations on this approach have been proposed. One, advocated by Herbert Kelman (among others), calls for increased efforts at action research, where social scientists directly participate in the development and implementation of action programs and help to determine the course of the program (Kelman, 1972: 198). In the case of the substantive use just described, the policy-maker or public administrator actually plans and initiates the policy, whereas Kelman suggests that sociologists themselves should participate in this function. Of course, this is exactly the approach that Myrdal recommends (Myrdal, 1968).

A more radical variant of this action approach to using sociology is proposed by Alvin Gouldner. Gouldner defines the role of radical sociology as helping "to overthrow the old order." He inveighs against the traditional uses of disciplinary knowledge and methods for policy purposes—i.e., enlightenment, evaluation, information and substantive contributions—dismissing all of them as instances of collaboration of the social scientist with "the present Welfare—Warfare State" (Gouldner, 1970: vii). He claims that sociologists have become part of the liberal establishment. Such a sociologist he calls a "liberal technologue" who "produces information and theories that serve to bind the poor and the working-classes both to the state apparatus and to the political machinery of the Democratic Party" (Gouldner, 1970: 500).[13]

These are examples of some of the main ways in which sociologists believe that sociology can be used for policy. Clearly, differences of opinion exist about which of these are appropriate or possible uses of sociology, what role the sociologist ought to play in bringing them about, and so on. Yet, underlying this discussion is the strong tendency to define sociology's place in policy largely in terms of what sociologists know and can do but, at the same time, not considering what policy is and what it requires. This tendency to begin with sociology is also apparent in the sociologists' treatment of another key aspect of applied, policy-relevant work, i.e., the procedures followed in executing applied research.

PROCEDURES FOR DOING APPLIED, POLICY-RELEVANT RESEARCH

How do sociologists execute policy research on domestic problems that they do for the government? Unfortunately, explicit answers to this question are seldom presented in the literature of applied sociology. Consequently, to analyze this topic we must rely on surmise and impressions one gains from studying sociological research done for application. Such impressions can be gleaned from discussions about a variety of topics including such things as the training of sociologists for applied work, the selection of sites within which to do policy-relevant research, the selection of sociologists for executing this research, and analysis of examples of "good" and "bad" policy research. At times rather clear impressions can be gained about how sociologists conceptualize and execute policy-relevant research; at other times the impressions one gets are blurred and imprecise. For this reason, we must approach a discussion of this topic in a tentative, gingerly fashion, recognizing that few conclusive statements about it are possible.

The actual research styles adopted by sociologists who do policy-relevant work for the government in applied work are every bit as varied as those followed by persons doing routine disciplinary research.[14] Different orientations to sociology entail somewhat different styles of research and different procedures—even different audiences of consumers. Important as these differences are, running through them are certain basic commonalities regarding basic criteria for judging the value of the research and for evaluating the worth of procedures that are adopted.

The paths that lead sociologists to become involved in such policy-relevant research are many. Sociologists are attracted to do research in applied areas for many reasons—among them personal interest, a concern about pressing social issues, career opportunities and money—and are drawn into such work in a variety of ways. Yet, once a problem for study is decided on, the procedures that are followed thereafter are basically similar. The task of developing hypotheses and research designs to test them, as well as those involving questionnaire development, data processing and analysis are almost always guided by disciplinary standards, interests, training and investigative procedures. Thus, after the question for research is settled on, one turns to the literature of theory and past research for guidelines in developing a concrete plan of research. Sociological theories, concepts and methods of research are, so to speak, "brought to bear" on the issue or issues of concern. Policy considerations are kept in mind, of course, but usually this means only that the questions that the policy researcher has decided to study in the first place are in some way related to policy problems. As a rule, it is only after the study is done and results have been compiled that one then confronts directly the question of the policy relevance in the research findings. Thus, in reality what brands many studies as "policy-relevant" or "applied" is *not the approach to research but the choice of the field and problem for study.* Much of the research done by sociologists for purposes of governmental policy is, in fact, nothing more than conventional sociological research on practical problems in fields of applied work. The purpose of this research is to advance knowledge about social aspects of problems and practices in these areas. The hope is that if sociologists and other social scientists succeed in furthering basic sociological understanding of the problem, public officials will then be able to use this understanding to contrive better social policies to deal with them.

Carol Weiss is correct when she states that, "University researchers are used to choosing their own problems on grounds that derive from the state of their discipline and its theoretical development. They tend to select problems that fit the methods that they know and prefer. They like to take the time to do responsible research, win the plaudits of their colleagues, and gain academic records through publications in prestige journals" (C. Weiss, 1976a: 224).

To this style of research, Archibald has given the label "academically-oriented" applied social science. Her description of it parallels our own in many ways. She writes:

> Such an expert may choose his problem *area* in terms of his applied interest, but his choice of hypotheses and design is determined more by his disciplinary interests than by demands of any real-world problem. . . . [He] does not directly grab hold of a particular policy problem and make it his central focus (Archibald, 1970: 8).

Archibald explains that while the sociologist may genuinely want to contribute to policy formation, he or she sees policy-makers as only one of several audiences. The academically-oriented sociologist still regards disciplinary colleagues or other scientists as the principal audience (Archibald, 1970: 11).

> He feels that social scientists have *some* responsibility to disseminate their findings—either that this is one fraction of each social scientist's responsibility, or that some portion of the whole social science community should take on this responsibility . . . . [The] kinds of data he collects, or the design or method of his research; for these he turns to the criteria of his discipline (Archibald, 1970: 12).

Archibald further explains that the "academic" social scientist sharply distinguishes his research from his concern for policy-relevance.

> While doing research, his orientation is that of the pure scientist. When the research is completed, his policy interest re-enters and he becomes concerned about communicating his findings to decision makers. He assumes that his findings can be *made* relevant, not that they *are* relevant, and that the problem is one of figuring out how best to communicate them to policy-makers (Archibald, 1970: 12).

Thus, the academic expert tends to be vague about who the client is, how to get material to the client and the expert's effect on the client.

The preference for this disciplinary-type of orientation toward applied, policy-relevant work in sociology is greatly reinforced by the manner in which sociologists are trained. No detailed study of the education and training of sociologists in America today is necessary to realize that nearly all of them are trained in university-based academic social science departments and that their education is heavily oriented to the study of disciplinary issues. A principal aim of American graduate education in sociology, of course, has been to train scholars for the job of advancing basic disciplinary knowledge and understanding of human society through careers involving scholarship, teaching and research. While it may not be assumed that all graduate students in sociology work exclusively in areas related to traditional disciplinary concerns (after all, some graduate departments promote and encourage students to become involved in research on issues of immediate social relevance), much of their training is designed to provide them with the skills needed to do competent disciplinary work. Ideally, if graduate programs are effective, this training will help to prepare the student for a career of teaching and research in an academic institution and to equip him to do the kind of scholarship suitable for publication in academic journals. It is assumed that he will join disciplinary assocations and that he will come to think of others in his field as a primary reference group.

Of course, there are graduate training programs in which policy-relevant research is encouraged. Yet, even here, the worth of such work is typically judged by conventional standards of disciplinary excellence. Gouldner expressed the dominant theme in this regard, which is that anyone who elects to do policy research must have his work pass muster *first* before an audience of professional disciplinary-oriented colleagues who will consider it in terms of its academic worth before passing it to an audience of policy-makers to evaluate and use it (Gouldner, 1957: 93). Howard Freeman agrees: "The position adopted by the social research field is that the major consideration in assessing the worth of studies, whether basic or applied, are theoretical relevance and methodological competence" (Freeman, 1963: 145).

To summarize, most applied research studies done today employ the methodologies and procedures of academic sociological research studies. Their aim is to advance basic knowledge about social aspects of problems in specific policy areas through research methods that are borrowed from the academic wing of the discipline. Indeed, much of this research is beamed more toward other academics than to those who can act to change policy; moreover, concern about the impact of specific findings on policy deliberations is characteristically secondary in the researcher's mind. It is for this reason that we claim a disciplinary focus in the execution of applied, policy-relevant work.

There is another aspect to this topic that deserves special emphasis. The procedures we have described imply a basic division of labor between the sociologist and the policy-maker and a set of assumptions about how the two will contribute to the overall process of policy-making. According to this conception, sociologists are to provide scientific understanding and technical expertise that policy-makers will then use to devise programs for ameliorating or regulating troublesome social conditions. But this division of labor depends critically on the veracity of a single assumption. The assumption is that the theory and method of sociology, when applied to the study of society and its institutions, will result in the type of information and knowledge about them that can be an effective basis for developing long-range programs of planned social change. In short, they are based on precisely the same assumption on which many proposals for enhancing sociology's relevance for policy are based.

Sociologists have not always examined this assumption carefully. A fair summary of the dominant view is that if the researcher takes note of a few special problems of policy-relevant research, he may then conduct his research according to rigorous disciplinary standards and expect that his work will be relevant to policy. Yet, the procedures that we have described for doing this research make no sense unless the assumption is made that the kind of knowledge that results from applying disciplinary theory and research methods to social problems is an appropriate basis for formulating social policies. It must be assumed that any significant addition to the store of sociological knowledge, if it is based on reliable social research, will yield insights that will be useful to policy makers in such ways as enabling them to understand their alternatives more clearly, to formulate better or more rational policies or to evaluate consequences of their decision-making more clearly. Unless this assumption is granted, the neatly coordinated division of labor between sociologists and policy-makers that is envisioned makes little sense.

Many sociologists acknowledge the existence of differences between "pure" and "applied" research, yet few of them regard these differences as important. That is, the differences, though acknowledged as real, do not render the procedures of pure research inappropriate for applied purposes. It deserves to be stressed that this belief is highly serviceable to the profession. It has enabled sociologists to do applied research on socially relevant issues by legitimating for this purpose the only procedures they know how to use, i.e., those which govern research of an academic sort. It also permits academics in sociology departments to maintain strong ties with "the real world" while producing research that their academic colleagues regard as acceptable and respectable. More than this, it provides a justification for requesting public money to support programs of basic disciplinary research and training. If the belief is justified, that is, if following the conventional disciplinary research procedures does provide studies, the results of which ultimately are useful in helping to resolve or ameliorate unwelcome social conditions, then we are justified in continuing to do *what we have been doing*. But, if it is found that the qualities which a body of knowledge must possess to be useful for policy purposes are not the ones yielded by disciplinary theories and research procedures, or, if the obstacles to translating the former into the latter are more intractable than we suppose, then substantial portions of the knowledge we now possess about these social conditions in our society that policy-making bodies are seeking to regulate may simply be irrelevant from a practical point of view. Therefore, conducting more so-called policy-relevant research in accordance with these procedures may simply lead to more irrelevant knowledge. Moreover, if this is so, then many of the proposals that have been made for increasing sociology's relevance to policy (to be reviewed soon) by merely strengthening the theory and method of the discipline are suspect, for it is possible and likely that more knowledge may not necessarily result in more *useful* knowledge.

The fact that we have chosen to raise these issues suggests the conclusions that we have reached after considering these matters. These conclusions are that the relationships of pure and applied research are complex and problem ridden; that in many cases disciplinary theory and research procedures result in kinds of knowledge about the world that do not easily fit with efforts to change it; and that this fact helps to explain why a great deal of the applied research done in sociology today carries no evident implications for social policy. Indeed, we reject as misleading the notion put forth by some that most pure research has some practical utility and that most applied research has interesting theoretical implications.*

In conclusion, we see that sociologists' ideas about how to use sociology for policy derive from the same disciplinary perspective informing their notions about ways of using sociology for policy. Both begin and both end with sociology, gaining their structure from disciplinary concerns. This being the case, it should not be surprising to learn that sociologists also turn to the discipline when considering how to do better what they are trying to do.

INCREASING THE USEFULNESS OF SOCIOLOGY FOR POLICY

In Chapter 1 we reviewed the status of efforts to apply sociology to policy, coming to the conclusion that applied studies seldom result in policy recommendations of any kind and that when they do, these recommendations are usually rejected by policy-making bodies of government as impractical, unrealistic or politically unfeasible. Sociologists have recognized this fact and it has prompted some to consider why this should be so and what steps might be taken to improve the relevance of sociolgy to policy. Numerous proposals have been made. Basically they entail two approaches to the issue. One seeks to strengthen the discipline—the other, to familiarize sociologists with how policy is made. Both proposals, especially the first one, reflect the disciplinary bias of which we have spoken—a fact which becomes evident the moment we look at what is being recommended.

---

*In Appendix A we explain in detail the source of our disquiet about these assumptions.

Strengthening the Discipline

Many sociologists feel that although sociological knowledge about American society may eventually provide clues for ameliorating national domestic problems, these clues will not be clearly revealed until and unless more and better knowledge becomes available. This appears with great regularity in the literature on applied social science and is illustrated by the testimony given by sociologists and other social scientists who addressed the Subcommittee on Research and Technical Operations of the Committee on Government Operations. Presenters argued that the physical sciences became relevant and useful for policy purposes only after the basic or pure research in each field had been carried out. They therefore argued that one route to relevance in sociology is for the government to establish a series of National Research Institutes to do basic research in the social science disciplines and that funds be appropriated to support university-based programs of pure research. Congress, for example, was urged to create new foreign area study units; to consider funding long-term research programs for the study of such problems as concept formation, logical problem solving, thinking and decision-making; and to find ways to encourage the use of social statistics in the development of theories of social change and the prediction of future social trends (House of Representatives, 1967: I, 207). Precisely the same ideas are presented in the final report of the National Science Foundation sponsored study, *Knowledge into Action*, which recommends the creation of some 20 Social Problems Research Institutes, each to fund research on a different national social problem (National Science Foundation, 1969). In both reports the argument advanced is that sociology (and other social sciences) cannot be expected to come up with solutions to national problems unless given the time and resources to accomplish basic research. For this reason, government must grant sociology the necessary financial resources it needs to do extensive baic research on the problems and conditions of American society.

Related to this is the further suggestion that sociologists also work to develop better theories about society and human behavior, a suggestion that implies that another cause of the discipline's lack of impact on policy stems from the fact that its theories are weak, underdeveloped and inadequate. Many of the proposals made to the Congressional Subcommittee on Research and Technical Operations previously referred to plainly reflect this notion, as does the National Science Study, *Knowledge into Action*. Moreover, the idea has been advanced in other contexts by such persons as Robert Merton (Merton and Devereux, 1949), David Easton (Easton, 1972: 98−99), Herman Stein (Stein, 1968: xiv), Joseph Spengler (Spengler, 1969: 457), Albert Reiss (Reiss, 1970: 290), Harold Orlans (Orlans, 1968: 153) and Otto Larsen (Larsen, 1975: 17). All of them agree that sociological theory must be improved before sociology can expect to have a greater impact on public affairs. Each one, however, has tended to emphasize a different point. For example, Stein and Spengler stress the importance of strengthening sociological theory per se, while Merton and Easton have stressed the theoretical integration of social science discipline. Reiss and Larsen call for the development of a general theory of society that is policy-oriented, while Orlans urges social scientists to begin to piece together the fragments of theory and knowledge about social problems to achieve an interdisciplinary social science synthesis. Differences in emphasis notwithstanding, such proposals rest on the common assumption that development of a genuinely policy-relevant sociology depends on development of more powerful disciplinary theory.

Attention has been given to graduate training. It is suggested that while the development of sociological theory and conduct of basic research would be enhanced by an infusion of federal money into the discipline, other steps must be taken as well. Among these steps is the further support and development for programs of graduate training in sociology and related fields. This idea is prominently taken up in testimony presented to Congress, in which several sociologists suggested that the government should increase support for programs of graduate training. They claimed that in the long run such steps would greatly improve the relevance of sociology in policy-making. This suggestion has several forms. Robert Merton recommended that sociologists who are interested in applied work be given an education which is multidisciplinary so that transsocial science research teams can be established to work on specific problems (Merton and Lerner, 1951). David Truman agrees, suggesting that interdisciplinary social science commissions should be established that are capable of making the social sciences more effective in the formation of policy (Truman, 1968a: 510). Moreover, he would also require public administrators to undergo extensive social science training as well. Lucien Pye proposes that the quickest way to facilitate the translation of theory into practice in the social sciences is to train persons to function as social engineers (Pye, 1968: 260). Finally, Harold Orlans has called for more strenuous efforts not only to train better the sociologists who are already doing applied research, but also to attract competent people into policy research during their graduate education (Orlans, 1968: 153).

These proposals illustrate the kinds of steps that sociologists believe must be taken to strengthen the discipline if it is to function effectively in policy-making. The presumption seems to be that as knowledge about society increases, sociologists will be able to gain a better idea of how to deal with society's problems through policy prescriptions. But such proposals entail an implicit diagnosis of the disciplines' relatively insignificant impact on policy. According to this diagnosis, it is the disciplines' immaturity and the inadequacy of its knowledge that are primarily responsible for this lack of impact. The implicit assertion is that our effect on policy has not been great because we do not have the knowledge that is necessary to enable us to propose meaningful policy initiatives to deal with social problems. There is the further presumption that as more knowledge about society and its institutions is gathered, we will be able to gain a clearer idea of how to deal with these problems through policy initiatives—thereby enhancing our impact on policy. This diagnosis betrays the strong inclination we have seen elsewhere for sociologists to "turn inward" toward their discipline for ideas about how to conceive and execute works of applied sociology. Moreover, there are reasons to doubt the diagnosis itself (J. Weiss, 1976: 234). Specifically, we question whether the proposals that it spawns, if implemented, could ever provide effective long-term solutions for the problems they purportedly address. We will now discuss our skepticism.

First, these proposals appear to be more relevant to some of the fields' problems than to others. Clearly, the adequacy of disciplinary knowledge is an important issue in an understanding of the first problem that we just discussed, i.e., why so much so-called policy-relevant research leads to no discernible policy implications for national domestic problems. To be sure, this is not the only reason why this is so, but it is important to consider. Yet, we fail to see how these proposals handle other aspects of the problem. Specifically, it fails to address the fact that where adequate knowledge exists, this knowledge has more often resulted only in policy recommendations—not enacted policy—and why so many of the recommendations that have been made are rejected by policy-making bodies as unrealistic, unfeasible or politically impractical. Although we believe that a basic strengthening of the discipline could not but help to enhance its relevance for policy, we are confident that the reasons for sociology's impact (or lack of) on public policy do not lie exclusively within the discipline and what it does or does not know. In fact, one can easily imagine a situation where, after all of the measures proposed to increase the discipline's competency were enacted, the government might not accept our advice. Clearly, a more encompassing perspective on the relationship of sociology to government is required to understand and explain its impact and lack of impact on policy, a perspective which grants a greater role to the consumers of our knowledge in determining what impact we have on policy than the present perspective does.

This is a principle quarrel we have with the accepted diagnosis for the problems of policy-relevant sociology today, but it is not the only one we have with it. We are also bothered by the fact that the diagnosis arises out of a concern to explain the instances in which sociologists have failed to be relevant without the consideration of whether it provides an equally compelling explanation for instances in which sociology has had an influence. By this criterion, the diagnosis is inadequate; it seems capable of explaining *only* the failures (or at least some of them)—none of the successes. Are we to believe that in those instances in which sociology proved serviceable in the development of social policy, its theories were adequate; its basic research complete; its programs of graduate training suitable; and its practitioners in regular and close communication with policy-makers? The assertion is dubious. For a start, there is little indication that any of the proposals that have been made are based upon lessons learned from cases where the application of disciplinary knowledge is regarded as successful. In fact, we know no instance of any mention of such cases. For another, some of the examples cited earlier when we discused the relative grounds for optimism and despair, refer to research projects in which sociologists drew upon certain bodies of research and theory which were also drawn upon and used in projects that are regarded as failures. Finally, even when this has not been true, it is difficult to see how these explanations for the shortcomings of attempts to apply disciplinary knowledge and methods of research to social policy shed light on those efforts that are described as successes. Thus, a troubling aspect of the prevailing diagnosis for the state of practice in this field is that it fails to explain convincingly and simultaneously the instances in which sociologists can legitimately claim success as well as those in which they acknowledge that they have failed.

Another reason to question the validity of this diagnosis of the problem is that, as Janet Weiss notes, many of the things proposed appear to be ad hoc in character (J. Weiss, 1976: 234). One gets the impression that many of the proposals do not arise out of any particular comprehensive grasp of the enterprise as a whole, but from a kind of "knee-jerk" response to specific, limited criticisms and problems that arise from time to time. Too often, no thought is given to the wider, long-range implications of the proposals made. Proposals for support of basic research have implications for arguments about the immediate relevance of sociology to social policy. Pleas to involve the ablest of sociologists in applied work have implications for the development of basic theory and the successful accomplishment of basic research. Suggestions for altering established programs of graduate education carry immediate implications for manpower and long-term implications for the field's development. And, in the appeals for more money, little recognition is given to the fact that since resources are limited, the investment of more money in one program implies that less will be available for others. In other words, what is missing in the sociologists' diagnoses is any consistent sense of appreciation of the full range of implications for our field of particular measures that are proposed.

Finally, certain linkages in the diagnosis that we have presented are left unstated. Sociologists have requested more funds for basic research, to develop basic theory and to expand programs of graduate education; but they have not always explained how any of these steps would handle the problems within the field. Specificially, we must *know* what grounds there are for supposing that more basic research and better theory will enhance the field's relevance for social policy. The question is seldom asked (much less answered) but it involves an issue too important and too basic to deal with only by implication and unstated assumption.

Again, we stress the point that whatever the criticism, it should not be taken to imply that we regard the existing diagnosis as worthless. We regard it limited and incomplete. It must be embellished and enriched with a perspective toward policy-relevant sociology that gives weight to the receptivity of government to sociological advice and counsel. We believe that such a perspective must provide serious attention both to disciplinary and to policy concerns, not to just one or the other. In this sense we do not understand the perspective that we will propose as a competing explanation for sociology's impact and lack of impact on policy, but as an extension and revision of the one that exists.

Communicating with Policy-Makers

Sociologists have not ignored entirely the significance of governmental receptivity to social science as a factor in determining the influence they have on policy. The issue arises occasionally in discussions of other steps that might be taken to enhance the relevance of the discipline in public affairs. It is noted that in many policy-relevant projects, the two parties will not discuss policy issues until the research is completed: this is believed to be responsible for some of the disappointments that have occurred. As a result, a number of people have called for closer collaboration between social scientists in the academy and those people working in specific policy areas from the time a research project is formulated until the time it is completed.

Walter Williams strongly advocates this idea (Williams, 1971: 65). In his book, *Social Policy Research and Analysis,* he devotes considerable attention to the problem of how to improve channels of communication between sociologists who desire to do research, meant to be relevant to social policy, and the policy-maker who searches for the sociologist to give advice. The same idea is emphasized by Orlans (Orlans, 1968: 153), Merton (Merton and Lerner, 1951), Coleman (Coleman, 1972: 18), Reiss (Reiss, 1970: 290), Larsen (Larsen, 1975: 17), and Lazarsfeld et al. (Lazarsfeld, et al., 1975: 40−46; 138−145). The feeling seems to be that close communication between sociologists and policy-makers can help the sociologist to develop a better appreciation for what policy problems to research, and, to acquire, in addition, a better understanding of the political and practical impediments to enacting policy recommendations that may be forthcoming from this research.

We salute these proposals as an important step in the right direction. Yet, at the same time, they convey little sense of what concretely must be done to open up lines of communication; what sociologists and policy-makers would hope to learn through such measures that they do not already know; what collaboration between the two parties might entail; and how it would change the way in which sociologists work. The answers to these questions are neither evident nor simple, but the response carries significant implications for the ways in which policy-relevant work would have to be conceptualized and executed. Our analysis is to indicate what we believe this proposal would entail and what are its implications for the discipline generally.

CONCLUSION

In conclusion, we recall what we said earlier, namely, that when sociologists think about work for application, they have a tendency to consider only sociology—not policy concerns. They turn inward with their discipline for guidance, concepts and ideas—allowing policy no voice at all or one that is heard only after the research has been done, but not while it is being formulated. We believe that this tendency in sociology to approach work for application in terms of discipline rather than policy concerns has had major implications for how effective results are. We will try to explain why we believe this to be so.

NOTES

1. For a highly useful conceptualization of this problem see Janet A. Weiss, "Using Social Science for Social Policy" (1976: 234—238).

2. Thus, Gans states that the sociological policy researcher can make a valuable contribution by drawing on "his understanding of society, the social process and the effects of deliberate intervention in the process to offer help to the (policy) designer" (Gans, 1971: 19). Herbert Kelman speaks about this use of social science when he talks about the need to "explore basic premises that govern the functioning and change of social and cultural systems" (Kelman, 1972: 198); and Elizabeth Crawford argues that sociology and other social sciences are ". . . suited for performing 'enlightenment' functions in society, that is, to reveal the basic conceptions and values underlying societal thought-processes in general and policy formation in particular. . ." (Crawford, 1971: 9). People in the field of policy science, such as Klaus Lompe and Yehezkel Dror, have recognized enlightenment as a contribution which sociology can make to social policy. Lompe believes that the most basic contribution the social sciences have to make to policy "consists in raising the level of general culture and the understanding of the social universe" among policy-makers (Lompe, 1968: 164); and Dror states that sociology may make many contributions to policy-making, including "a general educational" contribution by "sensitizing the policy-makers to social aspects of their operation" (Dror, 1971b: 147). Finally, in his book, *The Scientific Estate*, Donald Price argues that the main purpose of science (including social science) should be to educate policy-makers more broadly by opening up new questions for them to ponder (Price, 1965: 107).

3. Others mention this use of sociology as well. Robert Lane writes: "Since government often proceeds by listening to advocates of one group or purpose at a time, the continued emphasis upon alternative and competing benefits inherent in policy analysis (of which he considers applied sociology to be a part) is a useful corrective" (Lane, 1972: 80). Merton and Lerner mention it when they state that sociologists may initiate policy research to "sensitize policy-makers to new types of achievable goals (and) . . . to more effective means of realizing established goals" (Merton and Lerner, 1951: 303). The use of sociology to "display alternative policies" also comes up in an essay, "The Use of Social Science in Public Affairs," by C. West Churchman, who cites this as one of the primary uses of scientific knowledge in policy (Churchman, 1967: 29), and Klaus Lompe discusses it when he analyzes the use of a "decisionistic model" by sociologists engaged in applied research. The aim of this model, he explains, is "to point to several alternative courses of action" (Lompe, 1968: 163). Finally, Austin Ranney writes that the social scientist's professional knowledge and skill may be useful to policy-makers in "the identification, comparison and evaluation of competing policy proposals" (Ranney, 1968: 18).

4. See also Janet Weiss (1976: 236—237) and Pio D. Uliassi (1976: 241).

5. For example, see Janowitz (1972).

6. For examples of this kind of use of sociology see the volume edited by Lazarsfeld et al., *The Use of Sociology* (1967), as well as the volume edited by Demerath et al., *Social Policy and Sociology* (1975).

7. Also see Dror (1971a: 141). Dror identifies the empirical case study as being one of two main approaches the sociologist might take to using sociology in policy (the other is "abstract analysis"). He explains that the aim of the empiricial case-study is to use the theoretical and methodological knowledge of sociology to arrive at sensi-

ble policies and programs to deal with specific problems. In this way, sociology is able to contribute to policy by "helping the policy-makers to choose major guidelines for operations . . . [and] by providing specific intelligence and ideas applicable to concrete and detailed issues" (Dror, 1971a: 147).

8. For other dissenting views about this use of sociology, see Coleman (1972) and Cook (1975). Coleman argues that the goal of sociology in social policy "is not to further develop theory about an area of activity" but to do research (Coleman, 1972: 1), a position that we will explain in more detail later in this chapter. Cook, a social psychologist, writing about the use of social science in education states, ". . . an educational innovation cannot take some social psychological theory of development and apply it in school. There are just too many gaps between the abstract elegance of our few well-tested formal theories and the concrete problem-ridden reality of implementing change in complex settings" (Cook, 1975: pp. 1—2 of Chapter III).

9. Others have commented on this particular use of sociology as well. In an essay on sociology and social policy by Merton and Lerner, two of three functions of research mentioned are informational in nature. From the policy-maker's perspective, these functions of research are (a) persuasion, in which "objective data" are sought as aid in support of one's own position and (b) action, when policy-makers request research because they think they do not have sufficient information for "intelligent" action (Merton and Lerner, 1951: 302). In either case, Merton and Lerner recommend that conventional methods for conducting social research be employed to collect empirical data useful in the policy-making process. Howard Freeman states that "the core of applied research has been and continues to be the technical procedures and conceptual notions of the behavioral sciences" (Freeman, 1963: 144); and Yehezkel Dror speaks of the "tactics contribution" that sociologists can make to social policy "by providing specific intelligence . . . applicable to concrete and detailed issues" (Dror, 1971a: 147).

10. Herbert Kelman believes that one of the main contributions of sociology to social policy is research designed to assess effects and implications of new policies and action programs (Kelman, 1972: 198). He distinguishes two main forms that such research can take: conventional evaluation research on specific programs of social action and more long-range or analytic assessment of policies or programs (Kelman, 1972: 198). Harold Orlans also cites evaluation as one of several contributions sociology might make to social policy, concluding that social research "is indispensable to the evaluation and improvement of federal programs" (Orlans, 1968: 152). Others who see evaluation as an appropriate use of sociology in social policy include Charles Glock (Glock, 1961: 3), Howard Freeman (Freeman, 1963: 144), Yehezkel Dror (Dror, 1971a: 147) and Klaus Lompe (Lompe, 1968: 163).

11. For two examples of the use of evaluation research in applied fields of study, see Stuart Adam, *Evaluation Research in Corrections: A Practical Guide* (1975) and Leo Bogart, *Social Research and the Development of the United States Army* (1964).

12. Froman lists some of the criteria used in traditional classification schemes. They are substantive (e.g., labor, education); institutional (e.g., congressional policy, third world policies); target (e.g., farmers, working-class, Blacks); time (e.g., prewar, postdepression); ideological (e.g., capitalist, liberal); value (e.g., good, bad, dangerous); support (e.g., consensus, divisive); and governmental level (e.g., national, local) (Froman, 1968: 48). Other classification schemes proposed by social scientists include the distinction between issues of "style" and "position" introduced by Berelson, Lazarsfeld, and McPhee (Berelson et al., 1954: 199); Edelman's distinction between "material" and "symbolic" satisfaction as a basis for differentiating political processes (Edelman, 1960: 695); Huntington's distinction between strategies and structural issues of military decision-making (Huntington, 1961: 4—6); and Freeman's categorization of social policies based on the "peer," the "operating" and the "policy" systems (Freeman, 1963: 145). Theodore Lowi has proposed the tripartite classification of distributive, regulatory and redistributive

policies. He explains: "Distributive issues are those that give things away . . . regulatory issues are those that restrict available alternatives . . . and redistributive issues are those that take from one group of people and give to another . . ." (Lowi, 1964: 678). And, Lewis Froman proposes a distinction between "areal" and "segmental" urban policies—that is, policies that affect a whole country or region at the same time in contrast to policies that affect persons at different times (Froman, 1967).

13. Richard Quinney advocates a similar approach. In place of existing sociological theories that, according to Quinney, "justify the existing social order," he calls for the development and implementation by sociologists of radical social theory (Quinney, 1972: 317). Unlike existing theory, radical social theory "makes no attempt to stop with what is" (Quinney, 1972: 33). Instead, its aim is "what is seen beyond our experience . . . what I am proposing . . . [is] .. . a radical social theory [that] involves a fusion of the transcendental and the political . . . . The transcendental allows us to go beyond our experience; the political forces us to question our experiences and to act in a way that will alter them. Only through such a social theory can we meet the problem of our age . . . only a radical social theory can liberate us—sociologically and spiritually. Liberation is the true goal of social theory in our radical age" (Quinney, 1972: 340). The sort of active participation by sociologists in the policy-making process that Kelman proposes is consistent with the uses of sociology we have listed. It would seem that Gouldner and Quinney form a group apart, since they propose to destroy the system that others seem to be anxious to rationalize and perfect. Yet, it seems reasonable to suppose that Gouldner and Quinney would endorse the various uses of sociology we have discussed for their own purposes, just as liberal sociologists endorse them for theirs.

14. Kathleen Archibald has identified three basic approaches to applied policy-relevant social science research: the academic, the clinical and the strategic. For a discussion of three styles and various subtypes of each, see Archibald (1970).

3

We argued that applied, policy-relevant sociology lacks a policy perspective. However, this does not mean that the disciplinary perspective of sociologists is devoid of notions about

Conceptions of Policy in Applied Sociology

policy. In fact, the perspective harbors a full-blown theory about it. Here we wish to disclose these assumptions and ideas about policy, implicit in applied, policy-relevant sociology today.

APPLIED SOCIOLOGY AND SCIENTIFIC PLANNING

An important, often neglected fact about applied policy-relevant work in sociology is that whenever sociologists urge particular uses of sociology for policy, unwittingly, they are also advocating a method for "doing" policy. That is, when they speak of using sociology in policy to enlighten, to provide ideas and information, or to evaluate or to further understanding of policy and so on, they presuppose the existence of a method for conducting public affairs, which grants these functions to sociology. In other words, unless those who are responsible for making policy are willing and able to commit themselves to follow principles and procedures of a certain kind, there is little room in public affairs for sociology to operate in the ways envisaged by the sociologist.

What are these principles and procedures? Basically, they involve a commitment to rationality, a willingness to be persuaded by scientific fact and to be guided by reason, a basic commitment to devise policies based upon scientific determination of what is required rather than political determination of what is expedient, a conscious decision to undertake regular assessment and evaluation of programs and to agree to be guided by their results—in a word, a commitment to *scientific planning*. [1]

We state this point in a different way. If one asks: "How would policy have to be made and enacted in order to use sociology consequentially in ways envisaged by sociologists?" we immediately realize that something closely akin to a scientific planning approach to policy would be required. That is, unless policy is made in this way, the ways in which sociologists intend disciplinary knowledge and methods to be used make little or no sense at all. Thus, when pursuing applied research, the sociologist, usually inadvertently, gears the production of knowledge to a planning conception of policy which results in recommendations that typically can only be considered when governmental bodies are able and willing to embrace this concept when they execute policy. This is why we say that the sociologist's endorsement of particular uses of disciplinary knowledge, theory and methods in policy, which originate in the discipline and reflect what we know and are able to do, involve implicit recommendations, as well, about how policies should be derived and enacted. As we will see, later, these are really more than just recommendations: they amount to an entire theory of government.

These notions about policy are a deeply embedded part of the disciplinary perspective toward applied, policy-relevant work in sociology that we reviewed earlier. The imagery that they project about policy does not come from intimate familiarity with policy: it derives from the sociologist's views about such things as the uses that can be made of disciplinary knowledge and method, the procedures that must be followed to achieve these uses and so on. To us, it appears that sociologists have inadvertently invented pictures about policy to suit the conventional nature of sociological studies.

It is important to stress that the claim is not that sociologists are unfamiliar with the idea of scientific planning: many of them have written about it and some have made notable contributions to its basic formulations. Rather, our claim is that this otherwise familiar idea goes largely, though not entirely,[2] unrecognized in the context in which we are presently considering it. Thus, there is a robust sociological literature about scientific planning from which we shall be drawing liberally (along with writings by policy and other social scientists) to clarify what scientific planning is and what it entails. Our point is that in this body of literature and in the literature about work for application in sociology, the dependency of applied, policy-relevant activities as these are conceived and practiced by sociologists on the method of scientific planning is largely overlooked.

What is scientific planning? For one thing, it entails a commitment to be *rational, comprehensive, deliberate*. The policy designer is portrayed by Herbert Gans as a person who "works toward the achievement of a social goal by the development of programs that can reasonably be predicted to achieve that goal, accompanied by an optimal set of consequences" (Gans, 1971:51); and the policy process as a system—consisting of factors, information and research—each element interacting with the other in an explicit way to produce social policy (Bauer, 1968:3; Ranney, 1968:7).

We also emphasize a commitment to proceed in a *deliberate, stepwise fashion*. As Lompe points out, basic theories about policy propounded by policy analysts are based on the premise that a rational social policy can only be established through a "specialized step-by-step approach" (Lompe, 1968:169). Various strategies for doing this have been proposed. Lasswell's model for stepwise procedures (to be reviewed shortly) is perhaps the best known of these (Lasswell, 1971). More modest are Popper's proposal for "piecemeal social engineering" (Popper, 1963:259−265), Lindblom's strategy of "disjointed incrementalism" (Lindblom, 1968), and Etzioni's strategy of "mixed scanning" (Etzioni, 1968:283−288). The following explanation of disjointed incrementalism illustrates the essential logic and method implicit in most of these strategies:

> 1. Choices are made in a given political universe, at the margins of the *status quo*. 2. A restricted variety of policy alternatives is considered, and these alternatives are incremental, or small, changes in the *status quo*. 3. A restricted number of consequences are considered for any given policy. 4. Adjustments are made in the objectives of policy in order to conform to given means of policy, implying a reciprocal relationship between ends and means. 5. Problems are reconstructed, or transformed, in the course of exploring relevant data. 6. Analysis and evaluation occur sequentially, with the result that policy consists of a long chain of amended choices. 7. Analysis and evaluation are oriented toward remedying a negatively perceived situation, rather than toward reaching a preconceived goal. 8. Analysis and evaluation are undertaken . . . (Schoettle, 1968:151).

Weighing alternatives and evaluating consequences is also basic to scientific planning. Robert Lane writes that "the consideration of alternatives, including doing nothing, is an essential, hence definitional, part of policy analysis" (Lane, 1972:71). He adds, "Since government often proceeds by listening to advocates of one group or purpose at a time, the continued emphasis upon alternatives and competing benefits inherent in policy anlaysis is a useful corrective" (Lane, 1972:80). Dror also emphasizes this feature of policy-making; he says, for example, that policy analysis "provides heuristic methods for identification of preferable policy alternatives" (Dror, 1971a:14).

Scientific Planning entails the use of special *methods* designed to aid in the weighing of alternatives and in executing other "steps" in the policy-making process. They include such innovations as systems analysis, PPBS (program-planning-budgeting-system), operations research, linear and dynamic programming, cost-benefit analysis, and Delphi and other forecasting techniques—all widely accepted among social scientists in varied fields. Their role in achieving rationality in public policy is illustrated by economist Alice Rivlin's description of PPBS. She states:

> . . . it seems to me simply a commonsense approach to decision making. Anyone faced with the problem of running a government program, as indeed, any large organization, will want to take these steps to assure a good job: (1) Define the objective of the organization as clearly as possible; (2) Find out about the dollars being spent and what was being accomplished; (3) Define alternative policies for the future and collect as much information as possible about what each would cost and what it would do; (4) Set up a systematic procedure for bringing the relevant information together at the time decisions are to be made. PPBS was simply an attempt to institutionalize this commonsense approach in the government budgetary process . . . . It is regarded as a desirable way to make decisions (Rivlin, 1971:4−5).

Another feature of the method of scientific planning is the role assigned to *scientific experts* in the policy-making process, which is central. In this concept of policy-making, the scientific expert—including the sociologist—though never king, is nevertheless a key member of the inner court. This notion is apparent in the thinking of such persons as Gans, who defines the sociologist's role in policy as providing key "conceptual and theoretical inputs" (Gans, 1971:15); Price, who speaks of "responsible policy-making" as a process of interaction and exchange of ideas and information involving "scientists, professional leaders, administrators and politicians" (Price, 1965:67), and Harold Orlans, who states that "social research, that is, knowledge obtained by systematic empirical inquiry, is indispensible to the evaluation and operation of federal programs, to the efficient allocation of resources, and to intelligent political decisions" (Orlans, 1968:152).

Undoubtedly the most comprehensive description of the concept of scientific planning is accredited to Harold Lasswell, who is usually cited as having established policy science as a specialized field of study.[3] His ideas have had a dramatic impact on modern day social science conceptions of social policy, and a review of them imparts, perhaps better than anything else, the flavor of the scientific planning model of policy. For this reason we will consider Lasswell's work in some detail here.

Lasswell is optimistic about the methods and viewpoints of policy science. He states:

> The trend toward a policy science viewpoint—contextual, problem-oriented, multi-method—is a move away from fragmentation . . . . When properly linked with law and jurisprudence, political theory and philosophy, the new instruments of policy analysis and management provide tools of unprecedented versatility and effectiveness (Lasswell, 1971:xiii).

And, Lasswell's optimism is influential. His description of the "policy process" to which applied social science aims to contribute is the single most important elaboration of the conception of the ideal of rational policy-making.[4]

Lasswell describes the aims of policy science as concerned with "knowledge of and in the decision process of the public and civic order" (Lasswell, 1971:1). "Knowledge of" the decision process implies systematic, empirical studies about how policies are made and put into effect. "Knowledge in" the decision process requires "anticipating the needs of decision-makers and . . . mobilizing knowledge when and where it is useful" (Lasswell, 1971:1). In fulfilling both of these needs for knowledge, he adds:

> . . . the policy sciences must strive for three principal attributes. The first is contextuality: decisions are part of a larger social process. The second is problem orientation: policy scientists are at home with the intellectual activities involved in clarifying goals, trends, conditions, projections and alternatives. The third is diversity: the methods employed are not limited to a narrow range (Lasswell, 1971:4).

The policy scientist, then, is "concerned with mastering the skills appropriate to enlightened decision in the context of public and civic order" (Lasswell, 1971:13).

Lasswell provides a proposed model of the policy process; some of its features will by now be familiar. Lasswell posits the existence of participants holding certain values that they seek to realize by creating social institutions designed to affect the environment in desired ways (Lasswell, 1971:18). These institutions and institutional programs are products of a rational decision-making process that consists of a series of sequentially related steps. The first step, termed by Lasswell, the "intelligence phase," includes the gathering, processing and dissemination of basic information for the use of all persons who participate in the decision process. This is followed by phase two, "promotion," during which information dissemination is buttressed by political agitation. Promotion leads to the "prescriptive" phase (phase three) involving the creation of norms by passage of laws. Phase four, called "invocation," is the activity of characterizing a concrete situation in terms of its conformity or nonconformity to prescriptions passed in the previous phase. Phase five is the phase of application, or taking measures based on judgments of whether norms have been violated in a certain situation. Phase six is termination of the activity, and phase seven is appraisal, which involves evaluating policy outcomes (Lasswell, 1971:28).

Lasswell's concept of policy-making includes the familiar "step-by-step" feature, somewhat elaborated. He advocates a step-by-step problem-solving orientation at each stage of the process. Each of the steps of this technique corresponds to the emphasis on weighing alternatives and consequences noted earlier as a feature of the concept of rational policy-making. Again, Lasswell's version is elaborate. The problem-solving orientation which Lasswell urges consists of five interrelated tasks. The first task, *goal clarification*, aims at clarification as to what future states are desirable in the social process (Lasswell, 1971:46). *Trend description*, the second task, is the effort to understand to what extent past and recent events approximate the preferred end state. In this process discrepancies are noted, and an effort is made to determine how great they are and how and why they develop (Lasswell, 1971:48—49). The third task, *the analysis of conditions*, is the attempt to understand what factors have conditioned the direction and magnitude of the trends that are described (Lasswell, 1971:49—53). The fourth task of this problem-solving technique is the *projection of developments*. The aim here is to ask what the probabilities will be for goal realization for discrepancies in the future, assuming current policies are continued (Lasswell, 1971:53—55). Finally, there is *the stage of invention, evaluation, and selection of alternatives.* Here the policy scientist asks what intermediate objectives and strategies will help to achieve realization of preferred goals (Lasswell, 1971:55—57). Lasswell refines this last task with a subset of further questions. What policy goals are to be realized? What is the problem or set of problems in hand? What particular objectives have to be realized through the policy process? Assuming that objectives can be realized, what is the probability they will achieve the results aimed for? What decisions must be taken to achieve the effects that are sought? Who must decide what and how? What factors are favorable or unfavorable to achieving desired outcomes? What strategies will help to optimize these desired goals? (Lasswell, 1971:57—60).

Throughout the process, the appropriate methods, such as PPBS and systems analysis, are employed, when needed. Thus, "knowledge in the decision process" is achieved as a result of "knowledge of the decision process" and of how and where social science can contribute to it. The end result of Lasswell's proposed policy process is a social policy that is arrived at rationally, informed by logic and based upon scientific knowledge and methods. In short, his method is the method of scientific planning.[5]

Horowitz and Katz suggest that the "Lasswellian" ideal of a science of policy-making has "largely given way to a *de facto* operational view that the social scientist is primarily concerned with facts, while policy-makers are concerned with implementation" (Horowitz and Katz, 1975:9). Perhaps; yet the idea, nevertheless, remains as basic to the successful use of sociology in the forms and ways that sociologists envisage. For this reason, Lasswell's work is fundamental to any analysis of the uses of sociology for public policy. Rationality, long-range comprehensive planning, self-conscious reconsiderations, weighing of alternatives, the use of scientific research to acquire knowledge, systematic, stepwise pursuit of objectives, evaluation of consequences . . . these are the methods and procedures that are implicitly advocated for deriving and implementing policy when sociologists talk about using disciplinary knowledge in public affairs.[6]

Procedures for Scientific Planning

This conception about policy has given rise to special procedures for putting the technique of planning into practice. Fundamental to the procedures is a prevailing image of a certain type of actor; one, Etzioni explains who "becomes aware of a problem, carefully weighs alternative means to its solution, and chooses them according to his estimate of their respective merits in terms of the state of affairs he prefers" (Etzioni, 1968:254). Such a person, Etzioni describes as "comprehensively rational" in that he views the process in its entirety, paying special attention to relationships among system parts. In order to do this Etzioni suggests four things are required: "(a) *information* about alternative courses of action and their consequences; (b) *calculation* of the alternative outcomes in terms of their meaning for the various values, and for various combinations of means; (c) a set of *agreed-upon* values on the basis of which to select goals and to judge the consequences and alternative courses of action; and (d) an *exhaustive survey* of all relevant alternatives" (Etzioni, 1968:264). In other words, as Carol Weiss notes, "The researcher assumes that policy decisions are 'made' by some identifiable 'decision-maker.' If he (the researcher) could only get the word through to him, the decision-maker would pay attention" (C. Weiss, 1976b:226). It gives rise to a model of research in which, according to Uliassi, " 'Findings' have policy 'implications' that have to be 'communicated' to practitioners, who in turn have to 'accept' and 'implement' them" (Uliassi, 1976:241).

To implement a program rationally, such a person would presumably follow certain procedures. Initially, he would want (1) *to determine what the problem is* (Rivlin, 1971:4—5). Anticipating the necessity for using methods and techniques of social science research in this and other facets of the policy-making process, it would be necessary (2) *to define the problem* clearly and precisely. The next step would be (3) *to clarify the goals, values and objectives* of the social policies to be developed to deal with this problem (Rivlin, 1971:4—5; Lindblom, 1968:12). One would want (4) *to organize these in a hierarchical fashion* reflecting prevailing notions about how to attack the problem and how to arrive at overall priorities (March and Simon, 1958:137). Next, the policy analyst would (5) *list all of the possible* ways of achieving these *goals* and (6) *inventory the full range of consequences* that might reasonably be expected to follow from each of the possible alternatives he has conceived (Lindblom, 1968:12). These, in turn, would be (7) *ranked along a continuum* from the most to the least preferred outcomes (March and Simon, 1958:137). (8) *Estimates* would then be made of financial and manpower resources likely to be available to accomplish the objectives sought, and some determination would be made of the probable (9) *costs* associated with each of the possible courses of action (Rivlin, 1971:4). A (10) *procedure* would then be instituted to bring all of this information together at the time and place that a decision must be made (Rivlin, 1971:5), so that the policy-maker would be in a position to compare the costs and probable consequences of each proposed policy with the overall goals and to select the most realistic and most effective alternative leading to the preferred set of consequences (Lindblom, 1968:13; March and Simon, 1958:138). Once agreement was reached, the policy-maker would then draw further on the sociologist's skills for such aids as supplying information necessary for the (11) *implemention* of policy and (12) *evaluating* a policy's success. Such information, particularly that gained through evaluation research, would then (13) *be fed back* into the policy process so that action could be taken to correct unanticipated problems and to improve overall effectiveness.[7]

What do sociologists and policy scientists believe will occur if policies are derived and implemented in this way? What do they think this method of scientific planning will yield that other policy-making procedures do not? Although these questions are rarely discussed explicitly, we believe that several answers can be inferred from a close reading of the materials from which we have quoted. The first is that policies so derived will result in the development of courses of action, i.e., policies that will be better, more effective and more beneficial than ones developed by the haphazard, piecemeal methods of partisan politics (McGowan, 1976:244). The terms "better" and "more effective" apparently imply that these methods for establishing social policy will enable government officials to forestall potentially disruptive effects of existing conditions; that they will enable officials to allocate resources with a minimum of wastage; that the procedures employed will help to guarantee that a wide range of interests will be represented in establishing a social policy; that all of the ramifications of a given plan of action will be explored and known in advance; and that there will be achieved a situation in which the greatest number of benefits will be provided for the largest number of people. In other words, there is the implication that *such procedures will lead to more frictionless situations than we now have, situations that maximize the good and minimize harm done to those affected by them.*

These are the immediate objectives of planning. But, beyond them lies the further hope that such procedures will ultimately transform society into a more coherent political and national entity. As we will see in Chapter 4, Progressive intellectuals and politicians who originated the concept of scientific planning articulated this hope clearly. They thought that if social policies could be derived and implemented in accordance with rational scientific method, the results would not only be more effective solutions to the nation's problems, but also the development of social cohesiveness that industrialization was believed to have destroyed. As Wiebe points out, Progressives felt that a political system governed by continuity and regularity, functionality and rationality, administration and management would achieve continuity and predictability for the nation as a whole in the midst of otherwise chaotic social change (Wiebe, 1967:xiv). Although this utopian objective may no longer be regarded as completely realistic, nevertheless it points to a basic faith held by some of the advocates of planning, i.e., that this method will bring a greater degree of orderliness and coherence into our national life. No critical analysis of the method of scientific planning can be considered complete which fails to consider the veracity of these assumptions.

This method of developing and implementing policy is the subject of intensive analysis in the remainder of this book. It is therefore important to reiterate why we believe that analysis of scientific planning is basic to understanding applied policy-relevant work as this is practiced in American sociology today. Our argument is that if we ask: "What would a policy-making process have to be like in order for things that sociologists know and do to make a contribution to it?" we see that, as constituted, sociology could best contribute to what might be termed a scientifically-based system of planning. This phrase evokes images of policy-makers concerned with the collective good who are willing to listen to reason and be persuaded by facts. The commitment of the sociologist is to discover what is required in a basic way to solve problems and to express solutions in the form of comprehensive long-range plans and programs implemented in a logical, step-by-step fashion. There are connotations of exact and shared procedures. The sociologist begins by clarifying the nature of the problem and proceeds by stating the goals of social policies. These goals are organized hierarchically. Ways of achieving them are identified and inventories taken of the full range of consequences that might reasonably follow. Options are ranked by preference with accompanying estimates of costs and a procedure is defined for bringing together this information to a deliberative policy body so that a reasoned decision might be made.

The point that we are making is well illustrated by findings from the Caplan study (Caplan, 1976). Given the disciplinary manner in which so-called "policy research" is ordinarily conducted, Caplan inquires about the characteristics of utilizers that facilitate adoption of social science materials by them. Not surprisingly, he finds that when federal officials proceed in ways that grant room for rationality and science, social science knowledge utilization is high; when they do not, it is low. For example, he reports that utilization is most likely to occur when "(1) The decision-making orientation of the policy-maker is characterized by a reasoned appreciation of the scientific and the extra-scientific aspects of the policy issue" (p. 229) and when "(2) The ethical-scientific value of the policy-maker carry with them a conscious sense of social direction and responsibility" (p. 231). In other words, he finds that knowledge utilization is greatest when potential utilizers proceed in ways consistent with planning, that is, in accordance with the model of policy needed for disciplinary based social science research to have a voice in the policy process.

This is the model of policy that is complementary to the work and studies of applied sociology formulated from a disciplinary perspective. Therefore, the possibilities of such a sociology depend heavily on the possibilites of this model of policy-making, and we are therefore lead to examine the problems and possibilities of the method of scientific planning for clues to explain the success or failure of applied, policy-relevant work in sociology. Specifically, we would expect to find that sociologist's efforts to be policy-relevant are most likely to succeed (1) when those responsible for making policy in our society are able and inclined to adopt a scientific planning approach to policy; and, when they do so, (2) to the extent that it is actually possible to use this method in practice. Thus, to understand why efforts to use sociology for policy do or don't work, we must ask: Under what conditions is government likely to be receptive to adopting a planning approach to policy? And, when they are willing to try it, how well does it work? We will consider these questions in Chapter 5. Chapter 4 is devoted to an examination of the origins of the idea of rational planning and how it became a part of sociology.

NOTES

1. This is not to say that where policy-makers do not engage in planning there is no role for sociology to play in policy. Our point is that in this case the role would not be the one that sociologists intend it to be. If more familiar methods of partisan politics are followed instead of planning, sociology might still be used—not to make policy as it presumably would be in the case of planning, but as a resource to buttress and justify already hardened positions that emerge out of the give-and-take of political bargaining, to lend scientific credence to policy decisions arrived at by purely political means, and so on. We will have more to say on this point later.
2. It is misleading to say that all sociologists have overlooked completely the dependence of applied social science on the method of scientific planning. A number of the people do mention it explicitly when analyzing possible ways in which sociology may be applied to policy. James Coleman, for example, points out that behind the notion of using sociological methods for policy lies a particular conception of society. He describes it as follows:

> It has an explicit evolutionary mechanism built in, an evolutionary mechanism that employs scientific methods. In this conception of a future society, it will be a scientific society, in the sense of a society that uses scientific methods for changing itself. The relation of the policy sciences to such a society is a relation in which social science theory plays a small and secondary part, but methods of the social sciences play a central part. These methods, together with the institutional structure that insures their employment, constitute the feedback mechanism that such a society needs (Coleman, 1972).

> Herbert Gans acknowledges the same point when he states, "The distinctive quality of social policy is its aim for . . . programmatic rationality; it seeks to achieve substantive goals through instrumental action programs that can be proven, logically or empirically to achieve these goals" (Gans, 1971:14). Henry Riecken, former Director of the Social Science Research Council, also recognizes that applied sociology implies a special conception of governance when he states that social policy "implies a deliberate allocation of resources through means that are intended to achieve a chosen end" (Reicken, 1971: 180); as does Alvin Schorr, who, in his book *Explorations in Social Policy* (1968) states, "I was dealing with social policy in order to change it. The belief that change occurs creates a responsibility to say what a rational policy will be" (Schorr, 1968:6). Also see C. Weiss (1976b:226)

3. Without in any way belittling Lasswell's contribution to this activity, it is absurd to credit him with the discovery of a science dedicated to the rational approach to policy. The intellectual pedigree of this idea in modern history goes back at least to the writings of John Locke and Jeremy Benthan.
4. Although Lasswell's landmark essay on policy science was published in 1951, he has continued his work in the field since. The description that we will present is drawn largely from his book, *A Preview of Policy Sciences*, published in 1971.
5. Since Lasswell's original formulation appeared in 1951, others have elaborated and extended it. [See especially Macrae (1970, 1971, 1973a, 1973b, 1974) and Gil (1970).] Such an extensive body of writing cannot be reviewed here; instead we can only present examples taken from it. Frank Knight, for example, has tried to explicate what he calls "the logical scheme of divisions of data that must be known . . . to act intelligently in any situation" (Knight, 1957:156). His problem-solving technique differs only slightly from Lasswell's. He suggests that the actor must know:

> . . . the natural course of events, i.e., what happens if no action is taken; what concrete action is "possible" to change the natural course of events; consequences of each possible mode of action; and the actor must be cognizant of a scale of composite values in terms of which to compare elements of the consequences of courses of action among themselves with the element of the "natural" course of events (Knight, 1957: 156–157).

Another elaboration and refinement of Lasswell's work appears in *An Introduction to the Study of Public Policy* by Charles A. Jones (1970). Jones attempts to develop a policy approach to the study of political behavior. His model of the policy cycle uses Lasswell's main categories but he elaborates extensively on Lasswell's stages of "formulation" and "legislation" (Jones, 1970:110). His work then, is basically an adaptation of Lasswell's model to political science, with special emphasis on how substantive policy problems are acted upon in government.

The work of Mark van de Vall provides a third example. He describes the main stages in a proposed framework for conducting applied social research using the discipline of sociology. The first stage he terms "diagnosis" in which the discipline of sociology dominates "with its theory of societies, organizations, and groups and its methods of social research, measurement, sampling, and statistics" (van de Vall, 1973:9). The second is design, a stage dominated by the field of public and business administration, including "its theories of administrative behavior, methods of policy formation and cost-benefit analysis, use of heuristic models, games and systems theory, [and] management by objectives" (van de Vall, 1973:9). Policy science dominates the third stage, development (van de Vall, 1973:9–10). van de Vall also attempts to state the conditions under which the use of social science experts is optimal or minimal and the conditions under which any or all of this knowledge will be useful (van de Vall, 1973:11).

6. Of course, as we mentioned earlier, this method of conducting civic and public affairs is not always advanced in the same fashion. By and large, policy scientists recommend it explicitly. Because of their interest in the policy process itself, independent of what kinds of empirical data or disciplinary knowledge may influence it, they seem more cognizant of the extent to which actual present practices deviate from ideal procedures they have devised. In fact, almost all of the policy scientists we have cited at least imply, if they do not emphatically state, that the way social policy is presently conducted is misguided, irrational and illogical. The whole purpose of policy science, in their view, is to improve on this process, to streamline it and ultimately to perfect it.

Judging from their writings, sociologists seem to be less cognizant than policy scientists of the realities surrounding the making and implementation of social policies. Whatever sophistication we possess in being able to understand basic social processes, seems to be suspended when we try to analyze the policy-making process to which we wish to contribute. This lapse in understanding manifests itself in two ways. Some sociologists and other social scientists blithely assume that since, in their view, social policies ought to be derived and implemented rationally, they in fact are. In other words, some discussions about the uses of sociology simply bracket the whole question by assuming that policy-making is a rational process. Other sociologists have recognized that conditions are not quite what they should be; therefore they propose corrective measures. Yet, here the assumption is that because those making policy are reasonable people, corrections and improvements are simple to make. In either case, one cannot help but be struck by the naivete of much of this analysis.

7. For a fuller discussion of the steps and stages of the rational decision-making process, see D. Braybrooke and C. Lindblom, *A Strategy of Decision* (1963: Part I).

4

The idea of scientific planning in American society did not originate with Harold Lasswell; nor are modern day

Origins of the Impetus to Plan

sociologists responsible for introducing this notion into the discipline of sociology. The concept of "marrying" a science of human society to the method of rational public administration in an effort to control and direct social change is an old idea in America whose modern roots extend back into the late 19th century.

This concept, traces of which appear at the time the Republic was founded, was nourished by certain powerful intellectual, political and social forces at work in American society during the late 19th and early 20th centuries, eventually giving birth to a social movement that vigorously advocated (and eventually practiced) the use of scientific expertise and rational planning in governmental affairs. From the movement's very beginnings, social science played a significant role in it, for social science was assigned the important task of providing governmental decision-making bodies with information and insights about societal conditions.[1] At the same time, the movement played an important role in shaping the development of applied social science by supplying our field with many of its basic ideas and assumptions about policy—notions that were soon accepted by the social science community as the only "reasonable" way in which to conduct public affairs. Modern day basic conceptions about how to do applied social science were developed with this notion of policy in mind; most of our research methods and procedures were made to articulate with it. Recent research by sociologists and intellectual and social historians of American society has begun to shed important new light on this movement toward scientific planning and the role that applied social science played in it. The purpose of this chapter is to draw upon this research to disclose and explain some of the political, social and philosophical origins of many of the key ideas associated with the modern day planning concept, including the role that social science expertise plays in it.[2] Our aim will be to place the conceptions and practices implicit in applied sociology into a developmental perspective—a perspective that we believe is imperative to acquire if we are to understand the problems and prospects for policy relevant sociology at the present. We say this for many reasons; at least two deserve special emphasis.

First, acquiring a developmental perspective toward applied sociology will help us to correct common misimpressions implicit in many of the discussions about sociology in policy that are in print today. Among these are the idea that the idea of rational planning in government is derived entirely from science; that science dictates the methods and procedures of planning; and that planning as sociologists and policy scientists conceive it is a necessary, inevitable and logical outgrowth of the scientific ethòs. To be sure, in a certain sense these things ae true, as rationality, logic and empiricism obviously fit hand-in-glove with science, and there can be no questions but that developments that are taking place within science have had an important impact on the conceptions and procedures that guide sociologists and policy scientists in developing social programs today. Yet, science as such did not completely dictate the method; it played only a part in its development. The impetus to utilize scientific knowledge about society to aid in developing and implementing rational social policies did not spring full-grown either with the emergence of science or with the development of the science of human society. Indeed, in certain important respects the science of human society was called into being by persons who believed that rational planning was necessary for society's survival. How they arrived at this view; who they designated as "societal experts"; the role that these experts came to play in planning, and the particular conception of planning which they advocated—all of these are matters that cannot be understood by recourse to the general concepts of science alone. The particular ideas about scientific planning that social science adopted were shaped by political, economic and social changes, which took place in American society at the time it began to industrialize—changes that are clearly reflected in the version of the planning concept that eventually burrowed itself into the assumptive world of sociologists who were engaged in work for application. To understand the particular conception of planning that is implicit in today's applied sociology, as well as social scientists' conception of what their role is in this process, one must therefore examine the philosophical, political and social forces that shaped it.

Second, many discussions about the application of sociology to policy that appear in print today often proceed as if serious efforts to use sociology in public affairs did not occur until after World War II.

Almost entirely, the examples that are discussed and analyzed involve projects undertaken after 1950. The heavy reliance on examples of efforts to use sociology in policy that have occurred in the past quarter-century has resulted in a highly misleading and incomplete picture of applied sociology in American society. It ignores about 50 years of active experimentation involving the use of social science knowledge by government—years in which some of the most ambitious efforts to use sociology were launched and some of the most spectacular successes in applying disciplinary knowledge in public affairs were achieved. The record of accomplishments in applied, policy-relevant sociology is seriously distorted and the explanations for them are misleading when we label 1950 as the approximate date when the first serious attempt to use sociology in policy began. One purpose here is to examine efforts to use sociology in public affairs that were undertaken during the period 1900—1940, studying them for what they may tell us about the role of social science in planning and the conditions under which attempts by sociologists to be relevant to national policy have and have not succeeded.

Our discussion of the development of the planning idea is divided in two parts. In Part One we will discuss the development of the conception of scientific planning implicit in applied sociology; the impact it had on sociology; and the role that social science played in its development. Our discussion of these topics is divided into three sections. Section One reviews the main philosophical origins of the planning idea; Section Two examines the impact of certain changes in American society that were occasioned by industrialization and the implications these changes had for the development of the planning movement; and in Section Three, we discuss the impact that the planning movement had on social science and social sciences' contributions to it.

Part Two is devoted to a brief review of some of the main efforts made by social scientists to use the knowledge and methods of their disciplines for social planning from 1900 to the time of World War II.

Our discussion of these issues is not, of course, exhaustive. The story of how and why the planning movement developed in America and the impact it had on sociology are matters that are much too complex to discuss completely in the space we have allotted. Our discussion, preforce, must be general, and our basic aim is modest. Our effort is to reveal certain fundamental connections between contemporary sociology and the past—linkages that we believe have become blurred, yet which must be recognized if we are to understand more satisfactorily the state of practice of applied sociology today.

PART ONE: ORIGINS OF THE IMPETUS TO PLAN

In 1914, the noted journalist and social philosopher, Walter Lippmann, published a book entitled *Drift and Mastery* (Lippmann, 1914). He put forth for a wide popular audience the prospect of massive planned social change for a utopian America.[3] Lippmann's thesis was that in our national life *purpose* must be substituted for tradition and that conscious planning must replace idle drift. He wrote:

> We can no longer treat life as something that has trickled down to us. We have to deal with it deliberately, devise its social organization, alter its tools, formulate its methods, educate and control it. In endless ways we put intention where custom has reigned. We break up routine, make decisions, choose our ends, select means (Lippmann, 1914:269).

Lippmann believed that America needed *mastery*, not drift. He urged "the substitution of conscious intention for unconscious striving" (Lippmann, 1914:269).

Lippmann felt that mastery required scientific knowledge and scientific expertise ["to shape the world nearer to the heart's desire requires a knowledge of the heart's desire and of the world" (Lippmann, 1914:269)]. Such knowledge, he felt sure, could be gained through science, which he believed had reached such a level of development that it could now be used to study social life and to discover prescriptions for social action. He envisioned the creation of highly trained teams of disinterested professional experts who would be given responsibility for formulating plans for social change, and he thought of other teams of professionally trained experts in administration science who would be given the responsibility for implementing them (Lippmann, 1914:42–49). These experts, trained in university-based social science programs, would be hired to conduct the business of government in a disinterested, scientific way (Lippmann, 1914:10).

Lippmann's vision of a government in which invention and conscious experimentation would reign supreme would also be one of true self-government by the people. He felt that the greatest challenge to America, that which most threatened its growth and development, was neither oppression nor the malevolent designs of a plutocrat. It was instead "the faltering method, the distracted soul, and the murky vision of . . . the will of the people" (Lippman, 1914:xx).

Five years earlier, in 1909, Herbert Croly had voiced similar sentiments in his book, *The Promise of American Life* (Croly, 1909). "The fault in the vision of our national future possessed by the ordinary American," he wrote, "does not consist in the expectation of some continuity of achievement. It consists rather in the expectation that the familiar benefit will continue to accumulate automatically" (Croly, 1909:19). In place of this blissful attitude of complacency, Croly called for "the efficient regulation of public affairs involving the subordination of the individual to the national interest" (Croly, 1909: 23). For Croly, the automatic harmony of the individual and the public interest, the very essence of Jeffersonian Democracy, was an illusion. Vigorous national activity based upon scientific knowledge and expertise would be necessary to bring about a realization of the public interest (Croly, 1909:152). In this and a later book, *Progressive Democracy* (Croly, 1915), Croly advocated strong leadership and argued for the acceptance and widespread use of modern techniques of scientific organization to identify and mobolize better the national interest in the face of competing special interest:

> It is obvious that the development in this country of . . . such powerful and unscruplous and well-organized special interests has created a condition which the founders of the Republic never anticipated, and which demands as a counterpoise a more powerful organization of the national interest (Croly, 1909:131).

Both Croly and Lippmann emphasized the quest for mastery through planning. Both were confident that rationality, intelligence and science—above all, social science—would make mastery possible. They assigned to the scientific expert a central position in the conduct of public affairs. Using their concepts and research methods, social scientists would ascertain the will of the people and determine the wisest and best programs and policies; using scientific administration they would implement and evaluate these programs. Scientists, working together with enlightened public leaders who had widespread citizen support, would create master plans for social change in America.

This simple, yet awesome assumption of the new philosophy that these men espoused—that human beings could control themselves, their society, their environment by intelligence, knowledge and thoughtfully devised schemes of rational planning—constituted a virtual intellectual revolution in American society whose impact continues to be strongly felt today. The destiny of America, it held, was neither dictated by the past nor riding on an automatic escalator into the future; in place of these deterministic visions was a belief in the possibility of progress achieved through intelligent planning (Mowry, 1958:57).

Apparent in the philosophy brought about by Lippmann and Croly is a clear image of the modern day concept of scientific planning reviewed in Chapter 3. The ideas that these two men propounded were not entirely their own inventions. They derived from philosophical and sociological ideas about the nature of man and society that were developing in certain intellectual circles in American society during the late 19th and early 20th centuries. These ideas were broadcast to a society that was receptive to hear them because of dramatic social and political changes attendant with industrialization. These intellectual and social nutrients together shaped a major social movement in American national life—the Progressive movement—with a wide impact on literature, philosophy, social science, politics, government and other spheres of national life. What were these new ideas and to what were they reactions? How did the great social changes of the day shape them? What were the themes and ideals of the social movement that they created? And, how did these themes and ideals become assimilated into sociological thought? We will examine some of these questions in this chapter.

Section One: Intellectual Origins of the Impetus Toward Rational Planning

A new philosophy began to emerge in American intellectual circles during the late 19th century that supplied the epistemological foundations of scientific social planning and eventually gave birth to the idea itself. Termed "liberal social philosophy," this body of thought developed as a reaction against the formalism and determinism of dominant modes of thought of that day (White, 1949:12). To understand the new philosophy, one must understand something about those which it sought to displace.

The doctrines of formalism and determinism were implicit in the writings of many of the great European intellectuals and social philosophers of the mid-19th century. These principles were derived from pre-Renaissance ideas in which knowledge was conceived as something static; a thing unto itself that is created, transmitted and preserved for its own sake—and in extreme forms predicates a deep and lasting schism between thought and action. While formalism and determinism were 19th-century movements, many of their adherents drew upon this older concept of the separation of knowledge from action. The works of Durkheim, Spencer, Darwin and Hegel exhibit formalist and determinist qualities[4] and much scholarship in such fields as history, evolutionary biology, psychology, sociology, historical jurisprudence and economics was dominated by formalist and determinist theories. Guided by their precepts, philosophers, social scientists and other intellectuals sought to discover and clarify grand, irrefutable laws by which the social order operated independently of the actions of individuals. The main quest of each discipline was the discovery, by means of deductive logic and formalist thinking, of the general laws of the universe that compelled social life in human society to move in predetermined, unalterable ways. Most scholastics aimed only to discover these laws, not to alter them. In this view the social order in all of its aspects—historical, anthropological, sociological, political and economic—was governed by forces over which mankind had no control. According to this view mankind was viewed, to cite Mowry's apt phrase, "as a more or less controlled instrument of a Calvinistic scheme of predetermination, a Hegelian or Marxian dialectic, a Darwinian process of selection, or a Newtonian physics" (Mowry, 1958:19).

A number of American intellectuals of the late 19th and early 20th centuries resisted this formalistic, deterministic mode of thought seeking to end its domination over their fields of study. They shared a common conviction that abstract logic, deduction, mathematics and mechanics were inadequate to social research and incapable of containing the rich, moving, living currents that they perceived in social life (White, 1949:8). Some made especially important contributions toward drawing the main outlines of the "new" system of social thought. G. S. Morris and Charles Pierce, in philosophy, and E. B. Taylor, in anthropology, were among the first in their disciplines to deviate from formalism. These men in turn influenced such people as Oliver Wendell Holmes, Jr., John Dewey, Frederick Jackson Turner, Charles A. Beard, James Harvey Robinson, Thorsten Veblen, William James and James H. Tufts to mount an assault on formalism, an assault that took the form of criticisms of scholastic scholarship in their disciplines.[5] These criticisms eventually led to the development of an alternative social philosophy, a new philosophy that ultimately made possible, indeed gave rise to, the idea of rationalistic planning in public affairs.

What was it about the formalist, determinist way of thinking that was so unsavory to these American intellectuals? Morton White attempted to answer this question by scrutinizing the writings of various proponents of the new philosophy. The work of Thorsten Veblen provides one example. In an essay, "Why is economics not an evolutionary science?" (1898), Veblen criticized the way his colleagues were doing academic work in economics. He pointed out how they attributed hypothetical motivations to people, and hypothetical characteristics to economic systems, and then inquired in an abstract, logically rigorous way into the likely consequences for the economic system of actions motivated by these hypothetical drives. Veblen opposed generalizing about an ideal situation on the basis of logic or hypothetical speculation; further, he opposed the search for static natural laws and all that this approach implied about the manner in which a society's economic system operated.

Oliver Wendell Holmes, Jr., provides another example. Holmes was troubled by the way law was being studied for many of the same reasons Veblen was disturbed by the economists approach to scholarship. In *The Common Law* (1881), Holmes complained that the study of law in traditional jurisprudence was only abstract and logical. At that time, traditional syllogistic, Aristotelian logic was the principle analytic tool of jurisprudence. Holmes argued that although the study of law could be approached in this deductive, logical way, it should not be. Holmes claimed that other tools besides logic were needed to understand the law, not because the systems of logic were flawed but because they were irrelevant and misleading (White, 1949:16). White saw that James Harvey Robinson, the well-known Columbia University historian, leveled the same criticism against history. In *History* (1908), Robinson described work done by contemporary and past historians as "thoughtless" (Robinson, 1908:15)—created only for the purpose of "amusing, edifying or comforting the reader" [Robinson (1908) as quoted in White (1949:28)]. It is true, he notes, that historians go to great lengths to reconstruct the past as accurately as they can. For this he praised them, but then complained that the work stops here, leaving historians with nothing more than highly formalized records of past events devoid of any sense of orderliness or relevancy for the present. The result he described as a "dead formula rather than a living picture of the past" [Robinson (1908) as quoted by White (1949:29)].

The same complaint about formalism was made of scholarship done in other social science disciplines. White explains how the renowed political scientist, Charles Beard, brought the issue to the study of politics. In a lecture at Columbia University (presented with a companion lecture by Robinson on history), Beard argued that his contemporaries and predecessors had erred in their study of politics by their excessive attention to abstract "juridicial-formal relations" (White, 1949:30). He stated, "The jural test of what constitutes a political action draws a dividing line where none exists in fact." (Beard, 1908:5). Another example is John Dewey's impassioned attack on formalism for its assumption of a dualistic separation between the mind and the object of knowledge (Dewey, 1887), and for its excessively mechanical view of human beings, based on this analytical dissociation between mind and matter (White, 1949:18–21).

The criticisms of Veblen, Holmes, Robinson, Beard, Dewey and others[6] were not without precedent. For hundreds of years, scholars had debated the nature of knowledge; whether it was static (to be transmitted and preserved for its own sake) or a dynamic power (a power to control man's environment for his benefit) (Curti, 1956:6). The idea of knowledge as a dynamic power has a long history, too, beginning during the Renaissance with the natural sciences and the scientific method.[7] After all, Francis Bacon argued that theories should be formulated in a manner that would lend themselves to direct testing by empirical experience; implicit in that argument was the possibility of technological, economic and social advances brought about by applying science to everyday problems. In the American colonies, the boundaries between knowledge and action became further blurred, as intellectuals took up practical pursuits and practical men cultivated intellectual interests (Curti, 1956:11). Thus was developed an American tradition, exemplified by such heroes as Benjamin Franklin and Thomas Jefferson—that thought preceded and informed action, and that thought and action were integral parts of a single process.

And so, in the late 19th century intellectuals who developed the "new" social philosophy drew on a long philosophical tradition that was well established in America. They took up the old debate specifically as a reaction against formalism and determinism. Seeking a more compatible approach, they developed a bewildering array of "isms." Dewey preached the doctrines of "instrumentalism" and "pragmatism" (Dewey, 1888, 1891, 1899; Dewey and Tufts, 1908). First Veblen and then Robinson suggested a new approach to the study of economics and history called "institutionalism." William James coined the term "behaviorism" for a system of psychology he proposed to replace the earlier associationism; Holmes called for studies in "legal realism" and Beard and Veblen spoke of "economic determinism." And in each of the social science disciplines, "new" approaches were advocated. There was the "new" history of Robinson, the "new" psychology of James and Dewey, the "new" jurisprudence of Holmes, Beard's "new" politics, Veblen's "new" economics, the "new" sociology of Lester Ward and the "new" ethics of Dewey and Tufts.

It must have seemed as if the tidy coherence so characteristic of systems of social thought up to that day had been forever shattered by the explosion of "isms" and new approaches to academic disciplinary work. It is true that their ideas sometimes lacked internal coherence or were inconsistent with one another. Yet, in retrospect we can detect several repeated basic themes that unify these proposed doctrines and approaches. White identifies three particular commitments that stand out as important in the development of the later planning ideology. They are *developmentalism*, a commitment to explain phenomena in evolutionary terms; *naturalism*, a commitment to take social context into account in searching for explanations for events; and *activism*, a commitment to make disciplinary studies directly relevant to the understanding and conduct of life in complex industrial society. White summarizes them:

> Holmes is the learned historian of the law and one of the heroes of sociological jurisprudence; Veblen is the evolutionary and sociological student of economic institutions; Beard urges us to view political institutions as more than documents; Robinson construes history as the ally of all the social disciplines and the study of how things have come to be as they are; and Dewey describes his philosophy alternatively as "evolutionary" and "cultural" naturalism. All of them insist upon coming to grips with life, experience, process, growth, context, function (White, 1949:12–13).

These three commitments enabled American intellectuals to transcend what they regarded as the limitations of formalistic thinking. Their new perspectives, applied to traditional problems, raised entirely new issues and questions; their resolution led to a new philosophy about social life that ultimately produced that vision of science in planning which pervades the writings of sociologists today. The impact that these themes had on modern-day applied sociology becomes apparent when we examine further the writings of these pioneering intellectuals about these basic issues.

Developmentalism. The commitment to view phenomena developmentally, that is, to attempt to explain events by reference to earlier ones and to look to the past to understand the present, was characteristic of the new liberal social philosophy. (It was also characteristic of Social Darwinism, against which it purported to be a reaction.) Thorstein Veblen identified a significant weakness in the work of formalistic economists as the lack of "a theory of a process, of an unfolding sequence" that developed, or of an understanding of the principles by which it had evolved—questions that demanded the amassing of empirical evidence from contemporary society and from historical materials. In his essay on economics as an evolutionary science, he argued that such information must be compiled, then interpreted and rendered sensible by a theory that specifically explained the manner in which that economic system was unfolding.

Oliver Wendell Holmes, Jr., urged more careful attention to history to clarify the law. He began with the premise that abstract meaning, apart from context, is impossible: "It is not true that in practice a given word or even a given collection of words has one meaning and no others. A word generally has several meanings, even in the dictionary. You have to consider the sentence in which it stands in order to decide which of those meanings it bears in the particular case" (Holmes, 1881:203). Applying this principle to the law, Holmes argued that laws, rules, legal terms and procedures could not be understood apart from their context—which he defined to include a historical aspect. As he states in *The Common Law* (Holmes, 1881), "The law embodies the story of a nation's development through many centuries, and it cannot be dealt with as if it contained only the axioms or corollaries of a book of mathematics" (Holmes, 1881:1). Convinced of the value of such a developmental perspective for the study of the law, Holmes specifically advocated intensive study of the history of theories of legislation to explain the emergence of specific legal procedures and terms (White, 1949:17) and, at a more general level, he advocated an empirical, scientific study of the evolution of law (Holmes, 1881).

Central to James Harvey Robinson's work in the field of history is a concept of history as an account of how things came to be. He wrote, "It is one thing to describe what once was; it is quite another to determine how it came about" [Robinson (1908) as quoted in White (1949:29)]. Robinson's primary interest was in "how it came about," where "it" included the present as well as the past. With Charles Beard, he co-authored *The Development of Modern Europe* (Robinson and Beard, 1907), the aim of which was "to enable the reader to catch up with his own time" [Robinson and Beard (1907) as quoted in White (1949:45)].

The historical, developmental method was important to Dewey's philosophy as well. Dewey was committed to testing experience directly; he formulated basic principles of experimentation and employed them continuously in his own system of thought. He believed that the experimental method was evolutionary because it "called results into being." "The experimental process . . . is genetic," he wrote, "because it 'calls into being' certain phenomena as a result of experimental manipulation" (Dewey, 1902:111), an idea that prompted him to consider the study of history as a substitute for experimentation. He wrote, "The early periods [of the history of an event] present us in their relative crudeness and simplicity with a substitute for the artificial operations of an experiment: Following the phenomena into the more complicated and refined form which it assumes later, is a substitute for the synthesis of experimentation" (Dewey, 1902:112–113). The book, *Ethics* (Dewey and Tufts, 1908), which he and James Tufts co-authored, demonstrates the practical importance of the developmental perspective for their theory of morality. They examined earlier stages of moral behavior in the belief that the study and the understanding of simpler stages will improve our understanding of more complex moral structures.

This evolutionary, genetic perspective on the social world [White's term for it is "historicism" (1949:12)] affected the way academic intellectuals viewed not only the past but future events as well. Once they began to look at economic and political systems and social structures as developing phenomena, they speculated about the directions in which these were evolving. It is this speculation that made developmentalism so significant for the later emergence of the ideology of planning. *By viewing the future as an extension of a continuing process, it led the new social philosophers to conceive of the idea of manipulating the present to alter the future,* an idea which, of course, is prerequisite to conceiving the possibility of social planning itself.

Naturalism. A second commitment of the new liberal social philosophy was to view phenomena holistically, taking into account context and culture. One indication of this commitment was the effort among certain scholars to abolish artificial disciplinary boundaries. In his *Politics* (1908), the influential Charles Beard wrote:

> We are coming to realize that a science dealing with man has no special field of data all to itself, but is rather merely a way of looking at the same thing—a view of certain aspects of human action. The human being is not essentially different when he is depositing his ballot from what he is in the counting house or at the work bench. In the place of a "natural" man, an "economic" man, a "religious" man or a "political" man, we now observe the whole man participating in the work of government (Beard, 1908:6).

Beard thus urged that politics and government be studied, not in isolation, but in relationship to the larger historical, social and economic context. "Any study of government that neglects the disciplines of history, economics and sociology will lack in reality what it gains in precision. Man as a political animal acting upon political, as distinguished from more vital and powerful motives, is the most unsubstantial of all abstractions" [Beard (1908) as quoted in White (1949:30)].

James Harvey Robinson also sought to break down disciplinary barriers. He saw history as a tool to enable the reader to "catch up with his own time" (White, 1949:45). This use of history to explain the present, he called the "new history," contrasting it with history as a chronicle of the past—a mere recitation of what he called "royal and military intrigues." Robinson realized that the "new history" demanded an interdisciplinary perspective. According to White:

> The view that history can explain supposes that the historian is familiar with the laws of social behavior. . . . The historian must be familiar not only with the isolated facts and events which form a bare chronicle, he must also be familiar with those generalizations which help us infer the occurrence of the event we call the effect from its cause. For this reason history demands a greater familiarity with the social sciences, the disciplines which hope to establish important generalizations or laws of human, social behavior; and Robinson urged that all the social disciplines are indispensable allies of history (White, 1949: 49–50).

This insight is reflected in the research of many other writers who were working to establish "new" social science disciplines. For example, in *An Economic Interpretation of the Constitution of the United States* (Beard, 1913), Beard tried to correlate the growth of political institutions to economic processes. Beard and Robinson together sought to connect the past and the present in a more holistic way in their book, *The Development of Modern Europe* (Robinson and Beard, 1907). Holmes' view that the meaning of the law is determined in the process of use led him to study many aspects of society, including "the felt necessities of the time, the prevalent moral and political themes, intentions of public policy, avowed and unconscious, even the prejudice which judges share with their fellow men" [Holes (1881) as quoted in White (1949:16–17)]. And Veblen, decisively influenced by anthropology, propounds institutionalism, a doctrine that demands that the economist study the connection between economic institutions and other aspects of culture (Veblen, 1899).

By this commitment to context the new liberal social philosophy made possible a more holistic coordinated conception of human society and human events. Obscured by the earlier formalist thought, certain connections between separate spheres of activity now became apparent. In particular it was recognized that *actions taken in one sphere would almost necessarily have consequences in others,* an idea which gave rise to the "systems" concept which is basic to the planning approach to policy.[8]

This insight, and the evolutionary, genetic perspective that we discussed earlier, made two vital contributions toward the development of thought about planning. A third, which gave practical significance to the other two, was a commitment to participate in public programs of social action for the purpose of improving conditions in society. Certainly the possibility for this commitment to action is implicit in a commitment to explain events genetically and contextually, but the possibility became a reality largely through the writings of one man—John Dewey.

Activism. Dewey wrote a philosophy of pragmatism, which breathed new life into the conception that knowledge should be a guide to social action. He began with the idea that knowledge would have to be relevant if man were to survive; he set out to make philosophy a relevant activity. In *Ethics,* he explains his concern for the world of action: "When the whole civilized world is giving its energies to the meaning and value of justice and democracy, it is intolerably academic that those interested in ethics should have to be content with conceptions already worked out" (Dewey and Tufts, 1908:v). In order to transform philosophy into a relevant activity, Dewey had to reject a prevailing conception about the nature of knowledge itself. According to the "spectator theory of knowledge," as Dewey called it, there is a true reality and a separate knower and ideas are the knower's way of comprehending the reality that they mirror. In place of this theory, Dewey advocated a traditionally American conception of knowledge as plans of action projected onto the world (Curti, 1956). For Dewey, knowledge is a form of experience that begins when a person encounters a problem or puzzle and ends when the problem or puzzle is solved (White, 1949:130). Thus, Dewey believed that thought was stimulated or initiated by activity and knowledge was "a matter of the use that is made of experienced natural events, a use in which given things are treated as indicators of what will be experienced under different conditions" (White, 1949:138).

The adoption of such a conception of knowledge made possible a transformation of Dewey's own field of philosophy from a contemplative science of existence and analysis of past acts to "an outlook upon future possibilities with reference to obtaining the better and avoiding the worse" (Dewey, 1917:53). Part II of *Ethics* is devoted to a discussion of the relevance of philosophy to the world of action.

> If we can discover ethical principles these ought to give some guidance
> for the unsolved problems of life which continually present themselves

for decision . . . ethics at least ought to have some practical value . . . man must act; and he must act well or ill, rightly or wrongly. If he has reflected, has considered his conduct in the light of the general principles of human order and progress, he ought to be able to act more intelligently and freely, to achieve the satisfaction that always attends scientific as compared with conventional or rule-of-thumb practices (Dewey and Tufts, 1908:4).

In education, too, Dewey advocated relevance, which he hoped would lead to greater freedom. As White explains, the purpose of Dewey's "progressive education" was "to affiliate the school with life, to make it a 'miniature community' an 'embryonic society' . . . the aim of which is the development of social power and insight" (White, 1949:98). Throughout his system of education, Dewey emphasized the achievement of real freedom, by which he meant not merely freedom from bondage but "the positive control of the resources necessary to carry purpose into effect, possession of the means to satisfy desire, and . . . mental equipment with the trained power of initiative and reflection necessary for free choice" (Dewey, 1899:438).

As the possibilities for shaping the environment through the liberating experiences of progressive education became apparent to him, Dewey developed the view that the *aim of all knowledge must be to help reshape life in society for the betterment of mankind*. He called on his colleagues in the fields of philosophy, law, economics, history, politics, sociology and psychology to free themselves from formalist metaphysics and devote themselves to social engineering. He believed in the "larger application of the scientific method to the problem of human welfare and progress" (Dewey and Tufts, 1908:v), later contending that the *only* reason for engaging in scientific work of any kind was to control and direct the environment (Dewey, 1917:53).

Thus, Dewey replaced the 17th-century mechanistic view of people as helpless creatures controlled by the grand laws of nature and society, with the idea of an open, constantly changing world in which thinking and acting could make a difference. He was persuaded that very little would be impossible to achieve if man used his mind and intelligence creatively and adventurously, was guided by a moral sense and took courageous action (Mowry, 1958:19). Henry Steele Commager, in *The American Mind* (Commager, 1950) summarizes Dewey's contribution to liberal social philosophy:

. . . more fully than any other philosopher of modern times, Dewey put philosophy to the service of society. More, he formed a whole network of alliances—with science, with politics, with education, with aesthetics, all devoted toward advancing the happiness of mankind. . . . He illustrated in his own career how effective philosophy could be in that reconstruction of society which was his preoccupation and its responsibility (Commager, 1950:99).

Dewey's pragmatism exerted enormous influence. Everywhere the quest was for relevance. As White noted, Robinson and Beard tried to combine "a historical interest with a pragmatic reforming spirit. . . . Their study of history was not motivated by nostalgia for the past, but rather by concern for the future" (White, 1949:52). In *The Development of Modern Europe,* they sought to connect history and ethics with current problems of society: "Even if all of us cannot contribute directly to their solution we should regard it as our duty to grasp the main difficulties and dangers which Europe and the world at large now face, and to follow intelligently the discussion that goes on about them" (Robinson and Beard, 1907:375). They were greatly troubled by the fact that a large portion of the world's population lived in squalor, ignorance and poverty, and they urged the use of reason, knowledge and science to improve these conditions (White, 1949: 56−57). In a later volume entitled *The Mind in the Making* (Robinson, 1921), Robinson explained that until his time the methods of science and intelligence had been used only in connection with physical problems—not with the problems of human society and social life. He believed that the social sciences must be developed and used to arrive at solutions for the myriad evils and problems of the day (White, 1949:199).[9]

Veblen, Holmes and James were also deeply affected by Dewey. In *The Engineer and the Price System* (Veblen, 1921), Veblen sets forth a format for social change in which scientific research, informed by the evolutionary and contextual perspectives of liberal philosophy, would be fed into the system of morality in society (Veblen, 1921:138−169). Veblen's idea was that eventually the scientific outlook, dictated by the great industrial transformation of modern times, would be communicated to politics and law (White, 1949:285−286). As for Holmes, he expressed admiration for the qualities of men of action, proclaiming: "To make up your mind at your peril upon a living question, for purposes of action, calls upon your whole nature" (Holmes, 1920:224). For William James, the real worth of an idea was in its consequences. He preached that people found what was good by constant experimentation, but that the lesson that was learned was relevant only to a given time, place and condition since the world was always in flux. Thus the only guarantee of success in the midst of this changing world was constant thought, experimentation and creative doing and acting.

Outlines of the New Social Philosophy

By the end of the first decade of the present century, the outlines of the new liberal social philosophy had been drawn. White describes it as "anti-formalistic, evolutionary and historically oriented" (White, 1949:107). Above all, it was committed to developing and carrying out programs of planned social action. Its impact, which was dramatic, has been described in this way:

> It was not so much the logical coherence of these ideas that led people to accept their works as though they were synoptic with gospels; it was rather the way in which they all seemed to contribute to the advent of a more rational society. . . . Followers became pragmatists in epistemology; they tried to apply scientific method to moral and social problems; they sent their children to Progressive schools; they defended social justice and civil liberties by citing Holmes' dissenting opinions; they voted socialist occasionally; they hailed Robinson's history of the western world; they interpreted politics economically and poked fun with Veblen at conspicuous consumption and the leisure class. Dewey thought of science as socially productive, and Veblen seemed to refute classical arguments for *laissez faire*. Robinson was an ally in the humanization of society and knowledge; Beard punctured myths about legal institutions which blocked social change; and Holmes recognized the legislative power of the judge and challenged the view that law was a deduction from divinely ordained principles of ethics (White, 1949:237–238).

The final yield of these ideas was neither the planning method per se nor direct political action; instead it was a basic determination to try to come to grips with a society that was undergoing extraordinarily rapid change. It was the sociological forces at work in this society that were responsible for shaping this predisposition into a specific conception about how to do planning, how to conduct public affairs in ways that granted the scientific expert a role of great importance in determining what needed to be done. To understand this conception and the important role in it that was given to social scientific experts, we need to consider these forces that shaped them.

Section Two: The Social Bases of Support for Activism in America

The new liberal philosophy might have amounted to very little if allowed to stand on its intellectual foundations alone. After all, the relationships between its philosophical ideas and the later ideology of planning are tenuous. For example, a leap of faith is required to move from Dewey's pragmatism to Lippmann's call for a master plan for social change, or from Veblen's insistence on an evolutionary perspective in economics to his later call for a scientific society. Judged solely as a system of thought the new philosophy was incomplete. The impetus toward rational planning was there; its form was not. This it received from the effect of social forces at work in the society—forces that had primed certain groups to be receptive to the new ideas which led them to interpret and expand them in specific ways. To understand this, we must appreciate why this activist philosophy received the support of some segments of the American population and this in turn requires us to understand some of the social changes that were occurring in the United States in the late 19th century. The work of two historians—Richard Hofstader (1963) and Robert Wiebe (1967)—stand out as especially illuminating on these questions. Both men describe American society of the late 19th century as experiencing disruptive changes associated with industrialization. They point out that for most of the 19th century, America had been a nation of small, rather isolated communities, which functioned as more or less autonomous self-governing units that were oriented toward local issues and concerns. Community political autonomy and the restriction of weak communication systems ensured that the power to form opinion and enact policy was widely dispersed. Thus, the heart of American democracy at this time was local autonomy (Wiebe, 1967:xiii—xiv).

Closely related to this tradition of local autonomy was an indigenous Yankee Protestant political tradition, which demanded each citizen's constant and disinterested attention to and participation in public affairs. As Hofstadter describes it, this tradition held that "political life ought to be run . . . in accordance with general principles and abstract laws apart from and superior to personal needs . . ." (Hofstadter, 1955:8—9). It need hardly be added that this political tradition was relentlessly middle class. Again, quoting Hofstadter, the common feeling was that "government should be in good part an effort to moralize the lives of individuals while economic life should be intimately related to the stimulation and development of individual character" (Hofstadter, 1955:8—9). The system of local autonomy and the widely shared political traditions resulted in a sense of social cohesion. But this social and governmental system, and therefore the social cohesion it fostered, depended on the community's actual ability to manage the lives of its citizens and the widespread belief of its members that the community possessed the political, social and economic power to do so (Wiebe, 1967:44—75).

By the 1870s, the autonomy of the local community was all but destroyed; only the illusion of authority endured, and even that misplaced confidence in community power disappeared during the 1880s and 1890s (Wiebe, 1967:xii). In these years, of course, industrialization was underway and a class of newly rich industrialists gained influence. Further, immigration and migration dramatically increased the size of American cties. From 1860 to 1910 the urban population of America increased sevenfold (Hofstadter, 1955:173). By 1910 nearly one-seventh of the nation's population (13.3 million persons) were immigrants. Most had been peasants in southern and eastern European countries and their ways were unfamiliar to the native-born Yankee Protestant middle class.

Naturally, all groups in American felt the impact of these changes in various ways. But in the middle class, the sons and daughters of the Yankee Protestants felt that they had suffered the greatest loss of deference and power. They experienced what Hofstadter calls an "upheaval in status" (Hofstadter, 1955:135). This class of professionals, including many clergymen and academics, believed that they had lost much economic and political influence to ward bosses and industrialists. In the cities to which many of the middle class had migrated, they watched ward bosses gaining political control by catering to the needs of immigrants in exchange for votes. They saw industrialists swaying political leaders and exerting complete economic control over communities in which a single corporation controlled the flow of capital and could make or break the community by single decision. [10] Hofstadter sums up the situation: "The newly rich, the grandiosely or corruptly rich, the masters of great corporations, were bypassing the men of the Mugwump type—the old gentry, the merchants of long standing, the small manufacturers, the established professional men, the civic leaders of another era" (Hofstadter, 1955:137).

The clergy, academics and other members of the middle class felt that they were losing moral authority as well; the political traditions that they cherished were being displaced. Industrialists made decisions based solely on profit motive, without regard to other implications; newly arrived immigrants unable to speak English exchanged their votes for help from ward bosses. As Hofstadter explains it:

> The other [new] system, founded upon the European background of the immigrants, upon their unfamiliarity with independent political action, their familiarity with hierarchy and authority, and upon the urgent needs that so often grew out of their migration, took for granted that the political life of the individual would rise out of family needs, interpreted political and civic realities chiefly in terms of personal obligations, and placed strong personal loyalties above allegiance to abstract codes of law or morals (Hofstadter, 1955:8−9).

The values of this new political system were completely at odds with those of the native-born middle class, which preached disinterested citizen participation. To this native-born professional middle class, and to many other groups in America as well, it must have seemed that the nation had splintered apart and become a "society without a core" (Wiebe, 1967:vii). Lippmann's term, "drift," aptly captured the mood of those who had been displaced by urbanization, industrialization and immigration.

Reactions to these changes varied. Some people closed their eyes and turned their backs to change, clinging ever more tightly to the largely outmoded values of small-town America. Others advocated repressive measures against immigrants and other minority groups, whom they blamed for the nation's problems (Wiebe, 1967:108–110). Still others advocated various schemes for solving society's problems; though few of the schemes succeeded, they had the appeal of reducing complicated matters of industrial development to simplistic moral equations inappropriate even to an earlier time (Wiebe, 1967:75–110).

The growing clamor for national planning and rational policy schemes was one of the schemes that was proposed. It was put forth as an attempt to solve problems caused by lack of social cohesion; it offered the hope that the "drift" of an apparently aimless change could be mastered and replaced by predictability and continuity. It would happen something like as follows. The agent for mastery would be powerful government that could engage in long-range rational planning. This government would be run by political leaders who possessed the old-fashioned virtues—men who would be "well-to-do, well-educated, high-minded citizens rich enough to be free from motives of . . . 'crass materialism' . . . whose family roots were deep not only in American history but in his local community" (Hofstadter, 1955:140). Aiding these high-minded political leaders would be scientific experts with lifetime tenure as government bureaucrats. They would be able to specialize in a particular problem area, and free from petty passions and narrow ambitions; they would find solutions to poverty, ignorance and disease in America. Science would provide the foundation for intelligent social action and effective socal policy; scientific government would bring opportunity, progress, order and continuity to American society.

This concept of government that emerged represented a peculiar amalgam of traditional Yankee middle-class values and new philosophical ideas about the nature and purpose of knowledge which were supplied by intellectuals such as Holmes, Veblen and Dewey.

The appeal of these ideas to the native-born professionally trained middle class is not difficult to understand. With political values not unlike those of the old Yankee Protestant middle class, it proposed a scheme for dealing with modern problems. Appealing to the widely held belief that American society was failing because of the influence of crass, materialistic, political considerations on policy, and because of a lack of planning, this movement, by comparison, promised a well-functioning political system achieved through planning, rationality, high-mindedness and the use of scientific experts. It was thought that such a well-functioning political system would, in turn, automatically solve society's problems. In addition, the importance assigned to knowledge, science and intelligence in the ideal society is closely related to the upheaval experienced by the professional middle class. Those who possessed education, and those who provided education, would surely occupy highly influential and powerful positions in this system. Thus, those who thought they stood to gain the most in such a system became the advocates of it.[11]

Progressivism. The ideas and ideals of this new liberal philosophy were popularized in the writings and speeches of journalists and politicians alike. Especially influential in this respect were the works of Lippmann and Croly. Perhaps more than any other figures of the day, these two men helped to codify, extend and clarify the social and political implications of views which Dewey, Veblen, Beard, Robinson, Holmes, James and others were expressing, translating them into calls for large-scale scientifically conceived programs of public social action.[12] Through their efforts the basic tenets of liberal philosophy, which many educated members of the displaced middle class embraced, were soon transformed from a vague mood into a powerful movement for political and social reform. This was *Progressivism*, a social movement which flourished from the turn of the century through the end of the New Deal. Most historians agree that even though it died then, it left as one of its legacies that concept of rational, scientific planning that is a basic part of the assumptive world of modern day applied, policy-relevant sociology.

What did Progressivism stand for? What were the movement's themes? Three ideas stand out as especially significant. These are confidence, activism and a faith in scientific experts.

Confidence. This was the faith "that no problem is too difficult to be overcome by the proper mobilization of energy and of intelligence among the citizens" (Hofstadter, 1963a:5). To be sure, this optimism was always accompanied by anxiety about what *could* happen if events were allowed to follow their course unhampered, but implicit in such dismal prophecies was an insistant faith that Doomsday was preventable.

Activism. A second theme that pervaded Progressivism was *activism.* Progressives felt that social evils, of which they perceived many, would not remedy themselves if left alone; indeed, they felt that it was morally wrong for anyone to be passive and wait for things to take care of themselves (Hofstadter, 1963a:4). Herbert Croly, in *The Promise of American Life* (1909), stated bluntly that the future of the nation would not take care of itself, and that the people of America would have to be energized and motivated to bring about social progress through governmental action (Croly, 1909). At the heart of Progressivism was the idea, to borrow Lippmann's term, that the nation must end its policy of "drifting" and gird itself for the "mastery" of its own destiny (Lippmann, 1914).

To this end Progressives sought to arouse the citizens—to organize them in an effort to bring into being the political and social machinery necessary to cope with national crises. This promise of social progress was to be reached, Hofstadter explains, by "using the active power—by the exposure of evils through the spreading of information and the exhortation of the citizenry; by using the possibilities inherent in the ballot to find new and vigorous popular leaders; in short, by a revivification of Democracy" (Hofstadter, 1963a:5). Perhaps the best known example of such activism was the so-called muckraker, the journalist who exposed corruption, crime, waste, brutality and neglect in American life, hoping that his/her exhortations would arouse ordinary people to snatch political power from bosses and corrupt officials.

Faith in Experts and Science. The discovery of evil was one thing; its eradication another. Exhortation of citizens by muckracking journalists might create an environment conducive to change; mere exposure of evil would not tell newly elected leaders how to abolish it. A third theme of Progressivism, *the faith in experts and in science,* is introduced. Answers to the question of how to abolish society's evils would be supplied, Progressives hoped, by scientific experts. These experts—mostly social scientists—would conduct detailed studies of social problems in America and from the data design plans to solve them. These plans would be translated into legislation and the laws would be administered by "scientific managers" and professional administrators beholden to no one, but dedicated to carrying out these rationally conceived, comprehensive programs of planned social action. Weibe describes this facet of the movement:

> Progressives advocated the staffing of government bureaucracy with scientific experts who would be employed by the government for a lifetime and specialize in the solution of particular kinds of problems, or better, specialized aspects of them . . . . Expertise . . . meant immersing oneself in the scientific method, eradicating petty passions and narrow ambitions and removing all flaws in reasoning. The result would be a perfect bureaucrat who would give precisely accurate responses to questions raised within his (her) domain of specialization (Wiebe, 1967: 147).

Progressives embraced science, especially social science, as the foundation for intelligent social action and effective social planning.

From these three themes—*confidence, activism* and *faith in science and experts*—we can construct the Progressives' conception of how civic and public affairs ought to be conducted. Progressives envisioned a process of governance in which evil would be exposed through active investigations into social conditions, and vigorous dissemination of this information through social science research and through popular journalism as exemplified by the work of muckrakers. The exposure of evil would be accompanied by exhortation of citizens to wrest the power from those who had permitted evil to flourish. Once the people had gained power, they would, in turn, employ scientific and technical experts to investigate the wisest procedures for achieving social reform; to devise social legislation to accomplish reform; and to execute this reform as programs of social action. Throughout, action was to be guided by rationality, long-range planning, science and "the national interest."

The Development of Progressive Ideas About Planning: An Overview

Progressive activism had begun in the city, the meeting place of the new immigrants and the native-born Protestant members of the middle-class who had come from small towns and rural areas in search of new business and professional opportunities. These natives were shocked, not only by the political bossism of the city, but by the conditions of immigrant life: the overcrowding, dirt, disease, crime and poverty (Hofstadter, 1955:176). Many of the natives saw the immigrant as a victim of his ignorance of how government was supposed to operate and how American life was supposed to be lived. Their first response involved local programs of "naturalization and

Americanization" (Hofstadter, 1955:179). Settlement houses and churches joined in the effort to educate and Americanize the immigrant. [13]

Meanwhile the hidden realities of life in American cities were being relentlessly exposed by sociological research, muckracking journalists and by members of the literary wing of the movement. Novels and magazine articles by Ida Tarbell, John Fiske, Lincoln Steffens, David Graham Phillips, Ray Stannard Baker, Upton Sinclair and Walter Weyl (who, in 1914 joined Croly and Lippmann in founding *The New Republic*, for many years the house organ of the Progressive movement) dramatically exposed the evils of the society. Because of the growing number and power of newspapers, the muckrakers could call national attention to conditions in cities like Chicago and New York. In these journalistic accounts, "reality" became something of a dirty word. Hofstadter explains ". . .[reality] was hidden, neglected and offstage. It was conceived essentially as the stream of external and material events which was most likely to be unpleasant. Reality was the bribe, the rebate, the bought franchise, the sale of adulterated food . . . [it] was a series of unspeakable plots, personal inequities, moral failures which in their totality had come to govern American society only because the citizen had relinquished his moral vigilance" (Hofstadter, 1955:200).

The Progressives hoped that exposure of evil would result in social action. In the press, in churches, in classrooms and in political speeches, citizens were told that they had a personal responsibility to do something about conditions in society (Hofstadter, 1955:210; Mowry, 1958:38; Commager, 1950:216). Yet, clearly moral exhortation was not enough; political reform was necessary. The bosses must be driven from office and power given to the peple.

With few exceptions, efforts to achieve local reform through exhortation of the populace failed. This failure led Progressives to expand the scope and content of their original ideas, thereby adding new meaning to the concept of scientific planning. For one thing, the focus of planning efforts shifted from the local to the national level. Proponents of the idea of planning quickly learned that what happened in the city was largely determined by politicians who controlled the state. And those who worked on issues at a state level soon came to believe that coordination of activities nationally improved their effectiveness. Further, many problems confronting proponents of scientific planning were national in scope—conservation of natural resources, regulation of the activities of big business, controls on environmental pollution, electoral reform and tariff reform. The achievement of these and other reforms required a national effort. Finally, Progressives came to favor nationally coordinated efforts because they began to suspect that the forces opposing reform that were thought to be hidden and powerful, were nationally organized. Woodrow Wilson captured the suspicion when he wrote:

> Some of the biggest men in the United States in the field of commerce and manufacture are afraid of somebody, are afraid of something. They know that there is a power somewhere so organized, so subtle, so watchful, so interlocked, so complete, so pervasive, that they had better not speak in condemnation of it (Wilson, 1913:195).

In his call for a "New Nationalism," Theodore Roosevelt took account of these Progressive insights:

> The new nationalism puts the national need before sectional or personal advantage. It is impatient of the utter confusion that results from local legislatures attempting to treat national issues as local issues. It is still more impatient of the impotence which springs from overdivision of governmental powers, the impotence which makes it possible for local selfishness or for legal cunning, hired by wealthy special interest, to bring national activities to a deadlock. This New Nationalism regards the executive power as the steward of the public welfare (Roosevelt, 1910:29).

Thus, Roosevelt and other Progressives concluded that a strong national government was necessary to oppose the forces of evil and to implement reform policies. This call for strong national government posed a problem for the Progressives, as the movement was also strongly committed to government *by* the people. The 1912 Progressive Party platform, for example, defined the role of political parties as "to serve responsible government and to execute the will of the people" (Johnson, 1956:175). The Democratic and Republican parties were accused of selling out to an "invisible government" of corrupt business and corrupt politicians; in contrast, the Progressive Party proposed to restore government to the people through the reform of campaign practices and the extension of suffrage to women. Supporters of government by the people feared that a strong federal government might be more vulnerable to abuse. They faced a dilemma: without a strong government there could be no national program of reform; with a strong government came a greater potential for autocratic rule.

The Progressives' resolution of this dilemma brought to the concept of rational planning one of its most crucial ideas: *the idea of the neutral state.* Not only the individual political leaders and scientific experts who served in government would be neutral; the government it-self would be fair and even-handed in all situations. As Hofstadter stated it:

> The state must not be anti-business or even anti-big business: It must be severely neutral among all the special interests in society, subordinating each to the common interest in dealing out even-handed justice to all. It would be for neither the rich man nor the poor man, for labor nor capital, but for the just and honest and law-abiding man of whatever class. It would stand in fact where the middle class felt itself to be standing . . . in the middle on neutral ground among self-seeking inter-ests of all kinds (Hofstadter, 1955:232).

While the ideal of neutral government relieved anxieties about a strong federal government, it left unsettled a basic Progressive dis-agreement about what the phrase, "returning power to the common people," really meant. Theodore Roosevelt held a point of view about this question. Roosevelt envisioned an elite leadership of scientific experts and educated persons who would determine, not the people's will, but the wisest course of action for the nation to follow. Roosevelt believed that if the power to decide and implement policy were placed with a few professional experts, the decision-making and policy-making processes would be open and honest and the national interest would be served. In sharp contrast to this was a Populist view that insisted that the common people had the intelligence and capac-ity to recognize their own interests and to choose responsibly courses of action to meet those interests. Woodrow Wilson, who sharply criticized Roosevelt's view (Wilson, 1913:200−208), expressed this Populist view succinctly: "The people of the United States un-derstand their interests better than any group of men in the confines of the country understand them" (Wilson, 1913:63). He argued that the government of the nation must not be allowed to be lodged in any special group or to become a tool of any set of institutions. "I believe in the average integrity and the average intelligence of the American people, and I do not believe that the intelligence of America can be put into commissions anywhere" (Wilson, 1913:207). In Wilson's scheme of democracy, experts would use their knowledge only to help determine the people's will and to draw up and implement policies and programs to make this will a reality.

These opposing visions of how the public interest would best be served are of more than theoretical interest. They are reflected both in the styles of research and advice adopted by social scientists working with federal and state government from the administration of Theodore Roosevelt through that of Franklin Roosevelt, and have recurred regularly in public deliberations about governmental policy toward poverty, welfare, civil rights and education in the administrations of Presidents Kennedy, Johnson and Nixon.

Summary. We have tried to show that many of the basic notions involving the concept of scientifically informed social planning that were described in Chapter 3 derive from an historical pedigree whose recent past is centered in Progressive thought. The present-day version of this concept that sociologists embrace differs, of course, from the one that the Progressives originally proposed. For a start, the sociologists' conception of his role in the policy-making process is sharply altered: Progressives envisioned the social scientist as an architect of master plans for change, while today's sociologist is more inclined to feel that his role should be limited to research and proving technical knowledge. (The social and political bases of this redefinition of the role of the sociological expert is discussed in Section Three of this chapter. See pages 108–114). For another, the scope of involvement envisaged is different. For Progressives there were to be grandiose master plans for the whole society. No sociologist today envisages schemes quite so grand as these or, indeed, even a policy scheme for a given problem that is based on social science knowledge alone. Yet, the core concept that public affairs should be nationally and regionally planned and be conducted in a rational way and that political leaders should use the services of intellectuals and scientists freely to accomplish this goal, remains very much in evidence today. It is this basic idea that is the Progressives' legacy to modern day applied sociology.

Section Three: The Impact of Social Science on the Planning Movement

We have discussed the modern roots of the impetus to plan, and in the course of the discussion we have alluded to the influence that it had on sociology. However, this is only part of the picture for social science in general and sociology in particular had an important impact on the planning movement as well. Social scientists were instrumental in (a) helping to develop the movements main concepts and (b) helping to define the role that scientific experts would play in public affairs. Both of these issues must be explored to complete the discussion of how the modern day conception of scientific planning that we outlined earlier was originally developed.

Social science and the concept of planning. In certain respects the planning movement and social science were one and the same thing, as the concept of scientific planning had strong advocates among members of the American social science community. Members of this community who supported the idea, in addition to Veblen, Beard, Robinson, Dewey, Tufts, Holmes and others already mentioned, included such notables as political scientist, J. Allen Smith; economists, Richard Ely, Henry Carter Adams, Simon Patten, Frank Taussig and John Commons; Frederick Jackson Turner and Vernon Louis Parrington in history; and, in sociology, Lester Ward, E. A. Ross, Albion Small and Charles Horton Cooley.[14] This scholarly branch of Progressivism played an important part in the movements development, influencing its intellectual and political orientations in decisive ways. The sociologist, Lester Ward, was responsible for developing some of the movement's most basic ideas about governance and the role of science in social planning, and Albion Small was instrumental in devising concrete plans to implement them. The economist, Simon Patten, gave expression to Progressive ideas of social planning by applying them to the problem of poverty and the economist, John Commons, tried to work out a method by which to bring social science directly into government. It is beyond the scope of this chapter to present a detailed account of the full role that social science had in helping to develop Progressive ideas about planning in government.[15] It is our intention only to handle this question briefly, by illustrating the close affinity between Progressives and social science scholars as this is reflected in the writings and research of a few key social scientists of the day.

Lester Ward provides one of the best illustrations of this influence. The adverse reactions that the new liberals had to principles of formalism and determinism are mirrored in Ward's writings. As explained in Chapter 1, a formalistic, deterministic view of human society dominated the thinking of 19th-century sociologists. We saw how Herbert Spencer and William Graham Sumner led the quest to discover immutable social laws such as free competition and survival of the socially fittest—laws that they regarded as futile and immoral for anyone to attempt to alter. Ward challenged these ideas at every opportunity. The most ambitious assault he undertook was in his highly influential two-volume work, *Dynamic Sociology, or Applied Social Science, as Based upon Statical Sociology and the Less Complex Sciences* (Ward, 1883). Here he presents arguments against Spencarian sociology and offers his alternative of a "dynamic" sociology—an applied social science that might serve as the basis for planned social change.

The faults that Ward found with Spencerian sociology are precisely those which Dewey and others found with formalism and determinism in other fields. To some extent, Ward accepted determinism, but he did not agree with Spencer that it required noninterference in the course of events. He stated: "Because natural processes are genetic they [Spencerians] erroneously conclude that nature's way should be man's way . . . . They teach the natural as the proper human method, whereas the latter is necessarily an artificial method" (Ward, 1883:Volume I, vi). To Ward, the Spencerian conception of sociology was lifeless. He believed that unless it were replaced, "Sociology, which of all sciences should benefit man most, is in danger of falling into the class of polite amusements or dead sciences" (Ward, 1883:I, vii). Ward had a more than academic reason for challenging Spencerian sociology. Like the other academic intellectuals who were influential in formulating the new liberal social philosophy, he held an apocalyptic vision of what might happen to our civilization if allowed to continue to drift. He stated:

> This swarming planet will soon see the condition of human advancement exhausted, and the night of reaction and degeneracy ushered in, never to be again succeeded by the development of progress, unless something swifter and more certain than natural selection can be brought to bear upon the development of the psychic faculty, by which alone man is distinguished from the rest of the fauna of the earth and enabled to people all parts of its surface. The resources of the globe are not inexhaustible unless zealously husbanded by the deliberative foresight of enlightened intellect (Ward, 1883:I:16).

Ward often returned to this apocalyptic vision.[16] To prevent this threatened downfall of society, he advocated marrying "the vast emotional forces which are ever strong to improve society" (Ward, 1883:I, 21), but which invariably fail through lack of intelligent guidance, to "some truly Progressive system of machinery that should succeed in accomplishing the desired end" (Ward, 1883:I, 21). "American society," he wrote, "should not drift aimlessly to and fro, backwards and forwards, without guidance. Rather, the group should carefully study its situation; comprehend the aims it desires to accomplish; study scientifically the best methods for attainment of them; and then concentrate social energy to the task set before it" (Ward, as cited by Geis and Meier, 1977:7). He envisaged a "system of machinery" consisting of highly developed intelligence joined with facts about society systematically and carefully compiled through the methods of sociological investigation. The aim was to amass scientific knowledge about society and put it to use for the benefit of mankind.

Reason, intelligence and knowledge would be central to his plan at two levels. At one level, social and scientific experts would make available the existing knowledge or discover new knowledge through research on a given problem to aid in determining solutions. At another level, the universal education of the public advocated by Ward would ensure the entire nation's commitment to the use of knowledge and reason to benefit mankind (Ward, 1883:I, 25).

> Before progress can ever be achieved, the public sentiment must exist in favor of scientific education . . . [and] if by the term education there can be constantly implied the two adjuncts, scientific and popular; if the world can be made to embrace the notion of imparting a knowledge of the materials and forces of nature to all members of society there can be no objection to the employment of this word 'education' as the embodiment of all that is progressive (Ward, 1883:I, 26).

Ward believed that legislators should be trained in sociology. Legislatures would become arenas to amass and transform research into information that could be used to draft legislation. They would be "laboratories of philosophical research into the laws of society and of human nature" (Ward, 1883:I, 37). Naturally, the men and women who served in them would need to be thoroughly trained in dynamic sociology and committed to influencing the laws of human progress for the good of society (Ward, 1883:I, 56): "Every true legislator must be a sociologist" (Ward, 1883:I, 37).

In place of a deterministic sociology, Ward advocated a teleological sociology. Men and women would seek to improve society by the exercise of intelligent foresight. Using knowledge, they would take hold of the laws of nature that Spencer described and direct them to their own desired ends. Ward said it this way:

> To the regular course of the social phenomena as determined by the laws of evolution we must conceive added a new force limiting and directing these into special channels and for special ends. Its chief quality as distinguished from other forces is purpose. In short, it is teleological force . . . [and] . . . the source of this teleological force is to be sociology (Ward, 1883:I, 57).[17]

Ward's thinking, traces of which are apparent in the writings of Croly and Lippmann, was embraced by other sociologists, among them E. A. Ross, Charles Cooley, Robert Park and Albion Small. Small, in particular, worked to develop the discipline that Ward established in broad outline, continuing and extending Ward's emphasis on action. Small argued in *General Sociology* (1905): "From the human standpoint no science is an end in itself. The proximate end of all science is organization into action. The ultimate interest of the sociologist, therefore, is in turning knowledge of the social process into more intelligent promotion of the process" (Small, 1905:22). The sociologist should seek an intelligent framework within which to improve human conditions (Small 1905:655). The sociologist's purpose should be intensely pragmatic; his aim is to discover "not how the world came to be what it is, but how to make it what it should be" (Small, 1905:566). Paradoxically, in disagreement with Ward, Small argued that the path to ultimate usefulness led by way of disinterested scholarly research: he urged his colleagues to do their theorizing and research without regard to its immediate use (Small, 1905:645).[18] Once the basis for the new science was established, Small envisaged "middlemen" who would review the results of empirical research and assess their implications for social action. His definition of tasks is still evident in research and writing involving the applications of sociology to social policy. For example, Small felt that the first task facing sociologists was to amass enough information about American society to create a composite picture which would serve as a guide for social action. He explained this effort in a chapter entitled, "Social Achievements in the United States" (Small, 1905:718−727), in which he subdivided the American social structure into categories and then indicated the type of data to be compiled for each "cell" in his framework. This procedure was later followed by social scientists enlisted to prepare a report for President Hoover on social trends in the United States (*Recent Trends in the United States*, 1933), and, less closely, in the drafting of recent plans for compiling indicators of social change in America (Bauer, 1966).

Sociologists were not the only ones who developed and espoused the ideal of rational social planning. Economists, too, participated in it, a fact made clear in the wording of the preamble to the charter of the American Economic Association, which was drafted in 1885. It states: "We regard the State as an educational and ethical agency whose positive aid is an indispensable condition to human progress" (quoted in Mowry, 1958:22). This expression of the idea of teleological progress was aimed directly at the tenets of conservative economics as supported by such people as Arthur Hadley, John Clark and J. Lawrence Laughlin. They held a view toward economic development, which was both deterministic and laissez-faire. In contrast to this view, those responsible for forming the Association, whose ranks included Henry Adams, Richard Ely, John Commons and Simon Patten, charged that the laissez faire economic system was the cause of social inequality in America. They viewed evil as social—the product of existing social arrangements. But they also saw in the economic and social system the potential for good, because like many other social scientists and intellectuals, and in common with many Progressives, they believed that society was perfectable through the applications of scientific knowledge and understanding to the conduct of human affairs.

Their thinking is illustrated in Patten's *The Theory of Prosperity* (1902), a book with impact on many young economists. His thesis was that poverty was not an inevitable permanent feature of human society, but it was "an economic phenomenon that can and must be abolished. Moreover, the state is the only social institution with sufficient resources to deal with the complex economic and social forces that create poverty" (Patten, 1902:88). Patten believed that man could create enough material goods by harnessing nature to provide adequately for everyone. Through lectures, seminars, his *The New Basis of Civilization* (1907) and, later, as a political activist, Patten attacked the earlier determinist economic positions. His influence extended everywhere, including government political advisers, such as Edward Devine, an economic adviser to President Theodore Roosevelt; and to Francis Perkins and Rexford Tugwell (both students of Patten)—both advisers to Franklin Delano Roosevelt.

While Patten influenced government advisers, John R. Commons, a professor of economics at the University of Wisconsin, was actively applying economics and other social science disciplines to public affairs (Mowry, 1958:22).[19] He was himself an adviser to Robert M. LaFollette while LaFollette served as Governor of Wisconsin and United States Senator. Most important, however, was his work as a member and later Director of the Industrial Commission of Wisconsin. The Commission was established to provide the scientific expertise necessary for longrange planning in Wisconsin. Social scientific experts were to become familiar with problems requiring action, collecting pertinent data, suggesting solutions, and working closely with the public officials who would draft appropriate legislation and implement and administer it. Commons called the Commission, "a fourth branch of government . . . covering but not usurping the work of the three other branches" (Commons, 1913: 440). The Wisconsin Industrial Commission was the first statewide effort to use technical social science expertise for social planning, and the model of participation which Commons created is by now a distinguished tradition in the history of "applied" social science.

The pervasiveness of progressive thinking in American academia, and the debt owed its scholarly wing by the movement as a whole, is further illustrated by the fact that between 1886 and 1895, six academic social science journals were founded—all for the explicit purpose of providing professionally sanctioned outlets for the expression and development of Progressivist ideas. *The Political Science Quarterly, The Quarterly Journal of Economics, The Annals of the American Academy of Political and Social Science, The Journal of Political Economy, The American Historical Review* and *The American Journal of Sociology* were all created to serve as forums for publishing research and theoretical papers aimed at creating knowledge that could be used in policy. Through publication of articles in these and other journals, in books, and through teaching, research and consultation, social scientists sympathetic to Progressivist ideas about scientific rationality and planning in public affairs had an important impact on the movement's development.

Through the work of social scientists, the idea of planning in government gained definition and support both within and outside of the academic community. Academic social scientists provided much of the theory behind the planning ideology which was emerging, and helped to give direct expression to it.[20] It is accurate to conclude that social science influence on Progressive ideas about planning were perhaps as great as the influence that Progressivism had on the development of social science in the United States.

Interlude

Thus far in this chapter we have tried to illuminate some of the philosophical, social and political roots of the concept of social planning that is implicit in the theory and practice of applied social science today. We have seen how a new liberal social philosophy which was developed during the late 19th century provided the epistemological foundations for the subsequent development of a planning ideology in government, and how the basic themes of this philosophy—developmentalism, naturalism and activism—were interpreted, shaped and amplified by social forces unleashed by industrialization. Out of the complex interplay that occurred between the new philosophy and these forces of change came a new theory of governance termed, Progressivism. Progressives believed that change in American society could be controlled, made to develop according to the dreams and wishes of its people. The tool that would make this possible was the planning method, an approach to government policy-making based upon logic, reason, a long-range time perspective, a commitment to the common good and a deep faith in the methods of science to point the way toward stability, orderliness and realization of the common good. The fundamental conceptions about policy which sociologists today embrace are direct descendants of these Progressive ideas.

The analysis we have presented helps us to understand better where many of the basic ideas which modern-day sociologists hold about policy originated. What has not yet been made clear is where present-day notions about the sociologists role in the policy-making process came from. In Chapter 2 we discussed various ways in which sociologists believe that the theory, knowledge and methods of our discipline may be used for policy purposes. We cited the use of sociology to enlighten policy-makers; to provide substantive ideas and information that could be fed into the policy process; to evaluate ongoing programs; to study the policy process; and to engage in direct social action. Common to all but one of these (except the sociologist as political activist, a topic which is discussed on pages 47, 62) is the idea that the sociologist's role in this process will be confined to that of providing policy-makers with technical knowledge, information and ideas that they may elect to use in carrying out policy. In this division of labor, the policy-maker is responsible for electing the course of action to pursue and the sociologist is responsible for providing technical knowledge and ideas that may help him to make these decisions more wisely. The sociologist conceives his role in this process as an objective, neutral figure who uses the methods and knowledge of his/her discipline to answer "if-then" types of questions about proposed courses of action. This notion about the role that scientific experts should play in policy is not the only possible one that might be considered. In fact, it is greatly at odds with the one which such persons as Ward, Dewey, Veblen, Ely, Commons and Lippmann envisioned. All of these men saw social scientists as activists, critics of American society as then constituted and architects of its future. It remains for us to consider how and why this original definition of the social scientist's role in policy was abandoned, and supplanted by a role conception that is more narrowly defined, technical and advisory in nature. One solution to this puzzle is proposed by historian Mary Furner, who castes an especially illuminating light on the development of this aspect of applied sociology in America, adding new meaning to the point we raised earlier that in its relationships to government, it is government and not sociology that dictates terms and dominates. Furner's thesis is explained in the following section.

The role of the social scientist in the planning process. Many social scientists of the late 19th century strongly supported the basic idea of trying to direct the course of social change in American society through planning, joining in efforts to urge the government to use social science expertise more widely. Yet, beneath this broad umbrella of agreement were basic differences of opinion among them about the *precise* role that social scientists ought to play in policy-making and the manner in which their impact was to be made. Bitter disputes about these questions erupted among social scientists—arguments that took many years to resolve. The resolutions that were eventually arrived at helped to provide social science with a definition of its role in public affairs and guidelines for conducting applied, policy-relevant research, which correspond rather closely to the ones we described in Chapters 2 and 3.

In her excellent book, *Advocacy and Objectivity* (1975), Mary Furner presents a revealing account of how and why this particular conception of social scientists' role in policy came about. Furner recounts the history of the conflict between, on the one hand, conservative laissez-faire economists, most of whom were members of the academic community; and, on the other hand, members of the American Social Science Association (ASSA), a loose coalition of social reformers comprised of some academic social scientists who did not share the conservative convictions of their laissez-faire colleagues and various political activists. A laissez-faire ideology dominated conservative academic economics (and sociology). Furner describes the social science of the day as "a science of wealth . . . useful justification for entrepreneurs who were reaping the fruits of an expanding economy" (Furner, 1975:39). The academic wing of the ASSA rejected this idea. Its members consisted of men (many of whom were trained in German universities or influenced by those who were) who were taught the Bismarchian concept of "the positive role the state would play in governing the evolution of an economic system capable of spreading the benefits of industrialization to all classes" (Furner, 1975:48).[21] Laissez-faire and new school economists engaged in vigorous public debate on this issue, a debate that reached new heights of acrimony in the late 1870s and early 1880s, when new school economists began to emerge as dominant. As this occurred, economic conservatism began to lose its respectability within the profession, and more and more of its members became committed to the idea of placing economics at the service of state planning.

The emergence of Bismarchian ideas about planning, for all intents and purposes, put an end to serious debate in America between conservatives and liberals about the role that economics should play in the new industrial order; it did not put an end to dissent within this discipline. A new argument developed among those who had previously been united in their opposition to the laissez-faire position. Dissent now centered on the issue of what role the economist (or other social scientists) ought to play in the development of programs of social reform.

Two main positions emerged. One position was supported by economists such as Richard Ely, Richard Commons, Edmund James and, during the early years of his academic career, Henry Carter Adams; and sociologists such as Lester Ward and E. A. Ross. The other position was argued by economists such as Frank Taussig, Simon Newcomb and Henry Carter Adams (in the later years of his career); and sociologists Albion Small, Robert Park and Charles H. Cooley. The issue that divided the two camps involved the role social scientists should play vis-a-vis policy, as advocate or as objective expert. The issue reflected a deep tension in the profession between its members' zeal for reform and their need to amass knowledge about society. Those who adopted the advocate stance adhered to a Wardian conception of scientists' role in policy. Their position is exemplified by University of Wisconsin economist, Richard Ely. According to Furner, Ely held the view that:

> It is no longer necessary for economic thinking to be governed by assumptions that doomed most men to poverty. If the unbreakable imperatives of a pre-industrial system had made an equitable distribution of wealth and comfort impossible . . . no such a priori arrangement rationalized injustice any longer. Machines and new sources of power made it possible to transcend the grim Malthusian realities which may have existed in primitive societies. People could establish goals designed to place the welfare of the whole people above the customary privilege of any dominant class and then consciously direct society's various enterprises toward the achievement of these goals. Because advances in the economic system made a new social ethic possible, the obligation of designing a more humane system of economic relationships fell heavily on economists . . . . The responsibility for making these ethical judgments and articulating "what ought to be" defined the role of the new school economist (Furner, 1975:94—95).[22]

The economists' role would be to speak out against evils that resulted from established economic arrangements and to use his or her knowledge to propose new and revolutionary ways of overcoming them. Of necessity, such a scientific expert would have to make ethical judgments that would challenge basic values and threaten entrenched interests. Ely believed that this was inevitable; it had to be done in the name of the greater prize of meaningful and lasting social reform (Furner, 1975: 101–102).

The position adopted by the "objectivists" camp is exemplified in the writings of Henry Carter Adams, an avid supporter of the new state economics whose enthusiasm for advocacy waned after he became embroiled at an early point in his academic career in a major dispute that was triggered by his outspoken view on labor. Adams adopted a moderate position about the role of the social scientist in advising policy-making bodies. He argued that economists should abandon any claim to special moral authority. They should not place themselves or their colleagues in the position of advocating what should be done: instead they should adopt an advisory role in which they would agree to supply technical knowledge and policy recommendations for legislative bodies to consider. Furner writes:

> No longer did he (Adams) defend the economists' right to act as the conscience of speaking out against even the most firmly established customs if they impeded social justice. Instead Adams told his professional colleagues . . . that an economist ought to realize that tampering with institutions deeply imbedded in the historical life of the community was a risky business which might do more harm than good . . . . Academic economists might better limit their public statements to less controversial subjects and confine their attempts to influence policy to behind-the-scenes work as technical experts advising legislatures or operating government regulatory commissions (Furner, 1975:138).

Furner explains that the position which Adams espoused reflected the view that professional economists and other social scientists should "forego any activity, no matter how constructive, which might interfere with his main function of reasoned, impartial, disinterested inquiry. A university teacher's business was generating new knowledge and teaching unformed minds to think, not deciding controversial issues or putting on intellectual exhibition matches for cheering partisans" (Furner, 1975: 120).

This debate between the two camps raged feverishly during the 1880s and 1890s. Proponents of the objectivist position gradually gained the upper hand and eventually won the argument. According to Furner, what tipped the scales in their favor was not so much the intellectual merits of their case (proponents of both positions were equally skilled debators) as it was the impact that academic freedom cases of the 1890s had on the audience of professional economists and social scientists before whom the debate was being staged. In this decade, social scientists in the advocacy camp began to press publically for measures that directly threatened powerful political and economic interests. The most famous of these persons were E. A. Ross of Stanford University (who openly attacked Leland Stanford for exploiting Chinese workers in amassing his fortune), Henry Carter Adams at Cornell University, and Edward Bemis and John Commons, students of Richard Ely—both of whom taught at the University of Chicago. All four attacked vested political and economic interests with a vengence. Furner noted that in return for their criticisms of established economic and social arrangements, these and other men found themselves facing efforts at retribution (Furner, 1975:143). These ranged all the way from "subtle suggestions that they curb their more radical teachings to heavy-handed measures aimed at urging them from the academic profession" (Furner, 1975:143). The academic freedom cases brought against these and other members of the advocacy camp created special problems for the social science disciplines involved, not the least of which was that they began to endanger the authority that professional social scientists felt they needed to have in order to validate their claim of expertise in the area of social and economic analysis.

The fate of those brought to task for their activism taught social scientists of the day a clear lesson: "Avoid radicalism. Avoid socialism. Avoid excessive publicity and refrain from public advocacy. When trouble strikes, unless there is certain assurance of massive support, accept your fate in austere and dignified silence. Above all, maintain a reputation for scientific objectivity" (Furner, 1975:204). She adds, "The academic freedom cases contributed to the gradual narrowing of the range of dissent that seemed safe for professional social scientists and threatened their freedom to continue working . . . . For better or worse, these troubles taught many academics to conserve their image and perserve their institutions, to prepare to defend themselves but avoid the necessity, to exert influences quietly as experts rather than noisily as partisans" (Furner, 1975:257–258).

The consequence of these developments she describes as a "progressive, liberal profession" (Furner, 1975:258), a profession that strongly supported an affirmative role for the state but became intolerant of activism and advocacy within its own ranks. Members of the social science profession were now expected to "channel their reform efforts through government agencies and private organizations where scholars could serve inconspicuously as technical experts, after the political decisions had been made, rather than a reformers with a new vision of society" (Furner, 1975:259). Most academic social scientists stopped asking ethical questions, turning attention instead to carefully controlled, empirical studies of problems that were narrowly defined by the state of knowledge in their discipline rather than by the state of society. More and more they came to accept the basic structure of corporate capitalism. "Abandoning their pretensions to a role as arbiters of public policy, they established a more limited goal: recognition as experts with . . . technical competence in a highly specialized but restricted sphere" (Furner, 1975:8). Furner further describes this new breed of social scientists as "a cautious gradualist who was willing to let men who wanted to be identified as reformers take leadership in applying social science to society. At best, the new . . . economist preferred to take an assignment as an expert . . . and give advice to be carried out by someone else, after the political decisions had been made. Even then he wanted it clear that he was providing specialist services in his professional capacity as a social scientist, not as a volunteer partisan prompted by reforming zeal" (Furner, 1975:160).

Thus, out of this dispute came a view of how social scientists should become involved in policy, what they felt their responsibilities were, how they hoped to perform their functions in society while at the same time trying to fulfill their own ambitions. It would be accurate, of course, to say that the dominant position that emerged was entirely and solely a reflection of the fear engendered by academic freedom cases. Clearly there was more to it than this; yet, the impact of these cases on the academic community is a major factor in explaining how the social scientist came to conceive his role as objective adviser and provider of technical expertise.

This particular conception has pretty much remained the dominant one in 20th-century American social science; this is not to suggest that the activist conception of the sociologists role in public affairs had died out completely. Every generation of social scientists has had its proponents of this particular view and on rare occasions they have managed to bring it back into great prominence within the field. As we will see in Part II of this chapter, the advocacy stance reemerged in the administrations of Herbert Hoover and Franklin Roosevelt and, as pointed out elsewhere (pages 47, 62), it continues to receive support today by such sociologists as Alvin Gouldner and Richard Quinney.

PART TWO: SOCIAL SCIENCE IN SOCIAL PLANNING: 1900–1940

Early Efforts

Sociologists and other social scientists were involved in a wide range of applied activities in which they sought to have the knowledge of their disciplines used to aid in rational planning. One of the first areas in which they became involved was planning for *national social insurance*. In 1907, the American Association for Labor Legislation (AALL) was organized to work toward developing a national program of insurance. The AALL sponsored scientific research by professional social scientists to provide the basis for drafting and implementing labor legislation and a national insurance system. John R. Commons and Richard Ely of the University of Wisconsin, Henry Farnan of Yale, J. W. Jinks of Cornell, and Henry Seager and Samuel McCune Lindsay of Columbia were among the economists and political scientists who helped to supply this movement with leadership and technical research skills. Their goal was straightforward: "To apply to legislation [in this area] the same study of causes, of processes, and of effects, that lies at the basis of new modern sciences" (Lubove, 1968:32).

The AALL was organized according to Progressive theories and principles. A commission patterned after the Wisconsin Industrial Commission (Commons, 1913) was formed including representatives of business, labor and other groups, as well as social scientists and other academic experts. The unique task of this commission was to discover the "general will" of the people. Through a systematic program of investigation and research, scientific experts would then discover plans of action that would be in the best interests of the country and the people. The experts would draft legislation; reinforced by the data collected and by their conviction that their efforts were unbaised, disinterested and altruistic, the experts and commission members would then urge adoption of their recommended legislation.

Lubove has described the type of research that social scientists contributed to the work of AALL (Lubove, 1968:45–52, 66, 71–76). To the modern academic social scientist who is interested in advancing understanding about human society and behavior, this research will seem mundane and uninteresting. Clearly, its aim was not to address theoretically interesting questions but to collect specific items of information that would help the AALL executive committee enact the legislative programs to which they were committed. In reading these reports, we find no indication that the authors sought to consider for their academic audience the theoretical implications of the research they conducted. The AALL's use of social science was narrow and pragmatic and, at times, it may even have been ethically questionable, as for example, when mandates were given to provide only data that supported particular points of view about the goals of labor legislation (Lubove, 1968: 66–90).

The AALL had an important impact on the subsequent history of social legislation in America, made possible in part by the participation of social science in the process of investigating conditions and proposing legislation. In 1914, for example, the AALL published a set of standards for health insurance schemes throughout America. In 1915 it drafted a model code, versions of which were introduced into the legislatures of 18 states by 1917. Moreover, statewide planning commissions were instituted in California and Massachusetts in 1917 to oversee the enactment of legislation and to discover through research and study the need for further legislative action; and shortly thereafter additional commissions were established in Connecticut, Illinois, Massachusetts, New Hampshire, Ohio, Pennsylvania and Wisconsin (Lubove, 1968:67).[23]

A second area in which social scientists became involved in the early decades of the 20th century was *Conservation*. The leaders of the movement to conserve the nation's use of natural resources included social scientists (especially anthropologists, economists and geographers) as well as engineers and scientists from the fields of hydrology, geology, forestry and agrostology (Hays, 1959:2). Hays describes the role of scientists in this movement in this way: "Vigorously active in professional circles in the national capital, these leaders [from the scientific fields] brought the ideals and practices of their craft into federal resource policy. Its essence was rational planning to promote effective development and use of all natural resources . . ." (Hays, 1959:2).

The impetus for this movement came directly out of research in the fields of science and technology in which its leaders were trained. Recent developments in these physical and social sciences seemed to promise unlimited opportunities for human achievement and social abundance. Yet the leaders of the Conservation movement realized that if society were left to follow its present course, the nation's natural resources would soon be squandered and the country would be poverty-stricken. Under the political leadership of Theodore Roosevelt (whose interest in conservation was both ideological and deeply personal), James R. Garfield (Roosevelt's Secretary of Interior), the intellectual leadership of Gifford Pinchot (Chief of the Division of Forestry in the United States Department of Agriculture) and W. J. McGee (a geologist, anthropologist and social philosopher), the Conservation movement became the main vehicle for educating private industry and the public about the scientific management of forests, water, minerals and other natural resources. The message was simple: "The use of foresight and restraint in the exploration of the physical resources of wealth is necessary for the perpetuation of civilization and the welfare of present and future generation" (Hays, 1959:122–123). The Conservation movement's methods were efficiency, rationality and planning; its goal, in the words of Richard Ely, an ardent supporter and regular contributor to research on conservation, was "the preservation in widespread efficiency of the resources of the earth."

The chief theorist of the Conservation movement was W. J. McGee, who was devoted to the concept of applied knowledge and social engineering. He believed, "The course of nature has come to be investigated in order that it may be redirected along lines contributing to human welfare" (McGee, 1909:35). He considered the Conservation movement as a monumental step in human progress because it involved "a conscious and purposeful entry into control over nature through the natural resources, for the direct benefit of mankind" (McGee, as quoted in Hays, 1959:124). With Theodore Roosevelt, McGee helped to establish the Inland Waterways Commission of 1907, which was devoted to developing a national policy of river development.

The singleminded devotion of McGee, Roosevelt, Pinchot and Garfield has been termed "The Gospel of Efficiency" (Hays, 1959), the goal of absolute efficiency in every realm of public affairs. Initial interest in forest lands, water and other natural resources, gradually expanded to other areas of national life involving human resources, business and labor. Roosevelt in particular urged business leaders to begin a national inventory of natural resources, which would contribute to planning for optimal future use. The impact of this attempt to inventory natural resources extended beyond government natural resources policy. Herbert Hoover, in the Commerce Department, was so impressed by the idea that years later, in his own Presidential administration, he encouraged a project to "inventory" the *social* resources of the nation.

The Conservation movement is important in the present context not only because it brought the philosophy of Progressivism and social engineering to bear on the problem of expending the nation's natural resources, but also because it demonstrated the achievements of which the new approach was capable. Hays states:

> The broader significance of the Conservation movement stemmed from the role it played in the transformation of its decentralized nontechnical, loosely organized society where waste and inefficiency ran rampant into a highly organized technical and centrally planned and directed social organization which would meet a complex world with efficiency and purpose (Hays, 1959:265).

Faith in this power of efficiency insinuated itself into other realms of national life: into professional academic societies, societies of engineers,[24] the farm labor movement, industrial management and municipal government. The possibility of applying scientific and technical principles to particular problems, and the use of scientific experts and disinterested administrative personnel to achieve planning, foresight and conscious purpose were the legacies of the Conservation movement.

Progressives, backed by social scientists, were active in many other national and local concerns as well. For example, the New York State Child Labor Committee of 1904 was influential in calling the public's attention to the problem of *child labor* and formulating legislation to reform practices in this area. This Committee drew heavily upon sociologist Robert Hunter's research report *Poverty* (1904), later described as the most searching study of poverty in the United States up to that time (Bremner, 1956:151). Social scientists active on the Committee included Felix Adler, Professor of Social and Political Ethics at Columbia University and founder of the Society for Ethical Culture, and Jacob Riis, a Columbia University economist whose extensive research on poverty included the photographic essay, *How the Other Half Lives* (1971). *Housing reform* through city planning was another area which attracted Progressives and sympathetic social scientists. The Progressivist-influenced aim of city planning reform was to organize the social environment of the city to permit each individual to attain his maximum physical, material and cultural development (Lubove, 1962:215). Contributing to the efforts at housing reform and urban renewal was the research of social scientists—Jacob Riis, Edward T. Devine and several other faculty members of the City College of New York.

The problems that blacks had in the United States also attracted attention. W. E. B. DuBois and Frances Keller were early figures in the struggle to recognize the problems of America's blacks, especially those who had migrated to northern cities (N. Weiss, 1974:10). An organization that supported social research on the plight of blacks in America was the Committee on Urban Conditions, a forerunner of the National Urban League. The Committee was formed by Edward Haynes, a black who got his doctorate degree in sociology at Columbia. Haynes urged "the professionalization of social service and the importance of scholarly investigation as the basis for practical reform" (N. Weiss, 1974:29). Emanuel Houston, a black who held advanced degrees in sociology and urban social research, served as the first Research Director of the Committee on Urban Conditions. [25]

Of the many organizations concerned with the problems of America's black population, the Urban League was the one which drew the most support from Progressives. The Urban League conformed in nearly every respect to the concept that Progressives had about how to improve social conditions in the country. Its leadership consisted of a consortium of academic intellectuals, social workers, philanthropists, reformers, public officials and representatives of the black urban masses. Committed to "the theory and practice of scientific social research as the basis for the ultimate adjustment of racial difficulties in America" (N. Weiss, 1974:216), the League undertook careful surveys of the conditions of urban living and work of blacks in northern cities. To carry out this plan the League established its own Department of Research and Investigation in 1921. The Department's first Director was Charles S. Johnson, a black who had studied sociology at the University of Chicago and served as Director of the Chicago Urban League study of the condition of blacks in Chicago (N. Weiss, 1974:216–217). Ira Reid, a product of the Columbia graduate program in sociology, assumed the post when Johnson moved to Fisk University in 1928. [26] The Department of Research was responsible for collecting, analyzing and publishing the results of research studies on the social conditions of blacks in American cities. Weiss states that the studies "were never prescriptive; rather, they provided the raw material with which local agencies could devise local programs to meet local needs" (N. Weiss, 1974:217). The data thus obtained were used by Urban League experts to plan and implement social reform in accordance with "the factual interpretation of authenticated data rather than emotional and sectional appeal" (N. Weiss, 1974:219). To disseminate the information more widely and to improve the general understanding of blacks and their problems, the League in 1923 founded the journal, *Opportunity: Journal of Negro Life*, which published research reports and other documents describing the social and economic conditions affecting blacks in the United States (N. Weiss, 1974:220).

World War I provided social scientists with other opportunities to use social science for planning. The war brought an upsurge of interest in national planning and President Wilson actively sought the aid of intellectuals and social scientists in this effort. Although much of the help he received was highly technical (mostly econometricians and psychometricians), some of it was global in its scope. The career of Edwin Gay, Dean of the Harvard Business School, illustrates this approach. Gay went to Washington just before the outbreak of hostilities to try to stimulate interest in the collection of statistics for use by policy-makers who were faced with the problems of imports, exports, shipping and planning for a wartime economy (Heaton, 1952). Gay's success made him a prophet of the Progressive ideal of a rational plan for American society. After the war, Gay helped to found the National Bureau of Economic Research (NBER), an organization of academics and men of affairs who attempted to redefine and coordinate research on the American economy. Then, in 1921, partly in response to the success of NBER and partly in response to President Wilson's idea of academic experts to help design a plan for world peace, Gay initiated a similar venture of scholars, businessmen and public affairs leaders to form the Council of Foreign Relations. He was also influential in shaping the early course of the Social Science Research Council, established in 1924 by Charles Merriman and others, to sponsor research and contribute factual data to governmental planning for social policies in the postwar era.

Social scientists were also involved in *industrial planning*. Early examples of this include Frederick Taylor's work on scientific management (1911) and George Harvey's manipulation of public opinion as a public relations expert for industrial corporations, city planners, labor groups and resource convervation experts (Mowry, 1958:19). Such eminent social scientists as Otis, Cottell, Hill, McDougal, Terman, Tichner, Yerkers, Roethlisberger, Dickson, Mayor and Warner were also associated with industrial use of social science for planning from 1900 to 1940.[27]

Some social scientists feel exhilarated by the growing use of social science made by government and private groups; others felt frustrated. For one thing, the problems on which they were being invited to work seemed to them to be excessively technical and specific; for another, in areas in which Progressives were not politically entrenched, most of the policy recommendations that grew out of social science research went unheeded. Expecting to advise the government on great national questions, social scientists instead found themselves being put to work on mundane, often intellectually barren questions of fact about one or another aspect of social life that involved some highly delimited area of local community affairs. This research was usually reported in a rather straightforward, factual statistical fashion to a small audience of local politicians and community leaders. Though most economists and other social scientists imagined themselves as objective technical advisers to government, this kind of mundane local activity was not exactly what they had in mind. The urge to make social science a tool of statewide planning became great; the problem *was* that the opportunity to do this had not yet presented itself to the social science community. No President or other national political figure of the day seemed willing to undertake the kind of planning venture that social scientists envisaged, nor was there the kind of strong, neutral centralized government willing to act in accordance with the findings of scientific research which applied social science required if it was to be effective. That is, this was true until Herbert Hoover entered the White House in 1928.

Hoover's Research Committee on Social Trends

Hoover came to the Presidency with good Progressive credentials. Trained in engineering at Stanford University, he had early developed a commitment to "scientific intelligence" or, as he termed it, "the new scientific order of life." In his public life in the Department of Commerce under Roosevelt, in the War Department and in the National Research Council under Wilson, his Progressive sentiments continued to grow.[28] Even his personal habits reflected a Progressive commitment. For example, Hoover meticulously adopted a disinterested posture in public life, even to the extent of declining to identify his political party affiliation until just before the 1928 conventions (Karl, 1969:353). His nonpartisan stance reflected the more general Progressive rejection of partisan politics as inappropriate for achieving reform.

Hoover planned an ambitious program of national social reform, with the specific immediate purpose of abolishing poverty and establishing what Progressives were already calling "a great society" (Karl, 1969:347). The method of achieving this purpose was familiarly Progressive. Specific legislation to bring about reform would be designed by a committee, which would base its recommendations on a comprehensive survey of the social needs of Americans—a national "social inventory." Reforms would be implemented by the executive branch of the federal government, which would serve as a clearing house and a central coordinating power, as well as the source of information to the larger public. In fact, Hoover envisioned a self-operating system of rational change much like the one proposed by John Dewey in *The Public and Its Problems* (1927).

Hoover's plan was breathtaking. Just as Theodore Roosevelt had sought to bring under government control the natural resources of the nation, so Hoover sought to bring under government control the social resources of the nation. And just as Roosevelt had relied primarily on natural scientists in the Conservation movement, so Hoover would rely on sociologists and political scientists in the movement for social reform.

A method based on earlier experience existed already for moving from social science research to social reform. According to Barry Karl, a historian who has written about Hoover's commission, the method consisted of three basic steps, which could be slightly varied as necessary.

> The first involved the definition of the problem by a core group of interested specialists and influentials. The second step would be the calling of a conference to broaden the association of interested people including three groups who might not have been involved centrally in the first stage: newspaper and magazine writers for publicity, philanthropists for financial support, and potentially concerned political leaders for the ultimate legal action. The third step would be the research survey in which experts would study the multiple questions under consideration, introduce new ones if necessary, and produce finally a full document containing all the information and interpretations on which reasonable men, presumably in government, would base programs for reform (Karl, 1969:349).

Hoover followed this strategy closely in his Research Committee on Social Trends. From the beginning of his Administration, he involved some of the most able academic minds produced by the social science departments of leading universities. Drawing heavily on the advice of Chairman Wesley Mitchell, an economist, Hoover also appointed to the Committee Shelby Harrison, a sociologist at the Russell Sage Foundation, trained at the University of Chicago; Howard Odum of the University of North Carolina; William Ogburn from the University of Chicago; Charles Merriam, a political scientist from the University of Chicago; and numerous other leading social scientists. He publicized Committee proceedings, exchanged information with relevant organizations and sought to broaden the thinking of all concerned. Believing that a populace informed about the need for national reforms would support such reforms, Hoover had on his staff Edward E. Hunt, a journalist with wide experience in the public service. Worth stressing here, however, is the vital role the Committee played in President Hoover's plans for reform, for he regularly consulted with Committee members (Ogburn in particular) about the economy, pending legislation and the Committee's findings.

The President's Research Committee on Social Trends began work on the first stage of the President's program for reform, the stage of data collection, in the fall of 1929. To avoid any suggestion of partisanship, Hoover insisted that federal funds not be used to support the work, which was financed instead by a grant from the Rockefeller Foundation. The survey was to present detailed data on such questions as: What are the nation's main social problems? Where do these problems lie? Why do they exist? What resources are available to deal with them.[29] The Committee was expected to accomplish its task and make its recommendations in three years, so that in the final year of his term of office, President Hoover could begin to put the plan for social change into action. To coordinate this stage of his plan, he proposed to create a new agency in the Department of Interior, the Center for Social Reform (Karl, 1969:364). In the interim he appointed Ray L. Wilbur, a medical educator who was also an academic intellectual, to head the Department of Interior and oversee the transfer and implementation of the Committee's results.

The final report of the Committee (about 1500 pages) was presented to Hoover in the fall of 1932 and published in January, 1933. It included chapters by such luminaries as Edwin Gay and Wesley Mitchell in economics; Robert Lynd and Edwin Sutherland in sociology; and Charles Judd and Leonard White in political science.

In certain respects, President Hoover's Research Committee on Social Trends represented a high point in the use of social science for social policy. It is true that it failed in the sense that its report was not published until after Hoover's terms of office had expired and, also, that it never succeeded in bringing closure in the form of policy recommendations to the mass of statistical data it had compiled and analyzed. Yet, it was the first major effort by a powerful, national political figure and a team of social scientists to plan social change on a grand scale and for this its place of importance in the development of applied sociology is justly deserved.[30]

Applied Social Science Under FDR

Another opportunity to put social science into practice in national planning on a grand scale occurred shortly after Hoover left office, as his successor, Franklin D. Roosevelt, was a passionate advocate of rational planning in government. Roosevelt attracted large numbers of social scientists to Washington during his first two terms of office—people interested in the nation's social and domestic problems and deeply committed to helping him implement long-range programs of planned social change. Sociologists and other social scientists set to work·researching and studying a variety of problems including poverty, housing, land use, population, employment and welfare. Perhaps the most interesting effort of all these took place in the Department of Agriculture.

Of all the major pieces of legislation proposed by Roosevelt in the first 100 days of his term of office, three stand out as particularly significant efforts at planning (Graham, 1976:28). These were the Tennessee Valley Authority (TVA), the National Recovery administration (NRA) and the Agriculture Adjustment Administration (AAA). Of the three, social scientists had by far the greatest impact on the third.

Two influential academic Progressives who applied the basic concepts of Progressivism and the methods of applied social science to the multifaceted problems of the American farmer were Milburn L. Wilson and Howard R. Tolley. Both came out of the "Wisconsin" background of university social scientists who actively contributed their expertise to government. Wilson himself was trained at Wisconsin in economics by John R. Commons; later, he studied at Chicago with the philosopher James Tuft (co-author with John Dewey of *Ethics,* 1908). Tolley studied with Willis J. Spellman, an agricultural economist who pioneered improved methods of farm management using the results of scientific research and knowledge.

Wilson and Tolley were not in sympathy with the view prevailing among agricultural policy-makers in the late 1920s. It was widely assumed that, unhampered by artificial government interference and regulation, nature would take its course: the weakest elements would be destroyed; the strongest would survive. Gradual natural progress would result (Kirkendall, 1966:21). Wilson and Tolley, in contrast, believed that the poverty of so many farmers was not due to inferior heredity or limited innate capacity: poverty was a product of the economic system. "These farmers are poor not because they have suddenly become shiftless and lazy but because their farms simply cannot be farmed at a profit" (Kirkendall, 1966:122). They called for direct government intervention to benefit the farmer. Their plan was to employ scientific methods and knowledge in the practical management of farms to achieve more effective use of land; to articulate farm production with regional and national markets; and, eventually, to rationalize the process of production nationally to conserve land resources and maximize farmers' profits. To carry out these plans, Tolley believed public agencies must be created to supply research information to farmers. Additionally, he saw a need for democratically elected planning boards that would formulate policy for the region they represented (Kirkendall, 1966:15–16). Wilson added the idea of using mass media techniques of public persuasion to familiarize individual farmers with proposed new methods of farming and with new regional farm policies. Both Wilson and Tolley, Woodrow Wilson Progressives, insisted on direct and active participation of ordinary farmers in the formulation and implementation of farm policies. They did not view widespread participation as a threat because they believed that rural people would see the utility of the knowledge and methods of science and the inherent wisdom of using science to make their farms more profitable.

In 1930, Wilson and Tolley cooperated with Minnesota Congressman Victor Christgau, an agricultural economist sympathetic to Progressive ideas, to draft and introduce into the Congress the Christgau bill, outlining a new farm policy. The proposed legislation would join social scientists and farmers in a planning process aimed at rationalizing a system that was presently developing a chaotic and wasteful way. In general, the bill proposed that "scientific and democratic methods . . . be called upon to produce profit for the business of farming, to plan more effective use of the land, and to serve the interest of both producer and consumer of farm products (Kirkendall, 1966:11). More specifically, the comprehensive bill called for many changes. One part would create an "adjustment program" to help farmers in each agricultural region to determine what crops they could produce most profitably by coordinating production with demand" (Kirkendall, 1966:8). Another part would greatly expand the research function of the Department of Agriculture and would ensure the widespread transmission of research results to local farmers by the proposed Agricultural Extension Services. The bill also called for local, regional and national planning boards with representatives of farming interests, academic researchers, business people and consumers who together would draw up and help to oversee the implementation of master plans.

Wilson and Tolley were joined in their fight for the Christgau legislation by Lewis C. Gray, another economist who had studied with Richard Ely at Wisconsin. Gray, too, was a Progressive who combined an academic background with a tradition of government service. He had held several academic positions before he joined the

Agriculture Department as Head of the Division of Land Economics (Kirkendall, 1966: 21). These three men lectured to farm groups all over America and lobbied in the halls of Congress, but so long as President Hoover opposed the program, they made little headway (Kirkendall, 1966:30−49).[31]

Franklin Roosevelt's campaign for the Presidency brought hope to the supporters of the Christgau bill. Among Roosevelt's "brain trust" advisers were two economists who were impressed by the proposed program: George F. Warren, an agricultural economist from Cornell, and Rexford Tugwell of Columbia who had studied with Simon Patten. Together they persuaded Roosevelt to endorse the Christgau bill.[32] According to Kirkendall, Tugwell commissioned Wilson himself to write the Roosevelt campaign speech that would present the program for central planning in agriculture. The speech was made, appropriately, at a meeting of Midwestern farmers in Topeka, Kansas (Kirkendall, 1966:46).

Within the first 100 days of Roosevelt's administration, the Christgau bill became law—the Agricultural Adjustment Act. Under its new Secretary, Henry Wallace, the Department of Agriculture instituted a national system of production controls for farming. The influence of these active and tenacious social scientists in government continued well beyond the first 100 days and for almost an entire decade. Wilson became Undersecretary of the Department of Agriculture in 1935, while Tolley continued to exert enormous influence on the Department's programs for rural poverty. Together they persuaded Secretary Wallace to appropriate funds for new university departments of agricultural economics and rural sociology. Moreover, the activity and influence of these and other social scientists attracted large numbers of eager young people to Washington to staff the Agriculture Department.

It was not necessary, however, for a social scientist to leave the university to help influence farm policies at this time. Social scientists were routinely consulted on farm policy and the Department of Agriculture not only funded research, it used the results in formulating regional farm policies. One example of the use of "outside" social scientists was the Department of Agriculture's Special Committee on Farm Tenancy, established in 1936 at the particular request of the President, to study the problems of tenancy on poorer farms and to draw up model legislation. Key contributors included social scientists Howard Odum, Charles S. Johnson, William Myers and Henry Taylor. The report of the Committee led to the passage of the Farm Security Act of 1937 (Kirkendall, 1966:126).

In some fields of social science, the Department itself assumed the leadership in the New Deal years. For example, in 1939 a new Division of Program Surveys was established to conduct attitude surveys among groups of farmers and to transmit the result to higher level officials. Secretary Wallace believed that communication with farmers could be improved and resistance to change reduced, if Agriculture Department officials took into account, in their client negotiations and policy formulation, the attitudes of the farmers they were supposed to serve. Under Rensis Likert, a psychologist trained at Columbia, the Division developed a methodology for doing sample surveys and, according to at least one source, it "assumed the leadership in introducing the sample interview survey as a basic social science tool and as an instrument of governmental policy" (Alpert, 1959:79–80).

To ensure that Agriculture Department employees were familiar with social science methods and approaches, Undersecretary Wilson arranged for courses and guest lecturers in sociology, cultural anthropology and social psychology. One guest instructor was William Ogburn, who spent a term at the Department lecturing on his theory of social change and its practical relevance for Department programs (Kirkendall, 1966: 189). Later, Wilson established within the Bureau of Agricultural Economics an entire sociology department with Carl L. Taylor as its Director. More than any other single person, Taylor brought the discipline of sociology into the daily operation of the Department. Taking issue with many of the assumptions that economists had employed, Taylor and his colleagues insisted that increased income would not of itself solve the problem of rural poverty. The Department would also have to consider the social and cultural aspects of rural life, including health, education, recreation and morale (Kirkendall, 1966:221). Taylor also encouraged the Department to consider in policy-making the point of view of the common farmer. According to one of Taylor's sociologists:

> While it might be possible to put new programs across by administrative decree backed by force this is not the American way. We must operate within the framework of the Democratic process. If the government employed scientists and the best thinking to gain an understanding of the people, then officials would shape and operate programs that would serve popular needs and desires (Kirkendall, 1966:186).

Finally, Taylor recruited highly qualified sociologists to work for the Department of Agriculture. Among those who did research for the Department with Taylor's encouragement were Walter Goldschmidt, A. L. Kroeber and Paul Taylor. In fact, during this period these social scientists were, according to Kirkendall, "the most influential group in farm policies" (Kirkendall, 1966:255). They were also influential in their professions. The fact that Carl Taylor was elected President of the Rural Sociological Society in 1939 and of the American Sociological Society in 1946 is one indication of the high esteem in which this work was held by academic sociologists.

In certain respects, the social scientists who worked in or with the Department of Agriculture during the New Deal acted out the ideal of the objective, technical expert—the trained specialist who applied his special expertise to the problems of a particular segment of the American population. In other respects, however, these social scientists embodied the ideals of the advocacy stance, for, far from being apolitical or neutral, they were committed to active political participation. Their style combined expertise with persuasion, pressure tactics and attempts to transform the established power structure in farm problems. They *never* hesitated to lobby in the halls of Congress to proclaim what ought to be and to seek support directly from the President in order to overcome resistance to their plans. While, under Hoover, social scientists were held in great esteem and had enormous potential influence, in the New Deal years they *actually* influenced all kinds of decisions about agricultural or farm-related policies of the United States government. Certainly, academically based social scientists have seldom exerted as much influence in government as they did in the first decade of Franklin Roosevelt's Presidency.

Conclusion

In this chapter we have outlined certain historical antecedents of the highly rationalistic conception of social policy inherent in much of the writing and research of present day sociologists engaged in doing work for application. On the one hand, there was an intellectual tradition of liberal social philosophy that sought to replace an earlier deterministic view of human affairs with a conception of society as an entity capable of being manipulated and controlled through reason and intellect. On the other hand, was a social tradition in which certain groups—mainly professionals and other victims of a status upheaval in late 19th-century America—sought to reinstate coherence and social solidarity through schemes of national social policy. These two movements merged to form a social and political movement that aimed at rationalizing social policy in American life through the use of social research and academic expertise. Sociologists and other social scientists began using their technical expertise to do research on the myriad problems of American society—at first working at the local level and through private organizations to effect change. Gradually, at the instigation of political leaders, these activities became more ambitious and national in scope, culminating in a series of impressive research ventures undertaken in the Administrations of Herbert Hoover and Franklin Roosevelt.

We learn important things about applied sociology when we examine it developmentally in its historical context. For example, we see that in a certain way sociology became fixated at an early stage of development, binding itself tightly to a particular model for conducting governmental affairs. And, like most other fixations, this one too became so interwoven with other things that it has blended into the background of our work where, as we saw in Chapters 2 and 3, it now resides invisibly. One important purpose of this chapter has been to attempt to explain how and why applied sociology as practiced today developed a dependency upon scientific planning methods. We also saw that sociology was called into "The Nation's Service" almost before sociology existed as a scientific discipline, and that it was invited to participate in councils of government even though it knew nothing about the problems being deliberated. To us, this highlights a very significant feature of social science use in public affairs: its ceremonial function. In the past, and, as we will see in Chapter 5, today as well, government sometimes invite sociologists to join in helping to make policy as a way of *appearing* rational, a way of trying to create the impression that it is efficient, rational and foresightful in conducting the affairs of state. And, if this is true, then it is the sociologist's presence that is important, not what he or she may know or have to say about an issue. This fact, in turn, highlights the significance of government in the relationship of sociology to it. This is the topic to which we now turn.

NOTES

1. In this chapter, we will speak of policy-relevant *social science* more often than policy-relevant *sociology*. The reason is that in the period we will be dealing with (1880—1910), separate and specialized social science disciplines were less evident than they are today.
2. It is important to state clearly what our discussion is and what it is not meant to be. We do not present it as a fresh contribution to scholarship in the history and development of social sciences in America. Our analysis is derivative from literature that has already been published in the fields of sociology and of American intellectual and social history. We do intend it to be a contribution to applied sociology. By clarifying the interactions of developments in sociology involving the use of disciplinary knowledge to public policy, and developments taking place in the larger social, philosophical and historical environment of which sociology was a

part, we hope to offer insights into the practices of applied sociology which are not evident in contemporary writings about it.

3. Ironically, in 1937, 23 years after the publication of Lippmann's *Drift and Mastery*, he rejected the idea of planning as totalitarian and published a grand rebuttal to the notion which he had earlier helped to popularize. See Lippmann, *The Good Society* (1937).

4. Occasionally strains of it also appear even in the works of Comte and Marx, even though both are devoted to closing the gap between thought and action.

5. In the case of Holmes, of course, the critique was of the way in which law as a practical activity was conducted.

6. Sociologists, such as Lester Ward, E. A. Ross and Albion Small, also took issue with the formalistic-deterministic mode of thought. Their views on this subject will be explained in a later section of this chapter.

7. For a discussion of these developments, see Elizabeth Hanset's *Perfection and Progress* (1975).

8. See pages 64–66 of text.

9. Robinson's advice to President Harding was indicative of some of the difficulties that subsequent generations of Progressives and sociologists would have in specifying concretely what was to be done. When asked to help devise a master plan of social change for America, Robinson wrote back: "I have no reform to recommend except the liberation of intelligence" [as quoted in White (1949:199)].

10. Railroads are the best example of this devastating power. A railroad company's decision to bypass their town or link it to the main line was a life or death matter for a community (Wiebe, 1967:11–43).

11. Mary Furner points out that what the movement recommended was a new kind of specialist: ". . . one who could analyze and guide social policy from the comprehensive, disinterested, ethical perspective which the ministry had once maintained, and speak with the authority which ministers had once commanded, but with a modern, scientific voice" (Furner, 1975:51).

12. Their influence extended to Presidents. Upon reading Croly's *The Promise of American Life* (1909), Theodore Roosevelt wrote the author: "I do not know when I have read a book which I felt profited me as much as your book on American life .... I shall use your ideas freely in speeches I intend to make" [as quoted in Hofstadter (1955: 97)].

13. For a study of the settlement house movement of this period, see Clarke A. Chambers, *Seedtime of Reform* (1967). Walter Rauschenbusch's *Christianity and the Social Crises* (1907) provided the theoretical and theological grounds for the "social Christianity" movement, which inspired church involvement in these programs.

14. As we will explain on pages 110–114, though all of these persons supported the idea of science in public affairs, they often disagreed violently about the exact role the social scientist ought to play in them.

15. For the reader who wishes to pursue this topc, we suggest several excellent historical studies that shed important light on these matters. These include Mary Furner: *Advocacy and Objectivity* (1976); Edward A. Purcell: *The Crises of Democratic Theory* (1973); and David Thelen: *The New Citizenship* (1972). We also recommend the essay by Dorothy Ross entitled, "The Development of the Social Sciences in America, 1865–1920" (1975). Other books worth reading are Lawrence Veysey: *The Emergence of the American University* (1970); Albert Somit and Joseph Tenenhaus: *The Development of Political Science* (1967); and doctoral theses by Frederick H. Matthew, "Robert E. Park and the Development of American Sociology" (1973), David Grossman, "Professors and Public Service, 1885–1925: A Chapter in the Professionalization of the Social Sciences" (1973).

16. See for example, Volume I, pages 704 and 706; Volume II, pages 15, 210 and 272.

17. Ward's treatise is devoted almost entirely to presenting arguments against the laissez-faire position and in favor of the concept of a sociology that could be used to

redirect the course of social change in desired ways. Like many other liberal intellectuals, Ward seemed preoccupied with the potential of teleological sociology to the exclusion of substance. His book is filled with suggestions about *where* knowledge might be applied; he says nothing about *what* or *how* knowledge should be used. He acknowledged that a great deal of empirical research would be necessary before the new science of society would help legislative bodies in long-range planning. He assumes, however, that once this knowledge is acquired, the details of how sociologists' knowledge will be used by legislators will automatically take care of themselves. This lack of specifics in Ward's work is characteristic of other liberal social philosophers. Robinson had spoken eloquently about the use of history to understand the present and to chart a course for the future, but when pressed to say exactly what this use was he could only reply, "the liberation of intelligence" (White, 1949: 199). Dewey, too, when pressed for specifics replied with generalities about "the method of cooperative intelligence" (White, 1949:244). Veblen set forth a series of concrete proposals but then he argued that his proposals could not be carried out at the present time (White, 1949:199). This characteristic irony of the new liberal social philosophy has remained a distinguishing feature of sociology ever since. On the one hand it is dominated by a pragmatic conception that science and knowledge should be used in bettering the living conditions of all mankind. Yet, just as they might be expected to present concrete, specific, detailed proposals for planned social change, advocates often offer only vague generalities.

White suggests that the vagueness of the early sociologists may be related to their commitment to the belief in an open and free world in which everything and anything was possible. Dogmatism of any kind was abhorred as limiting; after all, they had just had to overcome the dogmatism of formalism and determinism. Yet, as White notes: "a political technology does require a program. If we are to reorganize human beliefs and behavior by means of technology, we must know how to reorganize it, and at some point or other we shall have to ask which beliefs and which behavior we want to encourage" (White, 1949:244). Thus, dogmatism is inherent in social planning; perhaps for this reason early sociologists (and some contemporary ones, too) have often been explicit about the possibilities for change but vague about its content.

18. The basis of Small's disagreement with Ward's position is explained on pages 111–112.
19. Commons was one of the first academics to come out of the Progressive tradition of social scientists in public service. The landmark example of this is the close relationship established between the University of Wisconsin, where Commons taught, and the Wisconsin State government. The Governor of Wisconsin, Robert M. LaFollette, described his contribution to this relationship: "I made it a policy in order to bring all the sources of knowledge and inspiration of the University more fully to the service of the people, and to appoint experts from the University whenever possible upon the important boards of the state . . . a relationship which the University has always encouraged and by which the state has greatly profited" (Kirkendall, 1966:4). Charles Van Hise, President of the University of Wisconsin during the time of LaFollette's term of office, actively encouraged his faculty to follow the model of Germany, in which government made wide use of academic scholars. The results included active participation in the affairs of the state and nation by social scientists like John Commons.
20. Specific instances involving the use of social science research in planning efforts are discussed in Part Two of this chapter.
21. The impact of European social thought on the development of Progressivism in America—a topic which falls beyond the scope of the analysis presented in this chapter—was effected primarily through members of the academic community.
22. For a present-day version of this same position see our discussion of Richard Quinney's views on the use of sociology in public affairs, page 62.

23. For additional information about the history of AALL and of social insurance legislation in America see, Lubove (1968), Burns (1944), and Jordan (1916).
24. For a study of engineering during the Progressive era see Noble, *America by Design* (1977).
25. For further information on the involvement of sociologists in the work or organizations for the improvement of conditions for blacks in America, see N. Weiss (1974:29−46).
26. Johnson moved to Fisk in 1928 to become head of the social science department to train more black students in sociology and social work in order to increase the attention that academic social science paid to the problems of black Americans (N. Weiss, 1974:467). A secondary effect of this move was to create a firmer bond between social action programs and academic social scientists.
27. For a study of this aspect of applied social science, see Loren Baritz, *The Servants of Power* (1960). For a critique of Progressives from a radical perspective see Weinstein (1968).
28. The National Research Council was established in 1916 to serve as an administrative agency for the distribution and management of scientific research funds. The funds went to foundations to support scientific research and to hire experts to help make decisions and exercise control over the expenditures of government. In keeping with the principles of nonpartisianship, NRC was located in Washington to advise the federal government but was made independent of it by means of a permanent endowment.
29. In many respects the Research Committee on Social Trends exemplifies the type of approach to social science in government that members of the advocacy position had in mind. It is worthy of note that the social scientists role in the Hoover administration was determined by the President's own personal views about the scientists role in government, not the views of the social scientists who were involved. Ogburn, Merriam, Harrison and Odum were all well-known supporters of the objectivist position who were drawn to an advocacy stance by the politicians who sought their advice. This fact reminds us once again of the ways in which government has dominated in its relationships to social science.
30. As it was, Hoover's conception of procedure was one which would almost certainly have doomed the report to failure even if the social scientists had managed to present him with the promised master plan in time to act on it. Hoover feared coercive centralized government and refused to use the power of his office to mandate anything. Instead, he preferred to use the prestige of the office to persuade people to do voluntarily what scientists were hired to tell him was in the national interest. In the few years in which Hoover tried to implement this strategy, the results were an unmitigated disaster.
31. Although Hoover strongly endorsed agricultural planning, he found the program too dependent on big government, and in addition, he was offended by the Wilson−Tolley−Gray style of personal participation and lobbying.
32. For an excellent study of Tugwell and his contributions to the New Deal see Bertrand Stershner, *Rexford Tugwell and the New Deal* (1964).

5

A planning-based model for sociological inquiry is sometimes useful for policy deliberation. In a balanced account of

The Limits of Planning in Politics

government receptiveness to sociological inquiry this is an important point to make. The more powerful observation, though, comes from stating the point negatively: this method of inquiry is of limited use to policy-makers. To get beyond the method to one more appropriate to policy study, we need to understand the characteristics of the model and its deficiencies, and the limited circumstances under which planning-oriented studies are embraced by government. These tasks divide the chapter into two major parts. In the first, we examine the characteristics of the planning model and the major deficiencies, including the presumption of self-sufficiency and reliance on orderly procedure—both of which are at odds with the nature of political deliberation. We then consider the hoped-for outcomes of planning studies—rationality and stability—and find that the model fails in these respects if only because it overlooks basic political concerns. In the second part, we will take up the question of government receptiveness to sociological studies and learn about the limited circumstances under which these studies find any significant welcome from government. The stage is then set to take up the question of how to increase government receptivity in the next, and last, chapter.

PART ONE: THE LIMITATIONS OF PLANNING

To proponents of the method of scientific planning, the rationale seems obvious for approaching policy-making in the logical, comprehensive, scientific way they suggest. One has only to consider the alternatives, they point out, to understand why this is so. For example, early turn-of-the-century proponents of planning believed that the nation's affairs, both domestic and foreign, were in great disorder. National political life, they said, was dominated by two groups, both corrupt and both dangerous. One group was comprised of ward bosses, men who had created political machines in many of the nation's largest urban areas;[1] the other, of tycoons of industry and business—the Robber Barons of coal, steel, railroads, banking, commerce, oil and agriculture. Both groups were bent on amassing great political power and personal wealth while showing little apparent concern for the consequences that their actions might carry for other groups or for the nation as a whole. In the system of governance that evolved from the activities of these two groups, many national, state and local policies that were enacted furthered the interests of these persons and became law because they had the kind of political clout that was needed to enforce their will upon others. Advocates of planning felt that no vehicle existed for representing or enforcing the interests of those people—the majority—who did not possess political power or the economic resources to influence those who did. Missing was the Progressivist impetus toward the long-term consequences of proposed legislation. Instead, those with political power or great wealth were seen as free to plunder the nation's human and natural resources entirely for their own benefit, which was believed to be the detriment of the nation as a whole.

Many modern-day proponents of scientific social planning hold somewhat similar views. Although the extent of corruption and crass self-interest in government has not always been as great as it was during the era of ward bosses and Robber Barons, the modern-day system of partisan politics is viewed by its critics as yielding legislative programs that are often in conflict with what they perceive to be the national interest, yielding programs too weak and feckless to address major national problems in a meaningful way. One common complaint about this system has been voiced by James Coleman, the sociologist, who explains that in it ". . . the principal deliberations about what strategy will generate enough support to enable passage of legislation rather than deliberations about social consequences of the legislation . . ." (Coleman, 1973:1). Its weaknesses, it is said, are that politicians are more concerned with what Congress can realistically enact than with what is required to confront issues meaningfully, that the foremost concerns of most members of Congress and other elected officials are getting reelected and consolidating personal political power, not with furthering the national good.

In contrast to this partisan approach to governmental policymaking, the alternatives that Progressive intellectuals and political leaders first articulated, and which modern-day sociologists and policy scientists frequently embrace, seem intuitively to be a far more sensible, reasonable and fair way in which to conduct public affairs. Instead of pursuing what is seen to be the reckless and socially costly course of laissez-faire, self-interest politics or that of compromise politics that produces only watered-down, ineffective, weak legislation, advocates of scientific planning regard the rational, controlled procedures inherent in their approach as inherently and unquestionably superior.

They may be right, but we must not allow this fact—that the method of planning seems more reasonable when compared with other established ways of doing policy—to lead us to believe that the method itself is problem-free or that it is without its own special limitations. Although it may be true that in the abstract, the method of scientific planning is inherently superior to other methods of policy-making, we must not let this fact divert our attention from asking how it has fared in practice. We will turn to the literature of sociology, history and policy science for reports and discussions by those who have studied groups who have actually tried to use the method. This literature, though admittedly thin in places, does point to a provisional, but clear, conclusion: i.e., that in practice the method of scientific planning is neither problem-free nor always capable of achieving the objectives for which it is intended. In practice, it is found that the method poses special problems, ones that can be as vexing and complex as those posed by other approaches to policy.*

Deficiencies of the Planning Model

Efforts by federal governmental decision-making bodies to engage in scientific planning in a variety of different areas of national domestic life have raised serious questions about the method's utility. These questions raise three basic criticisms of the method. The first is that *the planning method is not* self-sufficient; it is heavily dependent upon the very system of partisan politics it is meant to supplant for resolution of the most basic questions of purpose and definition. Second, the method is often impractical because it entails procedures that are *incompatible with the basic reality of political life in American society.* Third, in practice the method has sometimes produced policies which are *irrational and disruptive* rather than rational and stabilizing. Taken together these three criticisms hardly discredit the method as such, but they do call attention to fundamental problems that are inherent in it. These problems, in turn, enable us to understand better why

---

*In evaluating our discussion the reader may find it helpful to keep in mind the various steps and procedures entailed in devising and executing policy according to this method, which were explained in Chapter 3, pages 69–70.

planning-oriented studies have been of limited value, and therefore why so little so-called "applied," "policy-relevant" sociological research is given serious attention by policy-makers.

The Presumption of Self-Sufficiency and Reliance on Orderly Procedure

In practice, the procedures outlined for devising and executing policy according to the method of scientific planning have proven to be incapable of standing alone. Those doing planning have discovered that this method does not provide them with clear definitions and conceptions of "the problem," realizing that to obtain these they must rely on partisan political processes. This dependence of the method of planning on the partisan political process for resolving basic definitional questions and questions of purpose is evident in most of the 13 steps of the planning process, outlined earlier. We will not attempt to go through the entire process step by step in order to make our point. Rather, we will concentrate our attention on several of them.

We have seen that a prerequisite to planning is a clear definition of "the problem" that a given policy is meant to solve or ameliorate. An important assumption is implicit in this notion, namely, that policy-making bodies who are engaged in planning are provided with clear and self-evident conceptions of what the problem is. This is not always the case. More often it is the case that such bodies are faced with "situations" that trouble or worry groups of persons in ways that are neither clearly specified nor adequately understood either by them or by the policy-makers given responsibility for dealing with these situations. More often what policy-makers confront is concern about situations that are inherently ambiguous, fuzzy, uncertain and ill-defined. Thus, many of the situations, defined by political leaders as requiring social action in the form of public policy, do not possess these features of orderliness, coherence and clarity of definition that they must have in order for policy-makers and social scientists to be able to determine and devise rational, logical policies for dealing with them. This point is illustrated by the following example.

Several years ago, the senior author of this book was asked to do a study of blindness and services for the blind in American society. The purpose of this study was to investigate the effectiveness of services for the blind in the United States with the objective of making recommendations for changing the system of delivery of services for the blind and for reallocating resources to the different types of service programs. A major difficulty encountered in trying to meet this mandate was to determine what "the problem" of blindness is. The author soon learned that while severe visual impairment is a condition that affects a million or more citizens in our country today and that most agree that lack of sight is a problem, the term "blindness" *itself* gives no indication of what this problem is. Is the condition of blindness a matter of physical disability or of social stigma? Is it a health problem or a problem of poverty? In view of the fact that nearly two-thirds of all people classed as blind are 65 years of age or older, is blindness a problem of visual loss or merely a facet of the normal aging process? Is it a physical problem involving an inability to relate to the distant environment directly? Is it a psychological problem of personality, or is it a sociological problem of interpersonal interaction between those who cannot see and those who can? One obvious answer is that it is all of these things and more, but this response does not suffice for the purpose of evaluating the adequacy of existing programs and recommending new ones. To approach the situation from a planning point of view it is necessary to know clearly, plainly and in advance what "the problem" is; yet, this is not something that is inherent in the situation or condition as such.

The same difficulty has confronted sociologists who have worked on all of the recent Presidential Commissions discussed in Chapter 1. For example, James Short states that most of the time during the first two years of work on the Violence Commission was spent trying to agree on a definition for "the problem" of violence (Short, 1975). This difficulty is also apparent in the case of the Commission on Civil Disorder. Lindblom explains the problem which faced this body in the following way:

> Rioting breaks out in dozens of American cities. What is the problem? Maintaining law and order? Racial discrimination? Impatience of the Negro with the pace of reform now that reform has gone far enough to give him hope? Incipient revolution? Black power? Low income? Lawlessness at the fringe of an otherwise relatively peaceful reform movement? Urban disorganization? Alienation? (Lindblom, 1968:13).

Here, too, one is tempted to answer, "It is all of these things." Yet, for the purpose of suggesting what policies the government might follow in order to curtail such disorders this answer will hardly do. Such social planning requires a clear, simple, direct statement of what the problem is; without this, the planning method cannot proceed.

The same basic difficulty occurs at other stages of the process as well. Once agreement has been reached on what the problem is (how this is decided will be discussed shortly), a next stage in the planning process would be to attempt to devise workable administrative definitions of it that are serviceable for purposes of studying the problem and for conceiving alternative policies for dealing with it. In this context, the term "serviceable" means clear-cut and precise: planning depends upon exact specification of the scope of the problem, the number of people affected, and the degrees and levels of severity at which it exists. Unless these are known, it is not possible to make informative statements about the benefits of alternative courses of action that might be taken. Also, a clear-cut, precise definition of the problem is required as it is impossible to conduct policy research on the problem unless the dependent variable, that is, "the problem," can be specified with enough precision to quantify it; In addition, administrative planning and program implementation will not be possible without the development of eligibility rules which cannot be formulated without a clear definition.

But to devise a workable definition is neither a simple nor a straightforward matter; there are as many different ways of operationally defining "the problem" as there are ways of conceiving what it is in the abstract. Clear and serviceable definitions do not, so to speak, reside in the problem. They too must be *created* by a process that involves the imposition of a certain amount of simplification and artificial orderliness on situations that are inherently untidy and complex. Moreover, in the process of trying to agree on what is a reasonable definition of a problem one soon discovers that it is impossible to say which one of the many possible definitions is "the best" or "the most rational" one to adopt. We can illustrate this with the example of blindness.

Many years ago it was decided that because blind people must purchase special services and have unusual expenses, some form of pension for the blind was required. In order to make preliminary decisions about the costs and administration of such a system, or to consider the possible alternatives, an estimate of the number of potential candidates was necessary, yet, no accurate estimate could be developed until clear criteria were established to decide whether or not a person was "blind." Thus, rationality dictated that there must be an explicit, precise definition of this term.

The problem in constructing a workable administrative definition of blindness was the decision as to whose point of view to adopt; there was no single definition that was "the most accurate" or "the best" one to accept. The standard of cost suggested one kind of definition; the standard of adequacy of services a second; the standard of practical administration a third, and the standard of personal well-being of recipients of services a fourth. Moreover, what was a rational definition from any one of these points of view—say that of cost—often appeared to be irrational from some or all of the other points of view involved.

The first definition of blindness that was considered was strictly in accord with the dictionary meaning of that term, i.e., the total and complete inability to see. But at least two problems would have arisen if this definition had been adopted. First, it would have excluded from eligibility for service a substantial number of people who are severely visually impaired but who nevertheless possess some small amount of vision. Excluded would be an estimated 50,000 people who possess enough vision to be able to discern light from dark, or vaguely to perceive the outlines of objects directly in their line of vision, and a much larger group—numbering in the hundreds of thousands—who, though they can see, possess a degree of vision so restricted that it seriously interferes with their ability to perform routine activities of everyday life (Scott, 1969:39−55). By any reasonable standard, these two groups of people seem to require assistance within the definition of "the problem" of blindness and should therefore logically be eligible for assistance; yet they would have been excluded if it had been decided to define this condition in the most clear-cut, straightforward and unambiguous fashion possible.

The second problem was brought about by the fact that total blindness is a rare event in the American population; by this definition the population eligible for blindness services would probably not have exceeded 50,000 people (Scott, 1969:39−55). Therefore, it would have been prohibitively expensive to develop an entire national system of services for such a small population. Clearly a definition based on the standard of the total inability to see would have been irrational from an administrative point of view. So rational considerations made it clear that the definition of blindness to be adopted should not be restricted only to persons completely unable to see.

Thus, the question arose as to where along the continuum of sight the line should be drawn. Administrative considerations dictated that the line must be drawn in such a way as to ensure that the procedures for determining if someone fell within the definition would be simple to administer. Cost and administrative considerations dictated that it be drawn in such a manner as to produce a population in need that would be large enough to justify creating a national system of services, but not so large as to strain severely the government's social service budget. Social service considerations dictated a line that would include all persons functionally restricted because of visual loss. Although the interests were rational, they were sometimes in conflict.

Once the decision was made to draw a line that defined blindness, a further difficulty developed. The visual acuity of people in our population approximates a bell-shaped curve, but the slope of the curve's angle drops sharply as one moves away from the range of normal vision toward the end point of complete blindness. In fact, at a point somewhere between ten to 15 percent of normal vision the curve's slope drops sharply so that wherever the definitional line is drawn, there will the largest proportion of "blind" people be found. For example, the definition of blindness that was adopted, the so-called "legal definition," stipulates blindness as one-tenth of normal vision (20/200th vision as measured on a standard Snellen chart) or less in the better eye with best correction. Because of the sharp angle of decline in the visual acuity curve of the population, nearly 60 percent of the estimated 1.2 million people who are blind by this definition possess a visual acuity of 20/200s. This means that in the population of people regarded as "blind" by this legal definition, a majority possess a considerable amount of usable vision and experience problems vastly different and often less complex than the problems of those who cannot see at all. (Two obvious examples are navigational mobility and the capacity to read the printed word.) The decision to draw the dividing line between the sighted* and the blind at one-tenth of normal vision was made largely for economic and administrative reasons: it was believed that this definition would guarantee a population of people large enough to justify federal investment in developing a national system of services. Yet, ever since its adoption, at national conventions of workers for the blind, in professional journals dealing with blindness and among the growing number of blind liberation groups, there have been recurrent discussions about the absurdity of this definition from a social and psychological point of view.

The case of poverty provides another example of the difficulties inherent in trying to arrive at an operational definition of the problem for purposes of planning. Here, too, there is wide agreement that poverty is a problem and that something should be done about it. Yet, consensus hardly exists on the question of precisely what the problem is or how to define it operationally. As in the case of blindness,

---

*Although *sighted* is an adjective, the term is taken from blind people who refer to those with sight in this way.

different criteria point to different conceptions and definitions of the problem and these are often in conflict with one another. Yet, there is no logical way of deciding which is "the best" or most sensible definition to adopt. For example, in discussing the proposed negative income tax, the so-called "poverty line" (the point at which the government would begin to pay the citizen rather than the citizen the government) was determined largely by estimating costs for a national program. The reasoning was that if the definition of poverty was too liberal, the costs of a national negative income tax would be prohibitive, not only because of the large number of people who would then be eligible for cash transfer payments from the government, but because of a loss of revenue to the government from the so-called "positive" tax structure. At the same time some experts had calculated that to provide a family of four with a minimally acceptable standard of living, an annual income of $8,000 to $9,000 was required. Yet, the "poverty line" most widely used in public deliberations about this program was only about 50 percent of this figure. Thus, a rational definition from the point of view of cost to the government appeared to be absurd from the point of view of families in need.

To summarize, clear conceptions of "the problem" and clear-cut operational definitions of it are not inherent features of most of the situations which policy-making bodies confront. Definitions must be constructed, and this fact poses difficulties that are not easily resolved. One must decide for what purposes the definition is to be used, and ultimately neither social science nor the methods of policy analysis can resolve this question. The situation is further complicated by the fact that what seems rational from one point of view often proves to be absurd from another. In short, in practice it has proven to be impossible to decide upon a clear-cut conception and operational definition of "the problem" by logic alone.

This raises an important question. If clear notions about what the problem is and how to define it are not inherent features of situations that are defined as troublesome and these situations cannot be derived logically, then how is it decided what the problem is and how it should be defined? Who decides this? Clues to the answers to these questions are provided by experiences that sociologists and other social scientists have had in doing policy-relevant research. Societal decision-making centers have no standard set of values, goals and objectives. About these matters there is usually disagreement; even where consensus exists, it is much too general and vague to permit a clear, exact conception of the problem to emerge (Etzioni, 1968:265). Moreover, if we consider this definitional question from the point of view of those who are directly affected by enacted policies, how one conceives and defines the problem is a matter of enormous practical consequence. For example, these decisions determine what kinds of resources will be allocated, to whom, for what purposes and by what means. A decision to define a situation of urban rioting as a problem of incipient revolution, or the condition of blindness as a problem of aging, carries policy implications that will be advantageous to some groups of people but disadvantageous to others. Every possible way of conceptualizing and defining the problem affects the interests of all parties involved. This serves to heighten the possibility for dissension and conflict, thereby further frustrating the emergence of agreement about the problem's "basic nature."

In this circumstance, science and logic have limited roles to play. Research and logical analysis may help to clarify options and perspectives, but neither can produce a basis for deciding what definition of a problem is best, for ultimately this involves deciding which group's needs are most deserving, and these questions can only be resolved by making value judgments, a task for which the scientific method is unsuitable.

How are such decisions made? In practice the only recourse a group has is to have the parties that are involved provide the necessary definitions. And, since they will likely be at odds with one another in approaching the issue, about the only way that consensus can emerge is through routine partisan political means. That is, the conceptions and definitions of problems that typically emerge in policy decision reflect what it is politically feasible, possible or mandatory to do. Policy-making bodies soon learn what government is willing to spend on the problem in question; what the public seems willing to pay for it; what the groups involved will stand for; and so on. In some cases, impressions about these matters spontaneously generate conceptions and definitions of the problem; in others, a conscious effort is made to adopt a definition that best suits the political realities of the situation. It is important to appreciate that even here, firm, clear answers to these questions are difficult to arrive at in advance. As a rule, they can only be settled by the familiar methods of partisan and interest group politics. Indeed, such methods have proven to be the only reasonable ones available for resolving conflicting claims and interests. It is for this reason that we conclude that the method of scientific planning, far from a distinct alternative to the familiar methods of partisan politics, often depends squarely upon them for answers to the most basic kinds of questions.

This dependence of the planning method on partisan political processes helps to shed light on the problems encountered by sociologists who have worked on various recent Presidential commissions. In all five commissions, discussed in Chapter 1, fundamental conceptual and definitional problems were present, yet it is apparent from accounts written by those who did research for them that these problems posed a much less serious, intractable obstacle to the Commissions on Pornography, Population Control and Criminal Justice than they did to the Commissions on Violence and Civil Disorder. One reason for this is found in the specific charge that was given to each of the Commissions by the White House. In the case of the Violence and Civil Disorder Commissions, the White House sought clarification from experts about the nature of the problems. These Commissions were asked to *define* these problems and to propose policies for the government to follow. The charge given to the other three Commissions was different, for they were asked to clarify policy options available to the government for dealing with problems whose basic features had already been spelled out in the executive mandate. This enabled each of them to proceed to study the problem directly, whereas the Commissions on Violence and Civil Disorder floundered until agreement was finally reached on basic definitional matters. Thus, while the work of all five Commissions could not proceed until there was agreement on a definition of the problem, a factor which distinguished the simple from the difficult cases was the fact that politicians presented a reasonably clear definition of the problem in the former cases while in the latter cases they were asking experts to provide them with one.

Reliance on orderly procedures. We have said that a precise definition of the problem is necessary so that policy alternatives to deal with it can be devised to take account of costs, efficiency, feasibility, needs of affected persons and other such matters. According to the procedures for rational policy-making, these aspects of the problem must be measured and policy alternatives ranked according to their probable success in alleviating the problem. But once again the actual situation does not always fit the ideal model, for it may be impossible to measure relevant and significant aspects of certain problems or figure out how to give proper weight to them. For example, how does one quantify the meaning of stigma to a disabled person—or assign a number to it that would enable policy-makers to give weight to it along with other aspects of the problem? How does one quantify the moral indignation of those who wish the sale or distribution of explicit sexual materials banned—or the moral indignation of those who view censorship in any form as repugnant? There is no method known for measuring the cost to a family, a member of which is an alcoholic. Sociological research may be able to tell us how people in a population feel about these problems or how they are affected by these things, but research cannot account for specific weight to assign to them. This difficulty, in fact, proved to be one reason for the undoing of the Planning-Programming-Budgeting System, the highly rationalistic approach to the budgeting that Lyndon Johnson attempted to implement during his term of office as President.[2] As Otis Graham points out, a main problem with the method was that it "pressed every objective toward quantification . . . [even though] many benefits and even some costs cannot be quantified" (Graham, 1976:173).

Although such things cannot be quantified, this does not mean that they are insignificant in dictating which social policy will be followed. Clearly they are, for in the outcome of many policy deliberations their role has been central. But, if the factors are not quantifiable, then how do they enter into the decision-making equation? The answer is clear: the political process provides the solution. This is evident in the case of deliberations about pornography, where the magnitude of weight given to moral indignation about the sale of explicit sexual materials was determined by the political influence that outraged citizens could muster, and in the case of recommendations of the Commission on Population Control and the Future concerning abortion, where fear of moral indignation played a major role in the President's decision to reject it.

The final illustration we will present of the dependency of the planning method on partisan politics concerns the intended scope of the method. Most planning aims to be comprehensive, meaning that in deciding on policies to solve actual problems, decision-makers must allocate scarce resources for the society's greatest benefit among different competing causes. Thus, in the executive and legislative branches of government, decision-makers seldom have the luxury of considering only that which is the best policy for one problem. As Alice Rivlin points out in her book, *Systematic Thinking for Social Action* (1971), the real problem facing decision-makers is: "Which is more important, curing cancer or teaching poor children to read?" (Rivlin, 1971:50−51). While social science may be able to help measure the objectives of certain programs and how close society is to reaching them (Rivlin, 1971: 46−50), it cannot attach weight to these objectives. The question of which objective is more important for the society is political—not a matter for dispassionate rational scientific analysis. As Rivlin explains:

> Different programs benefit different people. Social action programs typically produce both private and public benefits. The first accrue to individuals, who are, for example, cured of cancer or taught to read, the second are diffused to others, who suffer less fear of cancer or enjoy the better life a literate society provides. The private benefits of different types of social action programs may go to entirely different groups of people. People who have cancer are not the people who cannot read. Even if we know that the benefit-cost ratio is higher for reading programs than for cancer programs, we could not necessarily choose to devote more resources to reading. The decision would depend in part on the value attached to benefitting cancer victims and illiterates (Rivlin, 1971:57−58).

These, it is clear, are political matters. The policy analyst or social scientist might succeed in clarifying some of the consequences that would follow for different groups or for the nation as a whole, of allocating monies to one cause or the other, or some mix between the two, but science cannot resolve the question of what the government should do.

Aaron Wildavsky emphasizes this in his critique of the previously mentioned Planning-Programming-Budgeting System (PPBS) procedure for developing the federal government's budgets. He points out that PPBS entails collecting data about program objectives and resources and making these available to decision-makers with the aim of coordinating allocation with objectives in a more rational way (Wildavsky, 1964:430). Wildavsky concludes, however, that one reason why the system has floundered is because, "The problem is not . . . how budgtary benefits should be mixed but who should receive budgetary benefits and how much . . ." (Wildavsky, 1964: 422). Posing the problem in this way makes it evident that these budget questions are inherently political. Thus, policy analysis and social science can be of only limited value in helping to solve them.

The method of planning must ultimately rely on partisan political methods to resolve basic definitional questions and questions of value, yet the two approaches to policy are not entirely compatible with one another. When efforts have been made to put the planning method into practice, many of its procedures have proved to be highly unrealistic in the day-to-day operations of government. Charles Lindblom points to one of the main problems in this regard. He notes that the policy scientists' notions of policy-making as a regular sequence of logically related stages does not accord well with the way in which most policy-making bodies are forced to operate in order to accomplish their assigned tasks. He explains that the planning conception tends to view policy

> . . . as though it were the product of one governing mind, which is clearly not the case. It fails to evoke or suggest the distinctively political aspect of policy-making, its apparent disorder, and the consequent strikingly different ways in which policy emerges . . . . A policy is sometimes the outcome of a political compromise among policy-makers, none of whom had in mind quite the problem to which the original policy is the solution. Sometimes policy springs from new opportunities, not from "problems" at all. And sometimes policies are not decided upon but nevertheless "happen" (Lindblom, 1968:3—4).

In the decision-making process, for example, the clarification of goals or objectives may not precede the choice of policy alternatives. According to Austin Ranney, "What we call goals or objectives may, in large part, be operationally dictated by the policies we can agree upon. The mixtures of values found in complex policies may have to be taken in complex packages, so that policies may determine goals at least as much as goal objectives determine policies" (Ranney, 1968:80). In short, the policy-science approach to decision-making, especially the fact that most of the decisions and policy-making activities that take place in our national and local political life simply have no clear-cut beginning or apparent end (Lindblom, 1968:4, 29).[3]

Another aspect of the political process that is in conflict with the method of scientific planning is the complexity and fragmentation of the process. Not only is there no neat stepwise procedure, but also as a rule there is no single identifiable "policy-maker." In most situations, power is held by numerous people and groups, no one of whom is strong enough to dominate (Lindbloom, 1968:29), and in certain cases it is impossible to ascertain who, if anyone, possesses power (Bauer, 1968:15). Power is diffused throughout different groups of people and it is fragmented by site as well. Policies are made at the federal, state and local levels, and within each of these, political influence is greatly dispersed (Lindblom, 1968; Polsby, 1971). Fragmentation of power means that in most cases policy-making is a cooperative, collective enterprise involving attempts to garner enough votes and power to enact a law. For this reason few policy proposals ever survive legislative deliberations intact. To gain support, *compromise* is necessary; as a result "theoretically" desirable courses of action, if they survive at all, may emerge from political debate in greatly rearranged and watered-down versions (Polsby and Wildavsky, 1971).

The Intended Outcomes: Rationality and Stability

A further problem with using a planning approach to policy within a partisan political system is in ascertaining what is and is not a rational course of action to follow. The policy-science conception of decision-making is one that places a high premium on rationality, yet in practice it has proven extremely difficult to state whether or not a particular course of action is rational or not. Lindblom illustrates the difficulty by posing a hypothetical case of a Congressperson who endorses four separate objectives but may actually vote against some of them to assure votes for others, which he/she views as more important or more feasible. He states the dilemma: "We cannot say that his turning against measures suited to some of his work is irrational, nor can we actually say that, taking all his ends as a group, he did not choose the wisest one" (Lindblom, 1968:109).[4] Lindblom goes on to list some of the complicating factors of real policy-making to further illustrate his point.

> To say that a policy was irrationally chosen would require . . . an investigation of all the circumstances of the choice including the time pressures under which it had to be made, the state of knowledge concerning it, the need for delegation, the appropriate method of cooperation, the possibility of partisan analysis of the issue, the relationship of the choice to other interlinked policy choices, the extent of disagreement of goals and even with such wide-ranging investigations, one will usually come up with disputed conclusions as to whether the choice was or was not well made, and whether it could have been made better. For we do not quite know which characteristics of policy-making we should call rational. In the present state of social science, a concept of rationality appropriate for judging a complex political system cannot be defined (Lindblom, 1968:109–110).

Another contrast between policy-makers' usual activities and the recommended procedures for rational policy-making is the important need for policy-makers to get things done. The planning approach to policy-making recommends complex analyses of a problem. We have said that during the early stages of the process, policy analysts who follow this approach would try to identify alternatives and specify their costs and consequences. For some types of problems this is feasible; for others the sheer task of measuring everything that requires quantification becomes excessively time-consuming. Indeed, in some cases analysis at this stage of decision-making can become so complex and time-consuming as to immobilize the policy-making process. Several examples of this difficulty illustrate the point. One is the efforts of Franklin D. Roosevelt to bring order to the national economy through planning. One measure he proposed was the National Recovery Administration. Basically the agency was an attempt to bring a number of industries together into a logical system of planned production. The idea was that firms that had been competitors would sit down with government officials to devise industry codes; specify production quotas for each firm; set industry-wide wage scales; develop and enforce common codes for unfair practices; and even set prices (Graham, 1976:28). To do this would have required an immense amount of information and technical skill, so much in fact that one economist, Mordekai Ezekiel, estimated that it would have taken ten years to develop the trained people and data to make NRA work (Ezekiel, 1939). Similarly, the form of analysis called for in the Program-Planning—Budgeting-System required a range of data that the government did not possess in most areas. As Wildavsky explains, the system "requires ability to perform cognitive operations that are beyond present human (or mechanical) operations" [as quoted in Graham (1976:174)]. Etzioni points out other facets of this same problem: "Most societal decision-makers most of the time have only a part of the information they would need in order to examine all the relevant consequences of the various alternative courses. As a rule, they do not even know what information would be necessary, and, hence, they do not know how much of this information they hold or its validity. Nor do they have the assets or time to collect more than an additional fraction of the needed information" (Etzioni, 1968:265).

There are other difficulties in adopting the planning method to the "real world" of partisan politics. In some instances measurement of outcomes and alternatives may be possible, but the costs are so great that the analysis would simply not be worth the time, effort and money needed to achieve the results (Lindblom, 1968:12). Moreover, in the analysis required to decide the single "best" policy, there can develop a conception of the situation so complicated and convoluted that if policy-making bodies were to take it seriously, they would be completely paralyzed. For those who are charged with responsibility for setting and implementing social policies, "less is more." In most situations, to take any course of action at all, some amount of simplification is essential. These tendencies for policy-makers to simplify matters and for policy analysts to complicate them are in contradiction to one another. Lindblom explains the problem: "To clarify and organize all relevant issues, to take an inventory of all important possible policy alternatives, to track down the endless possible consequences of each possible alternative, then to match the multifarious consequences of each with the statement of goals—all this runs beyond the capacity of the human mind, beyond the time and energy that a decision-maker can find to devote to problem-solving, and in fact beyond the information that he has available" (Lindblom, 1968:14). Some appreciation for a situation's complexity is essential in political decision-making, but beyond a certain point is paralyzing.[5]

The paralysis-inducing possibility of the planning model for policy-making is related to another aspect of conflict between this model and the political decision-making process. Policy-makers want to remain in positions of political power; to do this they must be reelected. They are therefore content not just to study a situation, but to take quick, decisive action (Coleman, 1972:3). In most instances they simply cannot await the results of dispassionate, comprehensive scientific analysis.[6] They have to act at the appropriate time on the basis of whatever knowledge is available to them, their own understanding of the situation, the political cross-pressures exerted on them and their own conception of what is politically feasible (Lindblom, 1968:15). Thus, for example, the failure of the social scientists on President Hoover's Commission to appreciate the policymakers' need for quick, decisive action led to a serious estrangement between them and President Hoover (Karl, 1969). While Odum, Ogburn, Harrison and Mitchell were guided by the methods and canons of academic social science in preparing their report on social conditions in American society, Hoover was pressuring them to provide him with results before his term of office expired and he faced reelection. Their *insensitivity* to his plight meant that these social scientists delivered their report, *not* to Hoover, but to Franklin D. Roosevelt.

Then, too, there may be political disadvantages associated with making a commitment to the long-term programs and policies that often develop out of a rational comprehensive approach to policymaking. Elected officials and other policy-makers must be extremely careful about committing resources for long-range programs because such actions severely limit their subsequent flexibility (Michel, 1973a). Obviously, such commitments limit policy options, but they may also limit political success, which depends to some extent on the ability to shift positions and invest funds quickly in particular projects. These

techniques of political survival are inconsistent with the establishment of long-range programs involving the commitment of resources
as fixed costs for extended periods of time. Political survival is also
aided by an image of competence, or at least by avoiding the impression of ineptness (C. Weiss, 1976b:225). Yet, as Michel points out,
long-range social planning entails embracing error as a positive virtue
(Michel, 1973a:228). He states, "All such policy, if it is to be humane
and responsive to reality, must be flexible with regard to reconciling
of goals and priorities and the means to realize them. Planning must
include an explicit moral obligation to turn from what goes wrong"
(Michel, 1973b:22). Yet the politician is in a stronger position politically if he appears to be wrong only infrequently. Thus, the policy-
maker's concern for reelection provides another conflict with proposals for rational comprehensive policy-making.

Finally, many of the proposals set forth by planning groups are
unacceptable for political reasons alone. Planners tend to recommend
the steps they think "must be taken to remedy a situation; politicians
look for steps they think can be taken" (C. Weiss, 1976b:225). The two
are not always the same. As a result, planners' recommendations are
sometimes politically unacceptable; for politicians to adopt them
would imply putting themselves into an untenable or disadvantageous
position (C. Weiss, 1976b:227). Examples of this are abundant. Some of
the most striking occurred during the Nixon Administration. During
his first term of office, Nixon was persuaded by Patrick Moynihan to
begin formulating a National Growth Policy by which growth and
development of all segments of American society would be orchestrated as part of a single master plan. Nixon embraced the idea
wholeheartedly, giving it prominent play in his first State-of-the-
Union message and instructing his domestic advisers to begin working
on its development. A Domestic Council was established, as was a
National Goals Research Staff, to work on clarifying National Goals
and social management. In 1972 *Report on National Growth* was published, in which many Council and Staff ideas were represented.
When confronted with the report, Nixon balked, for, as Graham explains, "on looking more closely at growth policy the Administration
had found it both conceptually more diffuse and politically more unset-
tling to elements of its constituency than had been foreseen" (Graham,
1976:226). In fact, the political difficulty created by such a policy became so acute that by the third year of his first term of office the
Administration, which had earlier heralded the wisdom of the idea of
developing a national growth policy, began to abandon it. By 1970, the
Administration had become totally disenchanted with the idea, so

much so for Graham to state that by that time, "The Administration wished it had never heard of growth policy" (Graham, 1976:228).

Two other examples of the conflict between planning and partisan politics are also provided by the Nixon Administration. One involved the Office of Science and Technology (OST); the other the Commission on Population Control and the Future. OST was established by the Kennedy Administration to evaluate government-supported research and development and coordinate policy implications that might flow from it. By the time that Nixon took office OST had grown into an elaborate agency that regularly supplied the White House with advice about a variety of national domestic problems. However, Nixon soon abolished the office for the simple reason that it did not give him the kind of advice his staff believed was politically acceptable. Graham states, "The White House Staff had not liked OST advice . . . because it was not 'packaged in a way they found helpful,' and in more clarifying words 'kept coming up with answers that . . . did not fit the political realities' " (Graham, 1976:230). Apparently the same problem lay behind his rejection of recommendations made to him by the Population Commission. Graham writes, "Readers of Nixon's population message of 1969 might have expected that the report would have his endorsement. Instead he politely thanked the Commission members, and in a few days chose two of the recommendations, on liberalized abortion laws and the availability of birth control information to minors, for specific repudiation. The President's negative public attitudes owed to more than this . . . (Moynihan's departure). It was an election year and he was trading a critical position on part of the Commission's report for Catholic votes in November" (Graham, 1976:232).

The sources of conflict between politics and planning can be illustrated in other ways. One involves an agency created in accordance with the dictates of the planning method which then found itself undermined by the political process into which it was thrown. The agency was the Reconstruction Finance Corporation (RFC) established during Roosevelt's second term of office. RFC was established to deal with credit policy. It was empowered to make loans to banks and industry, to purchase stocks in banks and other financial institutions, to finance public works and a variety of other things as well. Roosevelt envisioned the Corporation as a potent instrument for change. Graham describes its essential problem and ultimate undoing as one of becoming instead the instrument of select economic interests. "How could the RFC be given sufficient independence from political pressures of dubious or dangerous sort when it must also be a functioning and integral element in a system of national policies?" (Graham, 1976:47).

Caplan summarizes our point nicely when he writes, "The ultimate test of data acceptability is political. Rarely are data in their own right of such impelling force as to override their political significance" (Caplan, 1976:233).

There are two lines of research investigation in sociology that deal with some of the issues we have been discussing about scientific planning. One body of work deals with goal displacement and the other with prisoner's dilemma situations. The relevance of research on goal displacement to the present discussion is that it emphasizes the fact that courses of action that are prompted by completely rational considerations may have consequences which are utterly irrational and deleterious. The relevance of research on prisoner's dilemma situations is that it stresses the fact that individual and collective interests are often in conflict, so that rational actions of individuals can lead to collective ruin, and rational collective actions may promote conflict and instability by offending the interests of individuals.

Goal displacement. Earlier we stated that when policy-making bodies have tried to come to agreement about the nature of the problems with which they must deal, they have discovered that what seems to be rational from one point of view can sometimes prove to be absurd from another. This raises the possibility that the impact on a problem of policies that are derived rationally are not always necessarily rational, that the cumulative effect of actions taken on the basis of rational, logical considerations will necessarily be rational or desirable. Sociological research on goal displacement[7] provides us with some excellent examples of this fact. We will cite two illustrations to exemplify the difficulty that can arise.

The first example concerns a problem that developed in sheltered workshops for the physically disabled (Scott, 1967). When services for the blind in the United States became organized at the turn of the century it was widely believed that the best means for achieving full rehabilitation and personal fulfillment for blind people was employment. While emphasis was placed on job training and placement of blind men and women in commercial industry, it was recognized that some blind persons were so severely disabled as to be unable to compete effectively in commercial industry. An alternative was needed—an environment in which they could derive the therapeutic benefits of labor without having to meet competitive production standards. The sheltered workshops were created and designed to be social service organizations for commercially unemployable blind people and, secondarily, as temporary places of employment for able-bodied blind men and women who could not gain employment elsewhere. It was assumed that they would not be profit-making institutions and that to remain in operation they would have to be subsidized. The first real challenge to the fiscal integrity of this system came in 1929. The stock market crash and the subsequent depression forced many parent agencies to close while shops lost the support of many private benefactors who went bankrupt. At the same time many more people needed the services of the workshops, since many able-bodied blind people were laid off their jobs in commercial industry. In this crisis environment workshop managers met and conceived a logical plan to save their institutions from ruin by establishing a guaranteed market for their products. They convinced Congress to pass preferential legislation (the Wagner O'Day Act) requiring the government to purchase goods produced by sheltered workshops before turning to commercial producers to fulfill orders. The resulting orders for mops and brooms (the only two items then produced by workshops for the blind) helped to rescue these institutions from financial collapse. However, the number of mops and brooms the government purchased each year during the Depression was small, and filling the orders did not require the full-time services of even all commercially unemployable blind people, much less the able-bodied ones. Workshop managers realized that they would have to diversify. In 1937 they persuaded the Congress to amend the law to read "mops, brooms and any other items manufactured by workshops for the blind." Thus, with a guaranteed market and the freedom to diversify, the workshops survived the Depression.

Then came World War II, and with it huge governmental orders for the items that the workshops produced, which now included sheets, pillow cases, towels, undershirts and other clothing apparel as well as mops and brooms. They requested delays, fearing that if they did not fill most of the orders, the government might turn elsewhere for its supplies and the workshops might eventually be put out of business. Their fears were not unfounded, since mounting pressures developed from many sectors to repeal the preferential legislation and completely open up this potentially lucrative market to commercial suppliers. To boost production, managers tried to replace the commercially unemployable blind people in their charge with a work force consisting entirely of able-bodied blind people. They did this by building small craft shops to serve the unemployable clients and openly advertised for able-bodied blind people to apply for positions in the regular workshops. Managers were in sharp competition with commercial industries that faced a labor shortage and sought out able blind men and women to work for them; they simply could not hire enough blind people to keep pace with production demands. In addition, even a full work force of able-bodied blind people could not produce as many goods as production schedules required. So, managers decided that to meet government pressures for production, they needed to have a "mixed" work force consisting of both blind workers and normal, able-bodied sighted people. The enabling legislation specified that the percentage of the workshop work force that was sighted could not exceed ten percent, so at first only a few of the workers were sighted. Yet as both production and orders went up, so did the proportion of sighted people on workshop payrolls. By the middle years of the war, in many "sheltered" workshops for the "blind" well over half of the work force consisted of sighted people; in some almost no blind people were employed at all.

In reviewing these events it would be difficult to claim that each of the policies that were adopted were not logical or rational with the circumstances facing those responsible for keeping the workshops solvent. Yet, the end result was a preposterous situation in which able-bodied sighted people had displaced the blind people for whom these organizations were originally intended.

A second example of the irrational consequences that rational actions can sometimes have is provided by the case of low- and moderate-income housing built by the Urban Development Corporation of the State of New York. (*New York Times,* May 1, 1975.) In March of 1975, although thousands of potential tenants were applying for UDC units, 15 percent of the 17,000 UDC units stood empty; some had been vacant for years. The vacancy problem was caused, it seemed, by a large number of eligibility standards.

Taken individually, there were sound logical reasons for creating each of these standards. For example, a scale of need was established based upon the number of family members so that the housing would go to families who needed it the most. To this was added an income provision, involving a maximum salary—to ensure that only needy families could qualify for housing—and a minimum income—to ensure that maintenance and operating costs would be covered by the rent. Construction and maintenance costs rose unexpectedly, and as a result the minimum income had to be raised. Thus, by 1975, to be eligible for UDC housing, a family of four would have had to earn not less than $7,800 a year and not more than $9,100. This meant that the families who could apply had to come from a rather narrow band on the income scale. Similarly, what seemed like logical and reasonable restrictions pertaining to such matters as previous place of residence, age and sex of children sharing bedrooms, and history of substance abuse among family members, all combined to further delimit the pool of eligible families. As a result, there developed a situation in which were more units available than there were families eligible to occupy them, even though there existed an acute housing shortage among low-income groups.

These two examples raise the disturbing possibility that rational actions taken with respect to various separate aspects of a problem, or at individual stages in the development of programs to deal with it can result in the emergence of a final policy, the consequences of which are utterly irrational and deleterious in their effects. This fact should make us wary of any assumption that actions taken with rational intentions in mind will necessarily always produce consequences that are rational.

Prisoner's dilemma situations. But what if a more synoptic approach toward policy is adopted? That is, instead of deciding what is the reasonable thing to do for one particular aspect of a problem, or for just one stage in the development of a policy, suppose that one were to try to orchestrate all policies that apply to situations in their entirety in an effort to produce a maximally rational outcome. Wouldn't this effectively resolve the problem that is raised by these examples of goal displacement? Recent research on prisoner's dilemma situations highlights some of the possible problems that might then arise.

Prisoner's dilemma problems, an example of which follows, involve situations in which two or more participants in an activity are individually motivated to behave in a way that creates collective ruin (Luce and Raiffa, 1967:94–95). Research on prisoner's dilemma problems highlights the point that a perfectly rational course of action to follow from the perspective of a collectivity, that is, a policy that will guarantee the greatest benefit for the largest number of members of a group, often represents an utterly illogical course of action for an individual to follow, and vice versa. Light provides this example to illustrate the difficulty:

> Imagine yourself in a crowded department store, when suddenly a fire breaks out not far from where you are shopping. You must make a choice as to how to get out; as smoke starts to fill the room, you look nervously about, and notice that other people are doing the same. What are your choices? First, it is clear that if you bolt for one of the few exits,

while everyone walks calmly, you will certainly get out safely. On the other hand, if everyone else were to panic and run, while you remained calm and walked, you would stand a very good chance of being burned alive. At least, if anyone were injured or killed it would be you. Another possibility is that everyone, yourself included, tries to dash out. In that case, your chances would not be as good as they would be if you were the only person to run, but they would be better than if you just walked. Thus, no matter what anyone else were to do, your best bet is to run. Since everyone else is faced with essentially the same choices, it is likely that everyone would run for the exits. Thus even though more people (perhaps even everyone in the store) could get out safely if everyone remained calm and orderly, it is nevertheless clear that such order would be very difficult to maintain (Light,1975:1).

This example calls attention to the fact that what is rational and beneficial for the group as a whole may not always be a rational and beneficial thing for the individual and vice versa. This point, of course, is a familiar one to students of the economics of public good. One such analyst of this problem, Patricia Bowers, cites the following example to illustrate the tensions that can exist between public and private good.

Bowers poses a situation in which owners of neighboring apartment buildings are asked to consider the purchase of a device for their incinerators that can eliminate nearly all of the soot and foreign matter that results from the burning process. The basis for the possible course of action is a study which shows that up to half of all fallout from existing incinerators affects the residents of buildings in which they are housed, and the rest simply falls freely throughout the community. The problem is this. If an individual owner decides to install a more effective incinerator, half of the gain is dispersed throughout the community and cannot therefore be recaptured in rents. This will not be a problem if other owners install the device, since then there will be no fallout at all and rents can be increased accordingly. However, if there is any uncertainty about the behavior of other landlords, profit considerations may lead to a situation in which no one will buy the new device. As a result, all of them will end up in the worst possible situation: all refusing to cooperate and all desiring to install new incinerators, yet with everyone acting in a completely rational way (P. Bowers, 1974:94).

The point that these examples raise is that when one speaks about adopting a rational course of action to follow, one must specify the level in the system at which the criterion of rationality is to be applied, the reason being that a course of action that is considered to be rational and beneficial from the point of view of the whole may be an utterly illogical course of action from the point of view of individuals or subgroups of the whole.

This problem has been discussed in other contexts. James Buchanan deals with it in an essay entitled, "Private Decisions and Public Goods" (Buchanan, 1968:145−147), as does William Baumol in his book, *Welfare Economics and the Theory of the State* (Baumol, 1952). And Mancur Olson discusses it at length in his analysis of the logic of collective action (Olson, 1965).

Olson presents as an example the paradox that exists in the labor union movement of an extremely low level of participation in labor unions, yet overwhelming support given for measures that force members to support their unions (Olson, 1965:86). Studies show that less than ten percent of union members bother to attend meeting or participate in other union activities but that over 90 percent vote in favor of measures forcing them to belong to the union and to take substantial dues payments for the privilege of belonging. He suggests that there is nothing inconsistent or illogical in the two positions and that both are completely rational views even though the results appear irrational and illogical. He explains why. "If a strong union is in the members' interest, they will probably be better off if the attendance is high but an individual worker has no incentive to attend a meeting. He will get the benefits of the union's actions whether he attends meetings or not and will probably not by himself be able to add noticeably to these achievements" (Olson, 1965:86).

The problem raised by these examples emphasizes several facets of the relationship between individual and collective goals. They show that perfectly rational behavior of individuals in a system can have dysfunctional consequences at the aggregate level; that logically inconsistent and therefore apparently irrational behavior of individuals can be motivated by completely rational behavior; and that in any system of governance involving collective actions, decisions are often Pareto-like in the sense that utility for one person or group of people can only be achieved at the expense of diminishing utility for others (P. Bowers, 1974:84)[8].

If sociologists and others writing about the applications of social science to policy have glossed over this problem, at least some of the people who have had direct experience with the planning method have been acutely aware of the difficulties that arise in reconciling public and individual interests. One is John Whitaker, Undersecretary of the Interior under Nixon. Whitaker expressed the problem succinctly when he stated, "I think they are beautiful words

[Growth Policy], and when you try to get down to what they mean by it it is an extremely difficult problem, the center of that problem being . . . [deciding] who is going to grow" [as quoted in Graham (1976:226)]. Rexford Tugwell, a member of Roosevelt's brain trust, was another. In an article entitled, "The Principle of Planning and the Institution of Laissez-faire" published in the *American Economic Review* (1932), Tugwell wrote

> Those who talk about this sort of change [planning] are not contemplating sacrifice. They are expecting gains. But it will certainly be one of the characteristics of any planned economy that the few who fare so well as things are now would be required to give up nearly all the exclusive prerequisites they have come to consider theirs by right and that these should be in some sense socialized" (Tugwell, 1932:69).

Otis Graham has correctly identified this problem as "the seam along which the administration's (FRA's) planning government would tear, an intellectual pivot of the whole planning process: some would be required to give up" (Graham, 1976:26), for it was precisely this which proved to be the undoing of many of that administration's most ambitious efforts to plan. This is clearly illustrated by the example we cited in Chapter 4 of the participation of sociologists and economists in the United States Department of Agriculture in that department's attempt to forge a farm policy that stressed comprehensive scientific crop planning through soil-bank programs, quotas for individual farm products, and regional and national coordination of farm policy. The goals of this planning effort were to eliminate rural poverty while at the same time enabling wealthier farmers to earn a reasonable profit. But the goal of satisfying both groups ultimately proved to be impossible, and the policies adopted most often benefited poor farmers at a cost to wealthier farmers. Quotas, government control of products and coordination of individual farm output with regional needs severely interfered with the profits that could be earned by larger, wealthier farmers. For them a rational policy was one that would free them to grow and expand at will. In the democratic tradition of interest-group politics, they persuaded Congressmen from their home states of California, Oklahoma and Texas that academic intellectuals who were committed to "Communism" had gained control of the Department of Agriculture; eventually their dissatisfaction with Agriculture Department policies resulted in the forced resignation of large numbers of social scientists from the Agricultural Department in 1940 (Kirdenall, 1966:215–223).

Conclusions

Nothing we have said about America's political system is startling or new. It is merely a statement of facts about this system that any reasonably intelligent person possessing an elementary familiarity with it already knows. Why then do we make such a point of explaining the obvious? The answer is that in the context of discussions about the applications of sociological knowledge and methods to social policy, sociologists have tended to ignore these elementary facts about the political system in which their advice is given and the implications of these facts for the government's receptivity to it. A characteristic attitude of social science proponents of the rational planning approach has been to greatly underrate the significance of partisan politics for policy-making activities. Many of them have proceeded as though the normal operation of the American political system will somehow be suspended the moment that sociologists step forward with their scientifically based plans for action. An example of this attitude is supplied by the Hoover Commission on Recent Social Trends. Neither President Hoover nor his social science advisors were ever quite able to comprehend the fact that they were engaging in political activity when they were drawing up a scientific profile of the nation. Barry Karl describes Hoover and his advisers as the kind of politicians who were "committed to a new scientific order of life from the beginning—one in which 'American Democracy' would be pursued, but in accordance with a definition of Democracy that in some strange way omitted politics" (Karl, 1969:356).

One need not go back so many years for examples of this attitude. Couched in terms of the familiar problem of value-free social science, it is still very much in evidence today. Sociologists doing policy-relevant research are told that they must avoid allowing their own values to intrude into their research, scrupulously dissociating themselves from engaging in politics. Even assuming that sociologists could adopt such a value-free stance, this advice ignores the plight of the recipients of sociological knowledge—policy-makers, who *must* and *do* operate in a value-laden political environment. In this environment sociological research becomes a political resource, and it is in fact *used* in this way. Lost in many discussions of value-free social science is any notion of the significance of political realities for the success or failure of the sociologists' work in applied problems.[9]

It is naive of sociologists to imagine that policy-making bodies will automatically scrutinize scientific information for policy implications and then simply adopt them or that scientists can avoid what they view "as the sometimes nasty" political character of policy-making. In fact, the effect of policy-relevant research on social policy is largely dictated by the nature of the American political system. Social change in our society is not now and never has been dictated by scientific expertise; if anything, "social engineering" is more feared than welcomed by the American public; for this reason, politicians resist it. That there are political constraints to policy recommendations should lead us to recognize that the political feasibility of proposed courses of action is an important factor in assessing sociologists' recommendations and in determining the likelihood of their acceptance.

Some sociologists have recognized the importance of feasibility. A number of them have discussed explicitly the idea that success in applying social science to social policy depends upon an appreciation of the politicized nature of policy-making in our society. This is evident in the writings of such scholars as Herbert Gans, who, for example, states that, "A fundamental necessity of a policy-oriented social science is a model of the social-political process that is tailored to the needs of the policy designer" (Gans, 1971:29–30); and Howard Freeman who has written that, "The researcher accepts the commitment and obligation to be primarily responsible for the development of the research design and the selection of variables in applied studies, and . . . his obligations include orienting his research to the operating and policy system as well as the peer system" (Freeman, 1963:150). Another is Adam Yarmolinsky, who writes: "If he is to be really useful to the policy-maker or the policy analyst, the policy researcher must have a programmatic sense" (Yarmolinsky, 1971:209). Robert Lane suggests that policy analysts should be consumer-oriented in the sense of being attuned to the realities of the political system to which their work will be made relevant (Lane, 1972:83). Yehezkel Dror, writes, "Policy-relevant behavioral science materials must be presented in a language understandable to policy-makers and in easily accessible communication media" (Dror, 1971b:159), and Paul Taylor suggests, "That to be effective, social science must come to grips with the processes of decisions in order to understand the role of that game and to know the obstacles to acceptance of it" (P. Taylor, 1947:51).

These statements by well-known social scientists indicate that there is no shortage of awareness of the influence of partisan politics; at the same time, there is a tendency to dismiss this influence as a temporary problem that will disappear as sociologists expand their knowledge and theory about common social problems. This attitude is reflected in the writings of a number of people. Harold Orlans, for example, faults executive agencies of the government "for not enunciating sufficiently clear and limited goals" (Orlans, 1968:153) and Robert Lane complains that political structures rarely allow scientists to exercise influence to any meaningful extent (Lane, 1972). Dror recognizes the problem and proposes as a solution "a broad set of changes in the public policy-making system and in the behavioral sciences and in their mutual transition" (Dror, 1971b:156) before any genuine improvement in the use of behavioral science for policy-making can occur. He adds that what is called for "is not some incremental change here and there, but revolutionary redesign in the two systems and their interplay" (Dror, 1971b:156). Stein calls for a greater willingness by government to grant social scientists the status of "expertise beyond the kind of life experience and common sense judgment" (Stein, 1968:xiv) and James Coleman describes the American political system and process as "the greatest obstacle to the use of social science in public policy" (Coleman, 1973:1).

These commentaries reflect the inclination by sociologists and others to criticize the politicians' procedures as deficient in comparison to the model of governance endorsed by sociologists and to assume that the politicians' procedures are the ones that must change. Yet, years of progressive and reform pressures have not succeeded in changing the procedures used to devise and implement policy from their existing political nature to a highly rationalistic system of "scientific" government. It seems doubtful that this change will occur in the near future. In the meanwhile, if social scientists continue to view politics as "temporary," applied sociology as it is presently conceived and practiced will be unable to provide the important input into social policy desired for it by modern practitioners in this field.

There is an additional matter to be mentioned in this regard. Even if present political procedures could be changed, we should consider what kind of political system would be required in order to create optimal conditions for applying scientific knowledge to social policy. Needed would be a strong, centralized, enlightened authority with enough power to mandate long-term social changes and see them through to completion; command the resources needed to implement the desired programs; and plan and carry out regional and national policies even in the face of regional and other kinds of resistance. Whatever form such a system might take, it would almost certainly deviate in important ways from the concept of a representative democracy. William McCord alludes to this in posing the following dilemma: "[The applied social scientist] may endorse policies which he believes best serve the public interest, but the public may 'irrationally' reject the policy. . . . [Under these conditions] are policy scientists in favor of rational decision no matter how unpopular their base may be, or do they favor democracy, no matter how disastrous the consequences are?" (McCord, 1972:118).

Daniel Patrick Moynihan addresses this same problem but in a somewhat different way.

> The best of behavioral sciences would in truth be of no great utility in a genuine political democracy, where one opinion is as good as another, and where public policies emerging for legislative-executive collaboration will constantly move in one direction, then another, following such whim, fashion, or pressure that seems uppermost at the moment" (Moynihan, 1969:194).

Moynihan does not advocate the alteration of our political democracy, but he does point explicitly to the problem, ignored by many who criticize our existing political system for its failure to make use of social science knowledge in social policy formulation—that planning and participatory democracy are separate enterprises that are not always compatible.

At the heart of the matter, then, is planning and what it implies for the relationship between social science and government. Its presumptions, we found, are not those of government; its promise of politically desirable ends, most notably stability, are not often realized. Yet there are circumstances under which planning is useful. To gain a sense of these circumstances, to understand that they are indeed limited, we follow up on the uses of planning in the next section as we inquire into the variety of uses that government has for social science.

PART TWO: RECEPTIVENESS OF GOVERNMENT TO PLANNING

In this part of Chapter 5 we take the limited circumstances under which studies emanating from the tradition of planning have received significant attention from government. We turn our attention away from disciplinary concerns and details of the planning process to the nature of government. To aid us, several distinctions should be kept in mind. As a bridge between the topics we have discussed to this point and those we are about to take up, we should distinguish, at least, between expansive uses of sociological studies and more technical uses of sociological methods. We should avoid the singularly useless concept of "use," by which many mean the wholesale takeover of an approach or a seminal observation or finding in a completed piece of legislation or operating program. For we will see that as we consider the relation between branches of government and sociology studies, we will find that some take account of the discipline's knowledge and some may utilize techniques widely accepted in the discipline, but none ever adopts use directly—that is, without an intervening political deliberation that has its own life and its own requirements.

Specifically, we intend to discuss the Presidency and the Federal Bureaucracy, on the one hand, and the Congress, on the other, as they utilize planning-oriented studies. We will find that for the Presidency, outlook on the state of the country—relative crisis, relative stability—helps determine receptivity to sociological studies, as do such factors as ideological orientation and time in office. The Presidency and the Executive Bureaucracy may indeed be receptive to discipline knowledge, but receptivity varies greatly with time, inclination and the state of the State. For the Federal Bureaucracy, receptivity is, generally speaking, greater, with the qualification that it is receptivity to more narrow, or technical uses, that characterizes interest in sociological knowledge. Briefly, there is receptivity to measurement techniques and information—two sources that provide the means to carry out mandates and predilections. Finally, low receptivity characterizes Congress' relation to sociological planning-based studies, except for substantiating, supporting or justificatory uses for policy already formulated. There is some exception to this general pattern in the recent, more widespread and more technical uses made by the Congressional Research Service of sociological and other disciplinary knowledge.

Overall, we discover that there is no generalized, unremitting receptiveness within these branches of government to approach the development and implementation of policies in ways that leave significant room for social science perspectives. Indeed, if anything, the conditions under which federal institutions, singly or in cooperation, are able to make policy in this way are more exceptional than common, a fact which points to the disheartening conclusion that government's capacity to conduct public affairs in ways which grant a substantial role to sociology is very limited.

In this part of the chapter we emphasize government and refer back to the historical materials presented earlier. As is true of many of the other topics with which we have been dealing throughout this book, here too the information that is available is sparce, which limits us in terms of the kind of analysis that can be done on it. In light of the limited information available, our goal here will be to identify and illustrate some of the factors that appear to have affected governmental receptivity to social science and planning in the past and to show the role that these factors have played in the outcome of past and recent efforts to apply sociology to policy. We shall attempt to illustrate how receptivity to a social science-based planning approach to government has varied from one governmental policy-making institution to another, and we shall point to factors within the main policy-making institutions of government today that appear to enhance or diminish governmental receptivity to this approach. Our analysis is based upon published scholarly studies of planning efforts that have been undertaken within the executive and legislative branches of government; upon selected studies of policy and decision-making processes within these two branches of the federal government; and upon basic received wisdom about the operation of federal governmental institutions. We stress that we are not here attempting to present an analysis of the complete history of planning efforts undertaken by the federal government—only a selective analysis of them that is focused on aspects of planning which we believe help to illuminate the conditions under which government has been receptive to it and to the use of social science in conjunction with this approach.

Receptivity to Social Science and the Planning Method in Federal Institutions

There is, of course, no one single place within government where policy decisions occur. Instead, there are a number of different federal institutions involved and each of them is receptive to social science and planning, but in a different way. Here we will discuss just two of these institutions—ones that have traditionally played the central role in making and implementing federal policy. These are the executive branch, including specifically the Presidency and the permanent Federal Bureaucracy, and the legislative branch, including the Congress. Reflecting both the availability of published materials about them and actual usages made by each institution of social science and the planning approach to policy, we deal most extensively with the Presidency and more briefly with the Federal Bureaucracy and the Congress.

Planning in the Executive Branch

The Presidency. Presidential receptivity to social science and a planning approach to policy-making has traditionally been great. The reason is because the formulation of broad-based and extensive policy incentives is basic to a modern President's political success from the moment he announces candidacy for office to the time he seeks reelection. As candidate for office, a Presidential contender must propose new programs and policies for dealing with domestic problems that become campaign issues. When elected, the new President must present Congress with a list of legislative proposals. This program then becomes an issue affecting the mid-term Congressional elections. By the third year in office, the incumbent who hopes to be reelected must have a record of accomplishments to present to the American electorate; passage of a comprehensive legislative package is one visible sign the President can offer as evidence that he has carried out his campaign promises. Thus, political wisdom dictates that Presidents engage in some form of policy planning. Various methods are available for doing this, ranging all the way from crass partisanism to the Progressive-type schemes for altruistic planning in the national interest. Within this spectrum, the planning method has occupied a prominent position in Presidential policy initiatives; and, indeed, historically the White House has tended to be more receptive to planning initiatives than any other institution of the federal government.

This is not to say, of course, that all recent American Presidents have been equally enthusiastic and receptive to social science and the planning approach to policy. Presidents from Franklin Roosevelt to Gerald Ford have differed in this regard and their administrations have changed initial views about the method as a result of efforts to use it or because domestic crises have forced them to take immediate drastic steps to deal with pressing social problems. We can discover some of the factors that enhance or deter Presidential receptivity to planning and social science by studying the administrations of Presidents who have been amenable to this approach, comparing them to those who have not.

We shall mention a few of the conditions that we have found to affect Presidential receptivity to a social science-based planning approach to the development of social policy. The first set of factors bears on the question of Presidential receptivity to social science and the planning method *at the time the President enters office*; the second set of factors pertains to presidential receptivity to planning following the assumption of office. We also examine some of the *procedures* that American Presidents have used for employing social science expertise in policy in order to explain the form in which presidential receptivity to social science and the planning approach is most often manifested. Finally, we try to show how the receptivity perspective helps to illuminate some of the features of applied social science discussed in Chapter 1.

PRESIDENTIAL RECEPTIVITY TO SOCIAL SCIENCE—BASED PLANNING WHEN ENTERING OFFICE. Some Presidents have entered the White House strongly predisposed toward developing policies by the planning method and others have not. One of the factors that seems to distinguish the more from the less receptive Presidents is their perception about the state of American society at the time they take office. By and large, Presidents like Franklin Roosevelt, John Kennedy, Lyndon Johnson, and to a lesser extent, Richard Nixon, who entered office believing that the nation *as a whole* (as opposed to a political party or an office) was in a crisis, have tended to be more receptive to broad innovative policy approaches favoring the use of social science than those, such as Harry Truman, Dwight Eisenhower and Gerald Ford, who believed the nation was stable, healthy and on proper course.

Roosevelt took office in an atmosphere of extreme crisis. The stock market, having crashed three years earlier, showed no signs of recovering; businesses were continuing to fail at an alarming rate with few new ones appearing to take their place; a banking crisis, which had been gathering force in the months before he took office came to a head on inauguration weekend when every bank in the nation was closed; and, in his inaugural address, Roosevelt described a nation of people one third of whom were "ill housed, ill clothed, ill fed." In this crisis atmosphere, the belief took hold that something major and dramatic would have to be done, and done quickly, if the nation was to be saved from complete collapse. Roosevelt concluded that bold, far-reaching initiatives were required to put the nation back on course, and this conclusion led him to be highly receptive to a planning approach to policy.

Though less dramatic, there was nevertheless an aura of crisis as well in the administration of John Kennedy following his assumption of office. This crisis atmosphere came on the President slowly, as initially he was preoccupied with foreign policy. By 1963, he was able to give domestic questions sufficient attention to realize the extent of the nation's problems. Otis Graham explains what Kennedy and his advisers discovered:

Not even the Kennedy circle, keyed to the discovery of errors and mistakes in the way things were being done, had sensed [during the campaign and in the first year in office] how bad things really were, or even likely to get. Many social problems were both intensifying and converging. The country was on the threshold of a long-deferred confrontation with its racial history. It was coming to the end of a heedless spread of waste and consumption, and would soon have to live with deep anxiety about the way resources were used in American society. . . . Ahead lay urban riots, campus disturbance, alienation (Graham, 1976:127).

There quickly developed a sense of urgency in the White House about these problems and in this atmosphere, Kennedy set his top aides to work developing plans for new, broad-sweeping policy initiatives to deal with such things as poverty, civil rights, unemployment, education and other similar problems.

The perception of a crisis and the initiatives it spawned during the Kennedy years continued during President Johnson's term of office. Johnson actively sought the assistance of social science experts in efforts to plan national policies to deal with such problems as violence, urban unrest, poverty, civil rights, manpower, population, national growth and a host of other pressing matters. Though more subdued, Richard Nixon also brought to office something of a sense of alarm about the state of American society. Following his election, the feeling began to develop among top officials of his administration that American society was infested with serious social problems that showed every sign of worsening in the 1970s (Graham, 1976:189). This view led Nixon to seek the advice of Patrick Moynihan and other social scientists and initially, at least, to endorse their proposals for a synoptic national growth policy through which to redirect change and development in American society in the 1970s.

In contrast to these stances, there are the administrations of Truman, Eisenhower and Ford. A dominant theme in each one was the idea that American society was stable, healthy pursuing the right course; all three were generally unreceptive to the idea of planning in the domestic field. While each of these Presidents faced great problems when they took up the reins of office, none of them was inclined to characterize as crises-ridden the society as a whole. This is seen clearly in the Truman administration in which the President's view of America's domestic life was that of a time "to appreciate what one had . . . [and] to be skeptical of grand notions of social improvement" (Graham, 1976:93). Truman saw Roosevelt's New Deal as a set of gains to be defended rather than a mix of gains and unfulfilled aspirations in which the unfinished tasks would be foremost (Graham,

1976:93). Truman's attitude mirrored public perception of America as a nation on the right course and this belief led him toward a short-range, caretaker approach to leadership in the area of domestic affairs. In this climate, White House receptivity to long-range planning and development of bold policy initiatives in domestic affairs was slight.[10]

Eisenhower shared Truman's view of America as a strong, stable society following a steady course. He saw little wrong with it and, in any case, never believed that social reform was the business of government in the first place. The only bold initiative in domestic affairs he undertook was one designed to reduce the size of government to make it less intrusive in citizens' private lives. As for Ford, although the circumstances surrounding his elevation to office were certainly riddled with crises, during his brief term of office he was inclined to interpret Nixon's departure as a product of forces that in no way reflected on the inherent rightness and basic stability of American society. This view dominated his administration, during which it is generally agreed that the climate for planning bold new initiatives was rather cool (Graham, 1976:269).

Perception of crises in the nation's domestic life, then, has tended to make Presidents receptive toward a planning approach to social policy. Yet, this generalization must be qualified, for while crises may enhance Presidential interest in planning initiatives, the degree of their receptiveness to this approach depends on the understanding that Presidents have of why these crises exist. Arthur Schlesinger points out in his book, the *Age of Roosevelt* (Schlesinger, 1957), that American Presidents can be distinguished in terms of those inclined to explain crises in terms of flaws in the structure of American society and those who believed that crises are caused by the tendency of American society as constituted to function improperly. Presidents most inclined to adopt a structural view of crises—such as Roosevelt, especially during his first term of office; Kennedy, who revived the idea in 1963; and Johnson who continued it—are also the ones who have been most amenable to comprehensive initiatives carrying major political and social implications. Those who reject structural explanations—for example, Truman, Eisenhower, Nixon, by the end of this first term of office, and Ford—characteristically respond to perceived crises by recommending programs that amount to no more than fine-tuning of existing programs, avoiding proposals that carry far-reaching implications for change.

Roosevelt, during his first term of office, and Nixon, toward the end of his first term, provide contrasting examples. Both men shared the belief that America faced serious problems, yet their explanations for these were quite different. Roosevelt believed that the Depression that faced the nation when he became President had been caused by basic flaws in society's economic institutions; Nixon believed that the problems of urban growth, unemployment and population control (which he became aware of while in office) were the problems of a basically sound society undergoing unusual change. Roosevelt's structural diagnosis greatly enhanced his basic receptivity to the planning approach to policy while Nixon's diagnosis acted as a counterweight to his otherwise strong predisposition to implement policy in this way. Thus, while perception of crises certainly enhances Presidential receptivity to planning, the predisposition toward it is modified by the tendency of some Presidents to attribute national problems to structural flaws in existing institutional arrangements, and of others to explain them as relatively minor, difficulties stemming from the natural tendency of economic and social systems to be out of tune periodically.

Other factors have affected Presidents' receptivity toward the planning method as they have entered office. For example, previous efforts by past Presidents to conduct domestic policy using this method have sometimes affected a new President's willingness to consider it. It is generally agreed that the high repute in which Roosevelt held the concept in 1933 was a direct result of the fact that planning efforts made during World War I were widely believed to have been a major success, and that the low repute in which the idea was held in 1940 had resulted from the fact that earlier programs, which embodied the method, such as the National Recovery Administration of 1933, had failed (Graham, 1976: 93). Similarly, the failure of planning efforts during World War II had further diminished the method's appeal to policy-making bodies in the White House, so that when Truman entered office, he ushered in a 15-to-20-year period in which the planning idea in Washington fell largely on unsympathetic, deaf ears (Graham, 1976:95−100).

Ideological factors have also had an impact on President's receptivity to social science and the planning method. One reason for Truman's and Eisenhower's aversion to this approach in domestic affairs is that both of them felt that planning smacked of socialism, and the fear conjured up in the minds of many Americans of a world dominated by Communism made it politically inexpedient for either one to openly advocate this approach. Another reason why some Presidents have found the planning approach unpalatable is that they have been distrustful of scientific experts. For example, Truman felt alienated from the intellectuals and scientific experts who were pressing the government to do planning. As Graham notes, "Truman was never at ease with experts from outside the political world, especially academics" (Graham, 1976:102–103). Toward the end of his last term of office, Johnson, too, began to be distrustful of Ivy League intellectuals, in part, no doubt, because they were a source of opposition to his Vietnam policies; by the end of his first term of office, Nixon had come to distrust intellectuals altogether. In many instances, this attitude was accompanied by a strong inclination to reject the kind of bold new policy initiatives based upon the method of planning which is often equated with intellectuals, academics and members of the political left.

PRESIDENTIAL RECEPTIVITY TO PLANNING IN OFFICE. The factors that we have cited thus far are ones which have tended to enhance or diminish a President's receptivity to planning at the time he assumes office. Once in office, other factors come into play that modify this initial attitude, either intensifying it or transforming it entirely. One such factor concerns the perplexing question of *how planning is to be done*. The American Presidents who were most receptive to the planning approach when entering office—Roosevelt, Kennedy, Johnson and Nixon—all displayed remarkable vagueness about how to *do* planning in developing policies to deal with the problems they had promised to solve when campaigning for office. Graham explains that in the case of Roosevelt, "Neither the Democrat's history nor their candidate for the Presidency provided anything very clear or new as a remedy for economic collapse" (Graham, 1976:6). In his campaign, Roosevelt had promised to do "great" things, yet the planning idea he had in mind was "plastic and flexible and fuzzy at the edges" (Graham, 1976:14). The new President had no coherent recovery strategy; he came to office without any clear idea of what he would do. The same vagueness was apparent in the Nixon administration. Nixon stated publically the need for comprehensive planning, promising the nation a National Growth Policy in his first State of the Union Message. Yet, it appears that he had nothing precise in mind except the notion that solutions to big problems would require big planning. The same is true of Johnson and Kennedy, both of whom spoke glowingly about the need for planning, but were inclined to change the subject when pressed to explain specifically what they had in mind. Thus, all four Presidents were committed to an idea and an approach they were unable to explain clearly; and this strongly inclined all of them, on assuming office, to turn to social scientists and other experts on domestic affairs, for immediate advice about what specifically to do and how to do it. In each administration, responsibility was given to high-level social science advisors to conceive and work out details of national plans for dealing with poverty, unemployment and social unrest. Roosevelt relied on a Brain Trust of social scientists consisting of Adolph Berle, Rexford Tugwell and Raymond Moley to provide him with detailed ideas about how to plan a national economy. Kennedy invited numerous social scientists to Washington to lend substance and definition to his New Frontier program; and Johnson relied on a series of task forces composed of academic social scientists and professional administrators to become the architects and builders of his Great Society program. Richard Nixon hired Patrick Moynihan to advise him about what to do, and Moynihan in turn attracted numerous other social scientists to work on defining and developing a National Growth Policy to which the President had become committed. The point is that Presidential calls for a New Deal, a New Frontier, a Great Society or a National Growth Policy are merely commitments to develop comprehensive policy initiatives—not policy initiatives per se. For these, the President must rely on experts to tell him what to do and how to do it. Consequently, Presidential receptivity to social science-based planning efforts often reach their high water mark just *after* a new President enters office when he must begin to draw up legislation that details programs for dealing with initial crises. [11]

If the initial ardor of some Presidents for planning has been great, it usually cools with time. In fact, the closer a President comes to facing reelection, the less interest he seems to have in following a planning approach to policy (Graham, 1976:273). Richard Nixon was far more interested in considering initiatives such as a National Growth and Population Policy in 1968 than he was in 1972. Indeed, when the time came for him to face reelection, he had turned his back entirely on the idea of master plans for social change in America in the 1970s and he publically disassociated himself from several of the main recommendations of the Commission on Population and the Future. Roosevelt, too, became disillusioned with planning with time, even though he never abandoned the idea entirely. During his first four years in office he experimented with new institutional forms in an effort to transform the economic structure of American society. Yet, by 1938 he was increasingly content to take a purely fiscal approach to government and showed increasing impatience with advisers who persisted in proposing policies aimed at achieving basic structural changes (Schlesinger, 1957). A third example is provided by Eisenhower, who came to office in 1952 on a promise to reduce the size of government, but he abandoned his massive plans for this entirely by his third year in office.

The reasons Presidential receptivity to planning diminish with time have varied with one President to another. For some, it was the recognition that radical change carries political costs that they were unable or unprepared to pay; for others it was the discovery that long-term programs do not yield immediate benefits helpful to an incumbent desiring reelection to office. Another factor has been the recognition of how complicated the problem of planning is, as is the fact (to be discussed momentarily) that the permanent bureaucracy has seldom shared a President's objectives or enthusiasm for grand-scale planning, often taking steps to seriously undermine his efforts. Whatever the reason, the point is that the longer a President remains in office, the less receptive he becomes to social science-based policy initiatives.

Although a President may at the outset be receptive toward broad innovative approaches to social policy that favor social scientists, for obvious reasons any planning initiatives that are proposed must ultimately pass a rigorous test of political feasibility before they receive Presidential endorsement. This fact has major implications for Presidential receptivity to social science, for it effects *the way* in which White House based planning initiatives are developed and *the timing and manner* in which social science knowledge is introduced into them. As a rule, views of outside experts reach the President by a two-stage process. In the first stage, Presidential aides solicit a wide range of opinions and ideas from experts about the planning in question.[12] To this end they set up special organizational forms, such as study groups, task forces or Presidential commissions like the Commissions on Violence, Criminal Justice, Pornography and Population. These groups are charged with the responsibility for policy proposals and academics are frequently invited to participate in them. In the second stage, the aide in charge reviews the Commission reports with other presidential aides to consider their political implications and feasibility. What the President eventually sees are not the original proposals, but remnants that have survived the test of political feasibility. Clearly, the room for dispassionate consideration of what may be required to deal with a problem is greatest during the *first stage* of this than during the second, when concerns about political feasibility become overriding. Consequently, receptivity to social science-based planning efforts tends to be much greater early on in the process and diminishes the closer proposals get to the Oval office. Incidentally, this is precisely parallel to the tendency of Presidents to become less receptive toward a planning approach to policy over time, for in both cases the cold realities of American Presidential politics are responsible for the erosion of confidence in it.

An illustration of how this process works occurred during the Johnson administration. In 1963, Johnson, already confident of victory in the 1964 presidential election, decided that he should begin to prepare a comprehensive legislative program to offer Congress in its first session in 1965. President Johnson appointed Bill Moyers to establish and orchestrate a whole series of task forces to provide guidance in developing the "Great Society" programs. Moyers, in turn, conceived the idea of assembling some of the nation's leading thinkers into task force groups, challenging them to develop programs for the unemployed, the poor and decaying American cities. Their recommendations were to be the basis for the President's legislative program.

In all, 14 different task force groups were established, each composed of from 12 to 15 members of whom one half were government officials—the other half members of the academic community. On November 15, 1964, these task forces submitted reports to Moyers, who studied them and then turned them over to members of the President's cabinet (experts from the Budget Bureau) and key political aides of the President. Patrick Anderson explains what happened next: "These groups met for a series of sessions in Moyers' office to decide which ideas in the task force proposals had substantive merit, and, beyond that, were politically feasible. . . . Given the decision made and priorities set in these meetings, Moyers' office could begin to shape the final recommendations that would be presented to the President" (Anderson, 1968:332−333). Anderson's account of the procedures followed during the Johnson administration to develop legislation for Great Society programs suggests that while there is ample room for input by social scientists in the initial phase of the policy process, results must be carefully screened for political feasibility by key aides before they are transmitted to the President for his consideration. Moreover, this procedure strongly reinforces the view expressed earlier that the government dominates its relationships with the social science community.

Johnson administration procedures of using outside experts to help develop programs were patterned after ones that Franklin Roosevelt had used during his first two terms of office. As explained elsewhere, Roosevelt created a "Brain Trust" in 1932 to advise him in developing programs for the New Deal. The need for it came from Roosevelt's belief that traditional social and economic theories were being rejected by the experience of the depression and that he needed fresh ideas about national economic policy. The Brain Trust (Professors Moley, Tugwell and Berle) was brought together by the President with the advice of Samuel Rosenman, Counsel to then Governor Roosevelt, and D. Basil O' Connor, Roosevelt's former law partner. The task given to this group of academic social scientists, the Brain Trust, was to council candidate Roosevelt on academic theories pertaining to economic and social problems brought on by the Depression and to help him draw conclusions about policies to pursue. The Trust had a significant impact on candidate Roosevelt's campaign speeches and an even greater impact on the legislative programs he enacted immediately following his election to office. Perhaps the most notable examples of its impact are the National Recovery Administration, which entailed experimentation with economic collectivism, and the Agricultural Adjustment Administration, which entailed policies for ensuring the price of commodities by paying farmers subsidies for their crops.

Receptive as Roosevelt was to the idea of planning the national economy in ways consistent with new economic concepts, he was also a politician who realized that any legislative proposals by the Brain Trust would have to pass the test of political feasibility before he could endorse it. His position on this matter is nicely illustrated by the President's reaction to one of Rexford Tugwell's pet ideas to use the political campaign of 1932 as a forum in which to educate people about the principles of Keynesian economics. Tugwell writes, "Roosevelt's comment was that the thing I was being so eloquent about was one that most of the people he knew would reject—he said that I didn't understand about educating people; a campaign was not a dialogue or a program of adult education. It was a fight for office, and he meant a fight. The President, he repeated, could educate in the interest of his program, but a candidate had to accept the people's prejudices and turn them to good use" (Tugwell and Cronin, 1974:409–410).

Roosevelt was careful to institute a procedure to ensure that all legislative proposals suggested by the Brain Trust were scrutinized and approved by trusted political advisors before reaching his desk. After members of the Trust formulated their recommendations, they were turned over to a panel of high-level aides who were instructed to evaluate them for political feasibility. Original proposals were revised and modified accordingly; only then did Roosevelt see them. Thus, though highly receptive to the planning approach, Roosevelt, like Johnson later on, was keenly aware of political realities, using them as the standard against which all legislative proposals were evaluated.

Other Presidents have followed much the same procedures. Eisenhower, in 1951, for example, appointed a commission to establish National Goals for the 1950s (Archibald, 1967:334–335). Patterned after Hoover's Commission on Recent Social Trends (Eisenhower cited it as the model of what he had in mind when he announced the appointment of the Commission in his 1951 state of the union message), the Commission requested essays from 14 leading authorities in American life, six of whom were social scientists. Following its deliberations, the Commission issued a report, *Goals for America*, in which it set forth its vision of the future. Eisenhower received it with gratitude, but turned it over to his political advisers for their comments and study before reading it himself. They, in turn, urged him to reject the proposals, citing two reasons for their recommendation. One was that they found much of the discussion by the Commission to be impossibly broad, leading to no apparent or discernible policy implications. The second was that when policy implications did emerge, most of them proved to be politically unfeasible. Eisenhower accepted the advice of his political aides and the report was eventually buried.[13]

Thus, we see that by its nature, the Office of President is one that lends itself readily to the type of approach to social policy that is compatable with the use of social science for bold, innovative contributions which sociologists and other social scientists tend to favor. Unlike the Congress, which, as we shall see, draws on social science selectively to buttress positions rather than to define them, Presidential receptivity to social science typically assumes a much more open attitude. This attitude is often manifested as specially appointed Presidential Commissions that provide a concrete structure through which social science data and perspectives can be considered by policy-makers at the highest levels of the executive branch of government. Yet, at the same time, we see that even during periods involving the greatest receptivity by government to social science, political considerations affecting the Presidency provide the ultimate test for the success of any social science-based policy initiatives that are offered. The political feasibility of a proposal, as it affects the President, determines his response to any ideas he may receive from social scientists, indeed, if the advice they offer even reaches the Oval office in the first place.

This analysis helps to clarify certain features of policy-relevant work done by sociologists for the government. In Chapter 1 we examined some of the bases for optimism and despair among sociologists about the practice of applied social science today. Prominently featured in our discussion of optimism is the fact that sociologists can demonstrate a role for specific pieces of research in final reports drafted by Presidential commissions, task forces and study groups. A major reason for despair has been that Presidents have often rejected out of hand the very recommendation that sociological research has most influenced. The two most obvious examples of this are the recent Commission on Pornography and Obscenity and the Commission on Population and the Future. One reason for this is now clear. In both cases there was a great deal of room for sociological analysis to take place in the first stage of the process, when policy options responsive to the problem could be examined dispassionately; but in the second stage, when problems of political feasibility became overriding, the role of such analysis was greatly reduced.

In this analysis, Herbert Hoover is something of an enigma, as he comes closer than any other President in American history to turning basic decisions about policy completely over to social science experts. As we pointed out in Chapter 4, he believed that social scientists were in the best position to diagnose what was wrong with American society and to prescribe what to do about it. Unlike other Presidents we have discussed, Hoover attempted to set political considerations aside entirely. He believed that his role was to provide the moral and political leadership needed to introduce expert programs to the American people and to persuade them to support it. He apparently thought that if this could be done, Congress would recognize its duty to put aside petty political considerations and act in the national interest (Karl, 1969:347–412). This effort to put the planning method directly into practice by excluding politics from a political system based on participatory democracy was never tested, however, for Hoover did not receive the report of this Commission until after the outcome of the 1932 election campaign had already been decided.

To summarize what we have said so far, Presidents who have entered office believing that the nation was in crises have tended to be more receptive to developing comprehensive, long-range policy initiatives of the type that favors the use of social science knowledge and methods than those who believed that the nation was stable and on a proper course. The receptivity of those who entered office in crises was further heightened by their belief that such crises were due to structural flaws in national economic, political and social institutions, and was diminished in those who believed that the crises were due to minor or routine malfunctioning of institutions which they regarded as otherwise stable and sound. Idiosyncratic factors, such as fear of Communism or distrust of intellectuals has curtailed the receptivity of some Presidents to the planning approach at the time they entered office. We have seen that Presidents are most receptive to social science-based planning initiatives in the period immediately following their ascendancy to office, when demands to specify programs concretely are greatest; and that they become less receptive with time, as they begin to discover that long-range planning efforts entail political costs.

This analysis clarifies certain aspects of efforts by sociologists engaged in policy-relevant research during the past 40 years. Principally, it explains the extent and timing of heavy involvement by social scientists in work on Presidential commissions, task forces and study groups. All of these efforts were undertaken either during campaigns when the President was a candidate, or shortly after he assumed office and began to draw up legislative proposals on a large scale. We have seen that the enthusiasm for policy and social science was at its height in the years 1933–1936, in1963 under Kennedy, in 1964 just after Johnson was elected to his first full term of office, and in 1968 when Nixon became President. It also explains the timing of periods of great frustration for social scientists that have occurred either at the tail end of an incumbent's term of office—for example, the late New Deal years, during the last two years of Johnson's term, and the last four years of the Nixon administration—or when Presidents unreceptive to the planning idea in domestic affairs have come to office, as in the case of the Truman, Eisenhower and Ford administrations.

The Federal Bureaucracy, Presidential Control and Receptivity to Planning

"The White House," Otis Graham notes, "is in complete control of its visitors, but of almost nothing else" (Graham, 1976:169). The President stands on top of a cumbersome, bottom-heavy administrative structure, comprised of numerous Agencies, Offices, Departments and Divisions, all of them with special clientele, traditions and deeply vested interests that continually threaten to undermine the political management capability of the President.[14] For political reasons, if for no other, Presidential initiatives must therefore be taken to bring the executive branch of government under White House control, and *these initiatives sometimes result in policies and practices that directly and indirectly effect the President's receptivity to the planning approach* as well as his ability to execute policy in accordance with it.

The problem facing any President is that the executive branch consists not of one government working in consort—but of two governments in conflict. There is the "Presidential government" consisting of people from the world of business, universities, law offices and corporations who are attracted to Washington by the incoming President to work for his administration; and there is the "Permanent government," consisting of the standing bureaucracy with its own special interests and its characteristically conservative outlook on matters affecting it (Anderson, 1968; Cronin and Greenberg, 1969).

The influence of the White House staff on the top officials of the main Departments of the executive wing is, of course, immense. The Secretaries of each Department are appointed by the President and serve at his pleasure. If there are disagreements between the President or his immediate aides and the Department Secretary, they are usually resolved in the President's favor as he can replace the Secretary with another person whose term of appointment includes a guarantee to carry out policies dictated by the President. But the President has much less influence over members of the Permanent Civil Service. It is difficult, sometimes impossible, to fire them, and he cannot always arrange to have those who oppose him transferred elsewhere. This fact creates a serious problem for the President, especially since the Permanent Civil Service, although within the executive branch, can be as much in opposition to the President as is Congress. Moreover, the larger, often cumbersome administrative machinery that this permanent federal bureaucracy entails is far less flexible and easily shaped by the President than is the White House staff. Understandably, most modern Presidents have displayed limited confidence in the bureaucracy's response to their directives and have been strongly disinclined to entrust programs to the Permanent Civil Service that are deemed especially important to Presidential political success.

Speaking of the Roosevelt years, Rexford Tugwell describes the problem:

> The management of a bureaucracy comprising perhaps thousands of careerists will be at best, nominal; the agency heads will inevitably outmaneuver a politicians's intentions. The President's order transmitted through such channels becomes . . . mysteriously changed to suit the bureaucracy's preferences. Policies persist from one administration to another relatively unchanged. Resistance to change is also reinforced by the alliances between bureaucrats and the appropriate Congressmen. Altogether, it requires a most sophisticated and determined President to effect any changes at all (Tugwell and Cronin, 1974:290).

Every President, Roosevelt to Ford, has recognized the inherent weakness of the office, particularly in the area of domestic affairs. For all of them, the central problem has been how to control the bureaucracy, as managing the country seems forever delayed by the unsuccessful efforts to deal with the Permanent government (Graham, 1976:169). Arthur Schlesinger has graphically described this difficulty in the Kennedy administration. Under Kennedy the Presidential government consisted of liberal Democrats, people partisan to the President and his goals. The Permanent government that awaited his arrival in Washington was deeply entrenched. It confidently exuded the feeling that, as Schlesinger put it, "Presidents could come and Presidents could go, but it went on forever" (Schlesinger, 1957:567). This Permanent government wanted to go on doing things as it had been doing them all along, becoming deeply suspicious of the new President's intention and programs. "The Presidential government coming to Washington aglow with new ideas and a euphoric sense that it could not go wrong, promptly collided with the federal barons of the Permanent government, entrenched in their domain and fortified by their sense of proprietorship and the permanent government, confronted by this invasion, began almost to function . . . as a resistance movement" (Schlesinger, 1957:568). A central theme and frustration of Kennedy's brief tenure in office was his effort to bring this bureaucracy under control.

Roosevelt faced the same problem when he came to office, for he found the institution of President weak and unsuited to carry out his plans. He found major governmental functions dispersed throughout a myriad of agencies and departments, with no one, least of all the President, in a position powerful enough to coordinate them (Graham, 1976:105). Harry Truman found the same thing to be true, and in 1947 asked Herbert Hoover to chair a commission to investigate procedures for reorganizing the executive wing, as did Eisenhower, who convened the second Hoover commission on Executive Reorganization in 1953. The conclusions of the second commission exactly mirrored those of the first, i.e., that "the chief problem in American government was not waste but executive weakness" (Graham, 1976:108) with the President presiding over a government "divided," "diffuse," "managerially weak" and "unauthorative." Lyndon Johnson confronted the same problem that Roosevelt had faced earlier. He complained that the organization of the executive branch was exceedingly cumbersome, comprising much too unwieldy an instrument for implementing Presidential policies and programs. Nixon, too, complained about the intractability of the Permanent government, which he saw as "a politically oriented, tempermentally evasive, cautious bureaucracy, sprawling beyond his sight and comprehension, anchored to organized constituents and

Congressional committees and their elderly chairmen" (Graham, 1976:189—190).

This conflict between the Permanent government and the Presidential government creates immense problems for the President. In theory, he heads the Departments of the Executive branch, which employ the bulk of Civil Servants, and, by law, he must entrust them with responsibility for implementing the initiatives that are identified in the voter's mind as the President's program. Yet, to do so might invite political disaster, for, as we have seen, the President's political success depends heavily upon the effectiveness with which his programs are passed and enacted—matters that are far too important to be left in the hands of an antagonistic and conservative permanent Civil Service that the President cannot control. Every modern President has faced this dilemma, finding ways to deal with it. Some of the strategies they have used have led to policies and practices that have greatly enhanced receptivity to the planning method and the chief executive's capability for executing it.

The principal strategy that Presidents have used to gain control of the executive branch is administrative reorganization. The President's motivations for attempting to restructure the federal bureaucracy is to gain control of it so that it will become an instrument better suited to the pursuit of his political objectives. Typically, this motive is concealed by an ideology that stresses orderliness and the elimination of red tape in government. Plans are set forth to restructure and streamline government bureaucracy along functional lines, eliminating duplication of function, centralizing authority, and coordinating activities. Where it has been successful, the President's power and control over the federal bureaucracy has been enhanced. At the same time, executive reorganization has sometimes transformed this branch of government into an instrument well suited to the planning method. That is, reorganization can create the possibility for planning in the executive wing where none existed before. In turn, this potential has helped foster an atmosphere in which key aides of the President become highly receptive to proposals for policy initiatives based upon social science-based planning methods.

Every recent President has tried the idea of executive reorganization, even those who have been least receptive to planning in domestic affairs. Both Truman and Eisenhower, for example, appointed Herbert Hoover to head a special commission of governmental reorganization. Although neither President attempted to implement the findings of the reports they received, their motivations for commissioning the studies were clearly political, having to do with the frustrations of trying to gain control of the sprawling, formless government bureaucracy that they allegedly directed. Franklin Roosevelt was the first modern President to achieve a significant reorganization of the executive branch. When he entered the office, he immediately perceived that the government bureaucracy was far too clumsy and too cumbersome to entrust with his programs. He therefore reorganized the executive branch into six departments, assigning a key aide to coordinate federal programs in each one. Roosevelt had hoped that this streamlining of government would help to bring it under his control. His efforts in this regard, though comparatively modest, did have *the effect of greatly enhancing the administration's receptivity to planning*, for once the executive branch had been reorganized so that planning became possible, the natural desire of politicians and their aides to use the instrument they had created led them to look for ways in which to use it. The result was a flood of new programs familiar to students of the New Deal—proposals that attempted to deal with national problems through use of the planning method.

Although his achievements were comparatively slight, Franklin Roosevelt advocated radical changes in the reorganization of government. Roosevelt's ideas about reorganization lay dormant for nearly 40 years before they were resurrected, reformulated and implemented under the leadership of Richard Nixon. Nixon, like Roosevelt, felt a lack of control over the Permanent government. To remedy this, he appointed Roy Ash to develop a broad sweeping plan of executive reorganization. A two-phase plan was proposed involving the creation of two new superagencies directly under White House control: the Domestic Council and the Office of Management and Budget (OMB). The Domestic Council was an attempt to bring together into a single unit all agencies concerned with domestic affairs and to put them under the control of a single aide, John Ehrlichman. Its duty was to help the President decide what to do in the field of domestic affairs. The Office of Management and Budget was an attempt to coordinate and control the budgetary process. Under the direct control of key aides, its job was to help the President decide how to do the things his Domestic Council told him must be done. Nixon's intention in establishing OMB was to create a mechanism that would force agency heads to stipulate objectives which the President and his aides would then select from in accordance with plans formulated through the Domestic Council. They did this by instituting the system of Management by Objectives (MBO), in which agency heads were required to specify annual goals with accompanying plans and cost estimates. This method, which replaced Johnson's

Program-Planning-Budgeting-System, forced many agency heads to disclose plans, which Nixon was then able to control through veto power, while enabling him to hold others accountable for programs he wished to see implemented. [15] Though never put fully into effect, Nixon did succeed in achieving some streamlining of the federal bureaucracy and as he gained control of it, new opportunities for applying the planning method arose. For reasons already mentioned, Nixon ultimately turned his back on many of the ideas that were proposed, but this fact in no way negates our point that executive reorganization initially can help to foster an attitude of receptivity to planning. It did this by transforming the federal bureaucracy into a more effective tool for carrying out Presidential policies, while at the same time creating a machine ideally suited for the implementing of comprehensive policy initiatives. Then, in a classic illustration of the law of the hammer, the possibility for doing policy led administration officials to begin to look for areas in which it could be put to use. [16] Thus, Nixon's efforts to bring the federal bureaucracy under control led him to adopt strategies that transformed the executive wing into an instrument well suited to planning, and this in turn helped foster an environment that was conducive to its use.

Nixon was not the first American President to look upon the budgetary process as a way of controlling the Permanent government. Lyndon Johnson tried it as well through his much-heralded Program-Planning-Budgeting System (PPBS). As explained elsewhere in this book, [17] PPBS is a method of budgeting development that American industry designed to make the budgeting process explicit, objective and accountable. In it, programs must be justified by hard data and in light of alternative ways of achieving goals. Its purpose is to flush choices out into the open, identifying options for top management to follow. Robert McNamara first introduced PPBS into government in the Pentagon in an effort to make the Defense Department more manageable, less costly to run. Johnson saw at once that this system provided him with a way to gain control over the sprawling federal bureaucracy and, in August of 1965, announced his intention to put it into effect elsewhere in the federal government. In some respects it succeeded, for PPBS certainly helped the President to consolidate his power. At the same time, it dramatically transformed the conduct of government business in the process, creating many new opportunities for centralized comprehensive planning to occur. This opportunity was quickly seized upon by advocates of planning, who urged the President to begin thinking about National Growth policy, and policies for manpower, population, education, poverty and urban development. Johnson's use of PPBS, then, is another illustration of the fact that strategies, devised by the President to gain control of the permanent government, sometimes lead to changes in the federal bureaucracy, which transform it into an instrument well suited for planning, and this fact often helps to foster an attitude of receptivity of bold, far-reaching policy initiatives.

Executive reorganization and budgetary reform are two strategies that Presidents have used in efforts to gain control of the Permanent government. A third, which has also enhanced Presidential receptivity to planning, is the creation of new governmental agencies. The impetus for creating new agencies is clear. Since Presidents are loath to entrust important political programs to a permanent bureaucracy they cannot control, they may opt to deal with the problem by creating organizational shortcuts. The most common ways of doing this are to establish new agencies or to transfer activities formerly entrusted to the Permanent bureaucracy to the White House (Pressman and Wildavsky, 1973:128−132). *Whenever new agencies are created within the Executive office of the President, they are likely to become devices for implementing broad, innovative new policies.* This strategy, first used extensively in modern times by Franklin D. Roosevelt, is intended to free the President from having to work through established agencies of the Permanent government, thereby making it possible for him to implement policies that might be resisted by the Permanent Civil Service.

There are numerous examples of this. When Roosevelt came to office, an obstacle that threatened to undermine his program of measures to deal with the economic emergency was the fact that many members of the Permanent government did not agree with the new economic theories he espoused. Roosevelt's plan for reorganization of the executive branch we discussed before was an attempt to deal with one part of this problem, creating new agencies like the National Recovery Administration (NRA), The Agricultural Adjustment Administration (AAA), and the Works Projects Administration (WPA). In creating NRA, Roosevelt gave it the authority that had previously come under the aegis of The Departments of Interior, Labor and Commerce. As explained in Chapter 5, NRA was created by the National Industrial Recovery Act of 1933 to bring industry, labor and government together for cooperative joint planning for economic recovery. The collectivism implied by this legislation was based on economic theories that departed radically from prevailing doctrines of laissez-faire capitalism, a doctrine that had dominated the thinking of many people who were in key high-level Civil Service positions in departments of the executive branch of government (Leverett, 1935). By placing authority for economic planning in a single unit and staffing it with people sympathetic to his views, Roosevelt was able to create an agency that made economic planning possible. The WPA achieved the same thing. This agency was created to sidestep the established bureaucracy geared to an ideology of government assistance to the unemployed that was alien to Roosevelt's political goals. By consolidating authority for employment programs in a single agency and by appointing a trusted aide, Harry Hopkins, to run it, Roosevelt was able to overcome the problem of the Permanent government. Lyndon Johnson followed Roosevelt's lead in creating the Office of Economic Opportunity (OEO). The purpose of the OEO was to enable the President to cut across departmental lines to coordinate the entire package of programs contained in the Economic Opportunity Act. The act itself involved an approach to poverty that is "need-based" and "service-oriented" (Graham, 1965:234), which stood in sharp contrast to the dominant views of government bureaucrats at the time—based as they were on older concepts of welfare. Johnson endowed OEO with authority that had previously belonged to various agencies of the Permanent government and staffed it with people known to be sympathetic to his ideas.

When such agencies have involved bold initiatives aimed at dealing with domestic social problems, they have greatly increased governmental receptivity of the executive branch to social science-based planning. As word spreads about these programs, social scientists who are sympathetic to the type of approach taken are attracted to such agencies, and they seek out these agencies to work on developing new programs and see them through to enactment. For this reason, the tendency of Presidents to create new executive agencies can give a significant boost to White House receptivity to planning as well as to social science policy research. The creation by the President of a new office or administration within the executive branch is a clear signal that he is prepared to embrace the kind of approach to social policy involving bold new initiatives. This creates an atmosphere both receptive to social science policy initiatives and one in which opportunities for social scientists to have an impact on policy are great. In the past, the development of such agencies has often attracted large numbers of social scientists to Washington, sensing that the government is receptive and prepared to undertake the kinds of comprehensive long-range policy initiatives that social scientists typically favor.[18]

In summary, the conflict that is inherent between the Presidential government and the Permanent government over control of the federal bureaucracy has led several Presidents to devise strategies for centralizing power and authority that, in turn, helps to foster an environment which is conducive to planning. Presidents have tended to adopt three strategies to deal with this problem—executive reorganization, budgetary reform and the establishment of new agencies. We have tried to show how each of these enhanced receptivity to social science-based planning efforts among the Presidents using them, in the process, showing how receptivity to social science expertise for planning has been heightened as a direct result of Presidents implementing strategies introduced to give him control over the federal bureaucracy.

The Permanent Government

As with the Presidency, the receptivity to planning initiatives involving the use of social science expertise within the ten departments that comprise the so-called "Permanent government" is largely dictated by the functions that they are expected to perform. Traditionally, the Federal Bureaucracy has been responsible for two main tasks: it administers programs which have been enacted by Congress and signed into law by the President; and it is responsible for submitting proposals to Congress and the President for dealing with problems falling within its particular domain. The first task leads to the creation of a substantial market for the *technical* use of social science expertise within the federal bureaucracy; and the second task is primarily responsible for the existence of a market for social science that is based on planning initiatives. Since the primary focus of this chapter is on governmental receptivity to planning initiatives in which social science may play a role, we will discuss these first—more fully than the more technical uses of social science methods and information.

A major concern of each department and subunit of it within the Federal Bureaucracy is the development of programs and policies to cope with the particular problems for which the department is responsible. Planning is therefore a major aspect of the responsibility of most, if not all high-level departmental officials and the planning offices of departments of the executive branch are central to its overall operation. The necessity to plan is facilitated by the fact that the Civil Service is permanent, making it possible for persons so inclined to be able to adopt the kind of broad-based, long-ranged perspective that planning entails. As a result, the atmosphere within the federal bureaucracy is one that is broadly receptive to social science-based planning initiatives. This point is highlighted by certain data presented in Chapter 1 (pages 11–12) concerning federal support of social science research. We noted that in 1970 federal support for research and development projects of a policy-relevant nature stood at $38,487,000 and that total federal support for social science research, pure and applied, totaled $422,000,000 in 1971. Most of these funds were dispersed through particular agencies of the federal bureaucracy, indicating the existence of a substantial and widespread interest in social science within the Permanent government. It seems clear that on a day-to-day basis the extent of involvement and interest by the federal bureaucracy in social science-based planning efforts is rather impressive.[19]

The extent of this interest has been adequately documented by Nathan Caplan and his associates in a 1973 study of 204 persons in the upper level[20] of decision-making in the ten departments comprising the executive branch of the federal government (Caplan et al., 1975). These researchers attempted to gauge the extent and nature of social science research utilization in the policy formation activities in which these particular respondents were engaged. "Utilization" in this study means instances of use of social science in which "the decision-maker received . . . social science information and reported efforts to put that knowledge into use *even if this effort to produce an impact was unsuccessful* (emphasis ours)" (Caplan et al., 1975:xii). Caplan and his colleagues reported that they were able to document 575 instances of social science knowledge use in the 204 interviews which they conducted, of which at least 450 were clearly separate instances of use (Caplan et al., 1975:1).[21] The instances of utilization that respondents cited cover a wide range of policy areas including such things as organizational management, education, health, crime, communications, public opinion, management, welfare, marketing, employment, civil rights and minority affairs, the environment, housing, transportation, international relations, consumer affairs and recreation (Caplan et al., 1975:5).

The researchers reported that there is a high degree of interest in and enthusiasm for the use of social science knowledge in government. They find that 85 percent of the respondents subscribed to the belief that social science knowledge can contribute to the improvement of government policies and that 87 percent agreed that government should make the fullest possible use of social science information (Caplan et al., 1975:24). According to their respondents, the most critical impact that social science has is through "the application of the social science perspective, rather than through the use of hard information produced by social scientists" (Caplan et al., 1975:39). For example, respondents were asked for their views of the way in which social science knowledge was used by government. Ranked first by them was "sensitizing policymakers to social needs," followed in ascending order of perceived importance by "evaluating of on-going programs," "stating alternative policies," "implementation of programs," "justification of policy decisions" and "providing a basis for choosing among policy alternatives" (Caplan et al., 1975; 22). Finally, Caplan and his associates find that the greatest use of social science information in the Federal Bureaucracy occurred in the Departments of Interior, Housing and Urban Development, Health, Education and Welfare and Transportation, followed in order of ascending utilization by the Departments of Commerce, Justice, State, Defense, Labor and Agriculture (Caplan et al., 1975:16).[22]

The findings of the Caplan study point to the conclusion that receptivity to social science by those engaging in planning initiatives within the federal bureaucracy is probably great. While we would certainly endorse this conclusion, several important qualifications to it are required. First, it is important to recall that this study deals with instances of use where decision-makers reported that they had *attempted* to put social science knowledge into use even if their efforts to produce an impact were not successful (Caplan et al., 1975:xii), a qualification resulting in a finding exactly parallel to the conclusion we drew from our analysis in Chapter 1 that social science has had some impact on the development of policy *recommendations*, but that its impact on *enacted* policy is less extensive and apparent.

Second, it should be stressed that some of the findings that appear to indicate the extensive use of social science in government are based upon *attitudinal* items which do not necessarily reflect actual *behavior*. For example, the investigators report that 94 percent of their respondents had stated that social indicators data would be valuable in helping them to formulate governmental policy and to evaluate governmental programs in their own agencies, a finding cited to indicate the willingness of federal officials to use social science data in their work (Caplan et al., 1975:41). Yet, in a follow-up study done one year later, Caplan attempted to estimate the use of Social Indicators data for 1973 by these respondents and found that only 4 percent of them had actually made any use of them (Caplan and Barton, 1976). Thus, some of the apparent receptiveness of Federal officials to the use of social science in connection with policy-making efforts is more indicative of a hypothetical willingness to be guided by it rather than an actual effort to use it in specific situations.

There is a third qualification. As with the Presidency (and the Congress), the Permanent government's receptivity to planning initiatives based upon social science information and perspectives is mediated by political concerns.[23] As we noted in our discussion of the Presidency, the Permanent government has its own special interests to protect and these interests ultimately dictate what an agency's response will be to proposed policy initiatives. Caplan reports that his data show that "the consideration of whether or not a policy decision is politically feasible overrides any consideration of the relevant implications of social science information. In other words, social science data are not of such compelling force as to take precedence over their political significance not only with respect to the deliberate nonuse of data, but with respect to the deliberate use of data as well" (Caplan et al., 1975:35). In fact, so great is the weight given to political feasibility that about the only knowledge that governmental officials ever seem to actually use in connection with policy decisions is that which "either supports contemporary political positions or appears to have insignificant political implications" (Caplan et al., 1975:36).

This point suggests that the task of planning within departments of the Federal Bureaucracy entails two things—not one. Planners must not only come up with proposals that they believe will effectively deal with a particular problem, but proposals that will also help to ensure the continued vitality of the agency or department in which they are developed. For this reason, federal bureaucrats responsible for planning in executive agencies are unable to accept just *any* solutions that may be proposed. Instead they must develop a type of proposal that is responsive to the problem, yet sensitive to the political realities and vested interests of the bureau or office in question. This has often diminished receptivity to social science planning initiatives with the federal bureaucracy because these initiatives so often result in policies that are insensitive to the political needs of individual departments and offices.

The receptivity to narrow technical uses of social science research methods, techniques of measurement and procedures for information-gathering by the permanent bureaucracy appears to be great. We have said that a principal task of the Federal Bureaucracy is to implement programs enacted by Congress and the President; this task has helped to created a robust market for technical social science skills. Many of the examples cited in Chapter 1 in the section entitled "Bases of Optimism", in Chapter 2 in the discussion of proposed uses of sociology for policy, and in Chapter 4 where we reviewed the history of applied social science up to 1940—all have entailed this kind of use of social science. For example, we mentioned the extensive use made of the sample survey method as an instrument of government planning by the Division of Program Services of the Agriculture Department from 1932 to 1940. The same Department also made extensive use of techniques of attitude measurement and scaling techniques developed by Rensis Likert who worked for the Department for several years prior to World War II. Mention was also made of the use of social science data-gathering techniques employed during World War II by the War Production Board, the Office of War Information and the Foreign Broadcast Intelligence Service (Alpert, 1967:221; Horowitz and Katz, 1975); and of efforts to use social science research techniques to study national character and investigate topics relating to understanding of the behavior of foreign peoples (Alpert, 1967:220). Following the War, the Office of Naval Research funded a research on technical measurement problems relating to manpower, personnel and training, group morale and organizational structure. The activities of the Bureau of Labor Statistics and the Agricultural Estimates Division of the Department of Agriculture to compile data on wages, employment, commodity prices and other matters relating to the supply of labor also drew heavily on social science methods. In recent years the work of the National Institute of Mental Health to do research on mental health policies in its Laboratory of Socioenvironmental Studies has been a large consumer of social science methods and research techniques (Alpert, 1967:349), as were the now-defunct Office of Economic Opportunity and the Census Bureau, particularly in their joint efforts to develop new statistical series on the extent of poverty in America and the social characteristics of the poor. To these examples one can add the work on research methods supported by the National Science Foundation, the Office of Education, the Departments of Labor, Interior, Commerce, and Housing and Urban Development, and many other governmental agencies comprising the Federal Bureaucracy. These examples strongly reinforce the conclusions embodied in the report of the 90th Congress on the use of social science in federal domestic programs, that perhaps the most common use of social science by the federal bureaucracy is technical, involving the utilization of research methods and data-gathering techniques to provide information necessary to the conduct of governmental business.

Several conclusions emerge from this brief analysis of receptivity of officials in the permanent Federal Bureaucracy to the use of social science in conjunction with planning efforts in which they engage. The general level of receptivity to social science is high. This receptivity takes two forms: a use of social science perspectives to help sensitize policy-makers to social needs; and a more technical use of social science to gather basic information deemed necessary for the conduct of government business. The greatest impact that social science has on planning initiatives apparently occurs at the point of developing policy recommendations, but not in enacted policy. This particular conclusion is, of course, consistent with the analysis made of the Presidency in which we found that the test of political feasibility ultimately overrides all other considerations.

Planning in the Legislative Branch of Government

The Congress. The process by which the government decides on and carries out social policies is shaped by many factors; the constitutional doctrine of the separation of powers; the federal system that leaves substantial powers to state and local government; decentralized political parties; and the social traditions of different regions of the country. One result of the interplay of these and other factors is the dispersal of authority and power among numerous politicians and political groups. These conditions, which are characteristic of the American political system generally, are nowhere more evident than in Congress. Each center of special power in the legislative process is responsive to the demands and putative desires of different segments of the population. As a result, the passage of a piece of legislation by the United States Congress is nearly always the product of political compromise among interested groups. This fact has major implications for the extent of receptivity by Congress to social science perspectives and the planning method that is peculiarly political.

Congress has traditionally served the interests of special constituencies and these interests dictate the criteria that members of Congress use in evaluating legislative proposals. We have seen that social scientists are inclined to first define the nature and extent of a problem; then propose programs to deal with it. Members of Congress may also formulate proposals in this way, but of necessity they must scrutinize these formulations for political implications. They want to know: Who will be affected by a proposed bill? Who will be helped by it? Who will it hurt? They want to determine how proposed measures will affect their constituents; whether new programs and monies appropriated might be transferred into political assets and resources to bolster and consolidate political positions; and, if they are to support it, how politically feasible the legislation is. In short, before the members of Congress agree to support legislative programs, they must determine how these measures affect constituency interests (Polsby, 1971:67; Huitt, 1968:273–274).

Social science-based planning initiatives are seldom, if ever, developed with such concerns in mind. Therefore, it is largely a matter of chance whether the measures proposed will effectively satisfy the political interests of a majority of members of Congress. For this reason receptivity in Congress to planning and broad-based social science perspectives on policy has been traditionally quite low.

The generally low receptivity of Congress toward planning is further diminished by the fact that members of Congress are often weary of bold, new policy initiatives whose political feasibility is unknown and untried. Speaking of the Congress, Huitt notes that "low feasibility must be attached to whatever is genuinely new and innovative; especially if it can be successfully labeled as such, and more especially if it rubs an ideological nerve. What is most feasible is what is purely incremental, or can be made to appear so" (Huitt, 1968:273–274). As a practical matter, Congressional leaders are better able to muster the necessary support for *small* changes in existing programs than for *bold* initiatives of the sort that social scientists and planners are inclined to recommend.

The low receptiveness of Congress to social science policy research is further diminished by another factor that concerns what Congress is asked to do. As Dreyfuss noted (Dreyfuss, 1976:269), Congressional policy activity is of two types: legislative oversight and policy adjustment, and major policy initiatives. Most of the work of Congress entails the first type, i.e., making small decisions and incremental adjustments in programs and policies that already exist and they deal with this by delegating the work to special committees. Here the role of the Congress is to legitimate the policy proposals of others (principally the Executive) and not to change it. He explains that in 352 days of working time, the 93rd Congress enacted 772 of the 26,222 measures introduced (Dreyfuss, 1976:270). These included 39 appropriations acts involving thousands of program items. Nonlegislative issues, including Watergate, also consumed time. He therefore concludes that neither, "The members of Congress nor their principal staff advisors had the time or energy to consider fully the facts available concerning minor decisions. *Further research was not desired . . .*" (Dreyfuss, 1976:270. Emphasis ours).

Only a small number of major policy decisions ever come up before Congress in any given session, that is, the kinds of issues that many believe warrant the input of sociological policy research. But here the problem is that by the time such issues get to Congress, basic positions have already been defined, articulated and defended with data, so that significant debate about them is not possible. Dreyfuss writes:

> Such issues almost certainly will have been subjected to examination by a broad spectrum of commentators and the arguments of both sides will have been verified and criticized by the adversaries . . . [and therefore that] . . . major policy decisions treated by the Congress are rarely the result of congressional formulation (Dreyfuss, 1976: 271).

Dreyfuss concludes that whether the issue is great or small, "the circumstances of the congressional role are a rigorous application of policy research nearly impossible and practically unwarranted" (Dreyfuss, 1976:269) and suggests "the futility of attempting to introduce sophisticated policy research into the congressional decision process" (Dreyfuss, 1976:272).

Yet, members of Congress are not totally unremitting in this perception of social science planning initiatives, for there have been times in recent history when members of Congress have shown an apparent willingness to set partisan political concern aside to evaluate measures primarily on the basis of their suitability for particular problems at hand. Moreover, this has been true even when such measures have been directly counter to a member's own constituency interests. Two obvious examples of this are the overwhelming support that Franklin Roosevelt received from Congress for New Deal programs and the strong support Lyndon Johnson received from Congress for his Great Society legislation. The interesting thing about these and other such programs is that all of them were proposed during periods of great national crises, indicating that Congressional receptiveness to bold policy initiatives, like Presidential receptiveness to them, seems to be heightened by crises. Under these conditions, members of Congress appear to be willing to put aside strictly partisan concerns and cast votes in terms of beliefs about what the national interest requires. Of course, the pressure to do this can be enormous, for when the nation as a whole has lapsed into crises, values and norms which reinforce ideas about solidarity, cohesiveness and the general good become especially salient. Collective sentiments become foremost and members of Congress may be made to feel that it would be unpatriotic, inappropriate, even immoral, for them to place personal political gains before collective interests.

Of course, a Congressmember's motives for supporting measures responsive to collective problems during periods of crises may not be entirely altruistic. The reason is that payoffs associated with purely partisan actions probably diminish under conditions of collective crises, especially if the system of political rewards is altered by these crises. When this occurs, the marginal gains associated with self-serving actions can become smaller than those associated with actions perceived to be responsive to collective crisis. For this reason, members of Congress, acting out of purely personal concerns, may find it advantageous to support proposals in terms of their relevance for collective problems and concerns.

Indirect support for this thesis is supplied by recent research on prisoner's dilemma situations of the kind we described earlier in this chapter. Some of this research has sought to clarify the conditions under which individual members of a group will act in accordance with collective interests. John Light, in particular, has studied this problem in a number of small group experiments (Light, 1975). His data support four main conclusions. First, he finds that collective interests and the interests of individual members, though not always separate, do tend to be distinct. This does not mean that the two do not coincide at times, but he does show that it is not common for the two to be identical. Second, he finds that the conditions under which members of a group are willing to forego personal gain in order to cooperate for the benefit of the collectivity as a whole are exceptional. Third, the one condition under which individuals are most inclined to respond cooperatively and altruistically is when the integrity of the group as a whole is perceived to be in jeopardy. When this happens, individuals then display a tendency to think and act in terms of shared definitions about the greater good. Fourth, Light also finds that conditions must be rather extreme before a shift toward altruism occurs. In spite of the obvious problems associated with making inferences about national legislative bodies on the basis of small group research, Light's research findings do seem to be consistent with the attitudes and behavior of members of Congress toward planning initiatives in recent times.

We are quick to note that members of the United States Congress are not entirely unreceptive to social science and the planning approach to policy-making even during "normal times," for during the 20th century many Senators and some Congressmen have been among its staunchest advocates. Early in the century Senators Henry Cabot Lodge, Albert J. Beveridge and Robert M. LaFollette were strong proponents of the approach; and in recent years, Senators Henry Jackson, who has championed national planning for land use and energy conservation; Hubert Humphrey, who was a proponent of national growth policy; Walter Mondale, who has supported national planning in the social welfare field; Edward Kennedy, who has supported national planning in the health field; and members of Congress, such as Emilio Daddario, who has been concerned with the use of government supported research and development to aid national and regional planning efforts. Moreover, each of these persons, and other members of the Congress as well, have openly used social scientific expertise in their work.

Yet, this usage of social science in planning is heavily tainted by political considerations, for members of Congress who use social science for devising legislation have been inclined to use such expertise in an effort to *substantiate, support, and justify policy alternatives already formulated* rather than to use it to develop basic positions for the first plan. That is, social science has been used more often as a political resource by members of Congress than as a source of inspiration for developing legislation. As Carol Weiss points out, the most common use of sociological policy research in government is "as support and ammunition for a predetermined position. The advocate of a position latches on to research conclusions that legitimate his case and strengthen his bargaining power" (C. Weiss, 1976b:227).

An example of proposed legislation that received a good deal of publicity because of the supporting testimony of social scientists was the Child Development act of 1971, passed by Congress but eventually vetoed by President Nixon. Senator Mondale chaired the Subcommittee on Children and Youth, which aimed, in his words, "to identify and seek changes in arbitrary policies that place hardships on families with children; to develop policies that provide alternative ways of strengthening families; and to determine how we can provide the options and choices that families need to do their best job" (Subcommittee on Children and Youth, U. S. Senate, 1973:2). The "expert" witnesses invited to testify all presented testimony that confirmed the positions that Mondale himself had previously adopted. For example, in his testimony to the Committee, Dr. Edward Zigler, Professor of Psychology at Yale University, stated the need for a National Family Policy, which Mondale had articulated on many occasions before and which he expressed clearly in his opening comments at the hearings (Subcommittee on Children and Youth, 1971:80). Anthropologist Margaret Mead testified on the need for family impact studies, another of Mondale's main concerns (Subcommittee on Children and Youth, 1971:125), as did Urie Bronfenbrenner, Professor of Social Psychology at Cornell University. Clearly, those invited to testify were selected to justify Mondale's philosophy and lend supprt to a piece of legislation devised before this social science expertise had been formally invited. This is not to say that social science had no impact on the legislation, as Mondale is known to be generally conversant with social science and no doubt some of his ideas are influenced by it.

Ian Clark's study of Senate testimony on the supersonic transport provides additional support for this conclusion, that is, social science is used to justify established practices. He shows that the Senators who convened the hearings invited only those scientific experts who were certain to give testimony that supported their own position. Clark developed a list of seven principal issues surrounding the controversy and attached to each issue the names of individual social science experts (all economists) whose views on the SST controversy were known. He shows that invitations to testify were motivated by a wish to give scientific credence to already set positions. For example, Senator Percy, an outspoken opponent of SST, was responsible for having invited experts whose positions strongly supported the anti-SST position, while Senator Magnuson of Washington, a strong proponent of SST, was responsible for inviting economists whose views supported the project (I. Clark, 1974:416−432).[24]

Social scientists are not the only victims of "management" in Congressional hearings. Other "experts," scientific and otherwise, are commonly invited to present testimony before Congressional hearings because someone on the Committee recognizes a similar view. Moreover, members of Congress are not the only people who use Congressional hearings in this way. Actors outside of Congress—most often the President—may succeed in using Congressional hearings to gain support for political programs. A case in point is provided by the hearings on the Economic Opportunity Act of 1964. In the words of one commentator, the hearings "were carefully engineered and orchestrated by a well-organized administration lobby" (E. Graham, 1965:258). The witnesses were all selected because they were overwhelmingly in favor of the bill sponsored by the President. Walter Heller, then Chairman of the Council of Economic Advisors, was one such witness. He testified that a program that would solely redistribute income, "would not be an acceptable or effective solution to the problem of poverty . . . because it would leave the roots of poverty untouched and deal only with its symptoms" (Heller, 1964:26).

Heller's perspective and that of the Economic Opportunity Act reflected a conception of poverty as an exception in an otherwise affluent society, existing only in "pockets." This view implied that the causes of poverty were characteristics of the individual or those produced by his special (ghetto) subculture. It was criticized by opposing social scientists for ignoring the complexities of unemployment and the structural characteristics of the economy that relate to the distribution of income and wealth. These criticisms implied a preference for policies that would deal with income redistribution directly, rather than policies that sought to eliminate poverty by changing the attitudes, motivation and culture of the poor (E. Graham, 1965:234–250; Miller and Rein, 1965). However, this opposing view among social scientists was glossed over in the hearings on the Economic Opportunity Act and no counter witnesses were called to testify on this point of contention. The three academic witnesses who did testify against the proposed legislation "failed to offer constructive alternatives," as one author has phrased it, "dealing as they did with definitional problems, the need for research, and the concept of a welfare state" (Levitan, 1969:40).

Technical Uses of Social Science by Congress

The examples we have presented typify one kind of use made of social science expertise by the Congress. Another is a more technical use of social science data and research results in drawing up and evaluating legislative proposals. This use of social science has been greatly facilitated by a recent organizational innovation introduced into Congress in 1970. In the past, members of Congress have sometimes used social science knowledge to develop legislative proposals, but this has been sporadic and unsystematic. Recently, members of Congress generally have begun to feel a need for greater technical expertise early in the legislative process. In an attempt to improve the technical resources available to it, Congress, in 1970, reorganized and switched the name of Legislative Reference Service to Congressional Research Service (CRS). The Congressional Research Service is responsible for providing information on request to members of Congress and organizing reviews of past legislative activity. The range of topics canvassed by the Congressional Research Service is enormous, including energy needs, urban renewal, agricultural problems. child abuse, defense policies and manpower—to mention several. The Service keeps track of social science and other scientific reports on these subjects by surveying some 4,000 periodicals, many of them social science journals, entering them into a single bibliographic data base. Using this information, coupled with close inspection of legislative actions, the CRS provides technical and descriptive reports to Congress and supplies guidance on issues that Congressional committees should study. When Congressional hearings are held on pending legislation, the Service provides Committee members with memoranda on the purpose and effect of proposed legislation and on the nature and extent of the problem that the proposed legislation is intended to address. Preparing these reports often means making use of social science research, in the case of several housing studies that the Service provided to Subcommittee hearings on urban redevelopment in 1970 (Congressional Research Service, 1971:21).

In principle at least the Congressional Research Service provides a vehicle by which to bring social science knowledge and perspectives to bear on policy issues arising in Congress at the stages of initiation and formulation. To date its use by the Congress has been rather more narrow than intended. Thus far its function has been largely restricted to providing members of Committees of Congress with specific information as requested and not with broader perspectives on policy questions that arise.

The Service prefers to initiate more research on its own to address wider questions, making use of survey research information, in addition to responding to routine requests from Congress for specific information and expert consultation (Jayson, 1974:7−11). While it attempts to widen its role in setting the agenda that should govern the discussion of policies, analyzing alternative policies and pointing out the implications of particular formulations, the Congress (ever concerned with political realities) has indicated its preference to confine the Service to an informational and technical research role (Dreyfuss, 1976:272).

So, we find that there is a limited market in Congress for a kind of social science perspective and research, except during times of national crises when Congress tends to find social science more useful. Less restricted, but nevertheless limited, is the "market" for more technical uses of social science information, methods and data to draft legislative programs. At the moment, Congressional use of social science takes two forms: Congressional hearings, when social science serves as a political resource buttressing the positions of members of Congress on particular policy positions; and through the Congressional Research Service, which provides a vehicle by which social science knowledge and policy analysis is fed to members of the Congress before political positions have hardened. Overall, we find that Congressional receptivity to social science-based planning policy initiative is less than receptivity to it within the executive branch.

Executive−Legislative Cooperation

The process of making policy at the federal level of government has another aspect to it that must be considered, although briefly, because it carries important implications for overall governmental receptivity to planning and social science. We have said that each of the main federal institutions responsible for federal policy-making—the President, the Federal Bureaucracy and the Congress—is in some way receptive to planning initiatives and social science, but that its extent and form vary. But ignored in this analysis is the fact that enacting policy, no matter what method is used, requires these institutions to cooperate with one another. The President may suggest programs but these will never become law unless he gains support for them in Congress. Similarly, individual members of Congress who propose programs of their own must gain support not only from colleagues, but from the President, as well, if they are to become laws. Moreover, once enacted, a program's success may hinge on the willingness of members of the Permanent government or of a newly created agency to cooperate in carrying them out in accordance with dictates of the enabling legislation. This fact (that cooperation among the parties to federal policy-making is necessary for policy decisions to occur) greatly complicates the problem of governmental receptivity to planning and social science. The reason is that the need for cooperation adds an entirely new set of conditions that must be satisfied for any policy to be enacted, no matter what method is used. For cooperation to exist, there must be a basis for it. Among other things, this means that there must be executive–legislative correspondence, i.e., a situation in which the executive and legislative branches of government are controlled by the same political party; a mandate from the voters for the President and Congress to act boldly and in unison; and, as we have seen earlier, if the policy involves bold initiatives, national emergencies to shift politicians' natural inclinations to respond to measures in terms of constituency interest toward national interests and concerns. Clearly, these conditions have not been common in recent American political history. Only four Presidents—Roosevelt, Eisenhower, Johnson and Nixon—entered office with a clear mandate from the people and in only two cases—Johnson and Roosevelt—was there executive–legislative correspondence. The fact that the ability of government to conduct policy at all—whether it uses the method of planning or any other method it chooses—depends on the existence of conditions favorable to cooperation among federal institutions, further diminishes the capability of government as a whole to consider or enact bold policy initiatives derived from the social science-based planning method.

Conclusions

The analysis we have presented identifies and illustrates factors that help to create an attitude of receptivity in government to social science-based planning efforts, leading governmental officials to seek out social science as a resource in initiating, planning, implementing and evaluating social policies. We have shown how the features of different policy-making arenas of government, and the political contingencies with which each must deal affect the environment within which the relationship of government to social science transpires. Political considerations dictate the terms of the relationship, influencing how social science advice is interpreted and whose ideas and principles are accepted and rejected. In this highly politicized environment, social science information and social scientists become resources on which policy-making bodies may draw in an effort to further their political aims. Since each federal institution has a different role to play in the policy-making process, it must confront a different set of political contingencies, and consequently is receptive to social science in a somewhat different way. Congress seeks out scientific experts to buttress pre-established positions; the federal bureaucracy seeks out assistance principally to justify and refine administration procedures and only secondarily to do policy; and the President seeks assistance in developing comprehensive programs that are politically feasible. In addition, since all three must cooperate in making policy, additional constraints are added to the government's capacity to develop and enact policy by using the planning method. Finally, none of the federal institutions we described is apt to be receptive to ideas that imply curtailment of their power or authority. All of them are inclined to evaluate what social scientists have to say about a given problem in terms of its likely impact on their domain of influence.

Overall, then, within government, two main types of uses of social science occur. One of them is technical; the other is more expansive. From our analysis it appears that much wider use is made by the government of technical social science skills than is made of social science for planning. With respect to the latter it seems clear that there is scant room in Congress for such initiatives—none in the federal bureaucracy and in the White House. Yet, even in the most active case, the market for the most expansive forms of social science is limited. Social scientists are most relevant to the policy-making process as purveyors of methodologies and techniques; and they are providers of scientific justification for one position or another. They are less relevant as sources of intellectual advice about broad policy questions or researchers exploring the political implications and long-range consequences of proposed policy initiatives. This is because the political process is more likely to produce policies that imply a broad political consensus rather than to suggest new solutions to national problems that are substantial departures from present practices.

The receptivity perspective we have been developing in this chapter carries major implications for the practice of applying sociological knowledge and methods of research to social policy. It tells us that there is no generalized unremitting receptivity within the federal government to approach the development and implementation of policies in ways that leave room for social science perspectives. If anything, the conditions under which federal institutions, singly or in cooperation, are able to make policy in this way are more exceptional than common, and this fact points to the rather disheartening conclusions that the government's capacity to conduct public affairs in ways that grant a substantial role to social science is extremely limited, and that many of the frustrations that sociologists have experienced as a result of attempting to bring disciplinary knowledge to bear on social policy are attributable to the fact, not that the discipline is intellectually underdeveloped—though this is a factor—but because the government has been unable to conduct its business in ways that are compatible with the use of social science perspectives in policy development.

If this analysis is correct, it means that applied sociology as practiced today probably openly invites frustration and failure, interrupted only by occasional victories that result more from happenstance than design. This conclusion takes us back to the analysis presented in Chapter 1, in which we found that this precisely describes the present state of affairs in our field. In this respect, the analysis that we have presented in this and previous chapters has achieved its purpose, i.e., to explain why efforts by sociologists to apply disciplinary knowledge and methods to social policy have assumed their characteristic form and produced their characteristic outcomes. Our sole remaining task is to consider what, if anything, can be done to alter this state of affairs. We intend to make this attempt in the final chapter—next.

NOTES

1. See Chapter 4 for an explanation of these powers.
2. For a more detailed discussion of this system see page 66 of Chapter 3.
3. For a more elaborate statement about this conception of policy-making in American political life, see Lindblom (1968:5–11).
4. The problem which Lindblom has raised is dealt with further by James Coleman in an essay, "The Possibility of a Social Welfare Function" (Coleman, 1966), and by Kenneth Arrow in his book, *Social Change and Individual Values* (Arrow, 1951). For example, Arrow demonstrates mathematically that there is no procedure for com-

bining individual preferences so that they reflect the view of the citizens in a consistent manner when tastes differ.

5. Even if a policy group were willing to devote the necessary time and resources to this task, it is not clear that the calculations themselves can always be made. Etzioni explains the difficulty:

> First, this capacity assumes that . . . two . . . prerequisites have been met—that criteria for evaluation (or weighing of utilities) have been provided, and that information about the consequences have been made available. Second, this assumes that there is a limited universe of relevant consequences that can be exhaustively surveyed; actually, the universe involves future consequences and these are "open". That there is no adequate theory to account for cause and effect is well known (Etzioni, 1968:265).

6. Occasionally, a policy-maker may prefer to stall for time in the hope that a problem may solve itself or at least become less controversial. Under these circumstances, he or she may publicly favor careful study of alternatives and other policy-science steps. See Ravetz (1971).

7. For a discussion of this concept see Etzioni (1964:10–14) and Blau and Scott (1962:229).

8. This last point is a core problem to which economists and social scientists interested in the problem of public goods and collective actions have given a great deal of attention. See Bauer (1968:20, 99–104), Coleman (1966), Arrow (1951) and Baumol (1952). This research has sought to discover the characteristics of Pareto-optimal situations, i.e., situations in which benefits to the greatest number of persons are maximized at a minimum cost to those who are placed in a disadvantageous position by the actions in question. Also, for an interesting case study highlighting the limits of planning, see McGowan (1976:243–248).

9. This topic is discussed in detail in the next section of this chapter.

10. Except in the area of housing, where Truman believed a genuine crisis existed. See Chapter 6, pages 207–208.

11. This is true even of Presidents who have been otherwise unsympathetic to the idea of planning, for whatever impetus exists for planning in an administration almost always appears at the very outset of the term of office. The Hoover Commission on Executive Reorganization appointed by Eisenhower in 1953 and the Economic Summit convened by Ford shortly after he entered office are two examples of this.

12. For an example of how this process continues to operate in the Carter administration see The Week in Review, New York Times, April 2, 1978, "How Urban Policy Gets Made—Very Carefully," page 1.

13. It should be noted that ever since Roosevelt's first term of office, domestic social policy has received less of the President's time and attention than issues of foreign and economic policy. Responsibility for planning domestic social policies is therefore usually delegated to key presidential aides who often have great influence over decisions concerning domestic affairs. Roosevelt relied heavily on Henry Wallace for such help, Kennedy depended upon Patrick Moynihan, Johnson used William Moyers and Richard Nixon relied initially on Moynihan and later on John Ehrlichman.

14. For an interesting essay on this problem, see Cronin (1971).

15. For more detailed discussion of this plan, see Otis Graham (1976:204–218).

16. If you give someone a hammer, they will find something to hit with it.

17. See Chapter 3, page 66.

18. It should be noted that by working for agencies specially created by the President, social scientists often become alienated from policy planners who are members of the Permanent bureaucracy from whom the President removes responsibility for planning initiatives. Thus, factors that enhance receptivity to social science-based planning efforts in one branch of government may hinder it in another.

19. It should be noted that it is impossible to say from these data whether or not this interest is greater than, equal to or less than the interest in planning found in the White House and Congress, if only because the Federal Bureaucracy is vastly larger and more complex than the other two institutions. Moreover, the data Caplan amassed on use of social science by high-level federal officials does not specify the time frame within which the alleged use occurred, thereby making it impossible to state how extensive the interest is in such materials. Thus, although *expenditures* on social science research are much greater within the Federal Bureaucracy, it is not possible to convert these expenditures into per capita figures that would enable us to compare them with comparable data from the Congress and White House.

20. Fifteen percent of the sample were at the Deputy Undersecretary, Assistant Undersecretary or Assistant Secretary level; 27 percent were Institute Directors, Directors of Commissions or other general units or persons located in the Executive Office of the President; 33 percent were Deputy Assistant Directors, upper level administrators or Bureau or Division Chiefs; and 25 percent were agency personnel holding office of somewhat lesser authority.

21. See page 9 for a discussion of the meaning of the term "utilization" in this study.

22. For additional examples of the use of social science for planning within the federal government, see Hays (1959) for a study of programs of conservation and land use within the Department of Interior under Theodore Roosevelt; Kirkendall (1966) for a study of experimental programs involving regional and national planning initiatives in the Agriculture Department during the New Deal; Alpert (1967:220) for a discussion of programs to combat morale problems in the armed forces during the Second World War; Alpert (1967:227) and Horowitz and Katz (1975:6—12) for discussion of more recent planning initiatives within the Office of Education, the Office of Economic Opportunity and the Housing Office.

23. For an illustration of how this operates in the State Department, see Pio D. Uliassi, "Research and Foreign Policy: A View from Foggy Bottom" (Uliassi, 1976:239—243).

24. For another study of this type of use by Congress of social science expertise, see Kirkendall (1966). His discussion of the role played by two social scientists, Tolley and Wilson, in helping Congressman Christgau of Minnesota to formulate farm legislation is an excellent example of how this process operates (Kirkendall, 1966:11—29).

6

The conceptions and procedures underlying applied sociology as currently practiced
invite the frustrations and fail-

Toward a Policy–
Relevant Sociology

ures that have occurred. In this chapter, we intend to attempt an
answer to the question: What, if anything, can be done to make
sociology more relevant and useful to policy?

The question presupposes that it is desirable for the discipline to be
relevant; this, of course, is a controversial view. There are those who
say—with good reason—that the only proper business of sociology is
to study society and its institutions in order to understand them. If
the resulting knowledge proves useful, so much the better, but the
discipline's progress should not be measured by its real or imagined
impact on public affairs. We do not wish to challenge this view here;
indeed, there is much about it with which we agree. We are asking,
instead, a question which purposely does not join this issue; that is,
what can be done to make sociology more policy-relevant, assuming for
the moment that one would want it to be so. In answering this question we ask the reader to keep this point in mind: Relevance to public
affairs comes at a price, and no discipline can afford to become committed to policy-relevance without first examining the implications
this carries for its future development as a science.

One way to answer the question—what can be done?—is to ask
what control sociologists have over factors that affect the results of
their efforts to apply disciplinary knowledge and methods to social
policy. The answer is clear: We can have some control over these, but
we will never have a great deal. Obviously, certain things are beyond
the ability of sociology to affect or change. Barring some unusual
political development, it is certain that the government will continue
to dominate its relationships with sociology. Except for unusual
crises, political feasibility will remain the principal standard used by
policy-making bodies to evaluate proposals for change and change
will continue to be incremental, not revolutionary. These are "givens," so to speak, when one contemplates how to improve sociology's role in social policy.

There are other things sociologists can influence. For example, we can exercise some control over what we study and how we approach it. To some extent we can dictate the questions for research and the procedures for studying them. By carefully selecting variables for study, we can help to determine the form of the resulting knowledge. What we study and how we conduct our studies—these are the leverage points for improving sociology's contribution to public affairs.

We are quick to note that most of the factors that are "givens" are ones that influence more decisively the outcome of attempts to apply sociology to public policy than factors over which sociologists have some control. This has two immediate and related implications for sociology's role in public affairs. First, even in the best of circumstances, it will be possible for sociologists only *marginally* to improve their ability to contribute to social policy; and second, so long as politics and politicians dominate policy decisions in our society, sociology's role in public affairs will inevitably be *modest*. Grand-scale Wardian and Lasswellian schemes in which sociologists and politicians are partners must be abandoned for less pretentious approaches that are more closely attuned to political realities and less closely tied to academic and utopian concerns.

SOME THOUGHTS ABOUT A SOCIOLOGY FOR SOCIAL POLICY

One reason why sociologists doing policy research have so often missed the mark is not because they do not do enough research, but because they do not understand what kind of study is required. The key to developing an applied sociology that is more relevant to social policy than the one we now have is to learn what kinds of questions to study. This in turn implies a shift of perspective away from sociology toward policy concerns.

We have seen how sociological forays into the world of policy typically begin and end with disciplinary concerns. Sociologists have been prone to conceptualize applied research with disciplinary issues in mind, executing their research with the idea of satisfying an audience of professional colleagues. The questions they ask, the form in which they ask them, the manner in which results are interpreted, even the forums in which they are published reflect this practice. In this approach, policy and policy concerns are merely residual variables. We suggest that what is required to achieve greater policy relevance is a perspective and set of procedures that give greater weight to policy concerns from the outset and that make policy-makers a prime audience for the report. Our purpose in this final chapter is to explain in general terms what this shift entails and to illustrate the type of policy-relevant sociological study we propose.

The required shift in perspective begins with recognition of the fact that government dominates its relationships to sociology. Concretely what this means is that government can make policy without being *required* to seek the assistance of sociologists. That is, because politicians control, it is possible for them to engage in the task of making and implementing social policy without paying the slightest attention to sociologists. We sociologists may believe that government does its job badly if the expertise we possess is not used (C. Weiss, 1976:221); no doubt there is some truth to this claim. Yet, the base fact is that governmental policy-making bodies are under no official obligation to have us participate in the policy process or to listen to what we may have to say.

Formally, at least, this will always be true, no matter how much knowledge we possess or how sophisticated our research techniques may become. However, it is possible for sociologists to take steps to make it more difficult than it is now for government officials to ignore us. Indeed, a realistic goal of a policy-oriented sociology is to produce data, information or knowledge, which must be taken into account in the deliberation of policy; it is not to determine outcomes directly since, by definition, these must be arrived at politically. This can be done by studying questions and problems that are basic concerns of policy-making bodies, executing these studies with policy concerns foremost in mind. That is, rather than continuing to approach policy research from a disciplinary perspective, vaguely hoping that some of the resulting knowledge will prove useful, we must begin to study how the policy process actually works in order to discover what kinds of studies are required to produce knowledge that is directly relevant to it. Stated this way, the outlook is bright, since time and perspective are on our side. With our focus on basic, recurrent issues and our questions framed from a location outside of government, we can take a broader and deeper view of policy concerns, avoiding the transitory formulation of a political actor in favor of discerning what lies at the heart of a policy arena or issue.

What we are suggesting, and what our analysis indicates, is that sociologists must pay greater attention to the policy process to identify the issues and questions of greatest relevance to the work of those engaged in social policy-making. With these issues and questions in mind, sociologists can then use their methods and procedures to study them, giving policy-makers new insights and knowledge about them. The result will be a body of knowledge pertaining to matters central to social policy concerns. Policy-makers, of course, might continue to ignore us, but they could not ignore the issues and questions to which our knowledge pertains, for these are intrinsic to their work. To the extent that sociologists select problems for research with policy concerns in mind and supply information usable in a world geared for action, it will become more difficult for policy-making bodies to ignore what we have to say—and just that much more likely that we will have a meaningful role in their deliberations.

What constitutes a policy-relevant sociological study? The question is a difficult one to answer at the present time because specifying issues and questions for study depends on having an intimate knowledge of how social policy is made; this is not presently available to us (J. Weiss, 1976:234, Uliassi, 1976:241). Social science literature is generally unhelpful in this regard, for it seldom deals with policy explicitly, and when it does it often portrays the process, not as it is, but as social scientists wish or imagine it to be. To approach the topic meaningfully, we will address two major aspects of every piece of research, categories of analysis and procedures, and then, dissect, in schematic form, the differences between the studies we propose and what we might term "conventional studies." The organization of this chapter then, follows these three questions:

A. What is the nature of policy change and what are the recurrent categories in policy deliberation?
B. What changes in research procedures would be necessary to employ these recurrent categories usefully in our studies?
C. What are the major differences in choice of variables and conclusions as between policy-oriented studies and more conventional studies?

RECURRENT CATEGORIES IN POLICY DELIBERATION

In searching for basic guidelines for the conduct of policy-oriented studies, nowhere in the literature could we find a discussion of what it is that policy-makers deliberate when they deliberate policy. Of course we did find many case studies replete with examples of how policy was changed at the last minute by something accidental or haphazard (*New York Times*, April 2, 1978: Section 4, p. 1), but the enduring categories that help us organize ourselves from the outset for a study of a policy issues or a policy arena, unfortunately, could not be gleaned. We decided to take up the problem broadly, since our goal was to derive broadly applicable categories for analysis. The simplest way to proceed, we decided, was to trace legislative histories in broad sweep, allowing the categories to take form as we tried to discern patterns in rather large masses of data. We distinguished types of policies by types of policy arenas, while avoiding one category of arena (redistributive) that could conceivably cause unnecessary confusion for the tasks we had. Our choice of policy topics within the two areas of distributive policy and regulatory policy was arbitrary, making these choices based on what we thought we would enjoy reading. [1] In the area of distributive policy, we traced the legislative histories of housing and employment policies; in the area of regulatory policy, we traced the legislative histories of communications and labor-relations policies. We went to the primary sources, *The Congressional Record* and *The Congressional Quarterly Almanac*, eschewing any secondary discussions, since we wanted to avoid schemes of classification (if, indeed, any existed). To make the task manageable, we focused on post-1930 policy initiatives, although in some cases we compiled earlier data. Finally, because we hoped to draw out general categories, we tried not to become bogged down in excessive detail about individual policy action. Nonetheless, some substantial detail is unavoidable and necessary in the discussion that follows.

NATURE OF POLICY CHANGE

From our study we gained impressions about social policy-making in government. Of these, one in particular stands out as especially pertinent here: policies evolve incrementally. This, of course, is Lindblom's point (Lindblom, 1968:26−27). It is neatly illustrated by materials that we have gathered on one sequence in federal housing policy, which occurred between 1945 and 1969. During this time, several new housing laws were enacted by Congress, beginning with a major initiative in 1946. In that year the Senate Subcommittee on Housing and Urban Redevelopment of the Senate Committee on Postwar Economic Policy and Planning held hearings on the problems of housing in the post-war era. In its final report, goals were set forth for a national housing policy, which were to achieve an adequate supply of housing while maintaining the predominance of private enterprise. The report contained estimates of how many units of housing would be needed over what span of time to meet national needs; and it reviewed various mechanisms for financing their construction such as federal assistance, a Federal Home Loan Board and FHA aid to private enterprise. The Committee also advised government to offer incentives to encourage low-priced housing and in-vestment in rental housing, and it targeted certain problems, such as slum clearance and urban redevelopment, for special attention. The Subcommittee urged Congress to create a national housing agency and to give it funds for research on construction methods, housing markets and other matters basic to the housing problem. An adden-dum to the report was compiled following joint Senate-House hear-ings into the original Senate Subcommittee report. This report of the Joint Committee on Housing, which held hearings in 1947 and pub-lished its report in 1948, added to the list of issues already covered by the Senate Subcommittee—matters relating to federal aid for low-rent public housing.

Thus, by 1947, there existed a comprehensive plan for a national policy on housing. Yet the history of legislative enactments from 1947 to 1959 shows that the initiatives proposed in these hearings were enacted in piecemeal fashion over this 12-year period. Individual bills were introduced during this time that contained watered-down pro-posals for dealing with single elements of the overall problem. The most comprehensive of these was the Housing Act of 1949, which dealt with the question of public housing and private investment in housing for low-income families. In 1950, another bill was passed authorizing money for slum clearance and urban redevelopment. In 1951, a house bill was passed that sought to clarify the criteria used to determine how many housing units to construct and what standards to employ in making decisions about housing projects for individual communities. Bills introduced in 1953 and 1954 clarified jurisdictional responsibilities of a number of different federal housing agencies that had been created by the 1947 Housing Act. Bills enacted in 1956 and 1957 established guidelines for slum clearance and urban redevelop-ment projects that earlier legislation had authorized, and a 1959 legis-lative enactment placed firm limits on the extent of federal participa-tion in housing in response to President Eisenhower's mandate to curtail federal involvement in areas which he believed belonged in the private domain.

This example illustrates the common pattern of legislative enact-ment which is piecemeal, incremental and disjointed. Once basic po-sitions are defined, most policy-making activity then entails gradual elaborations, refinements and reinterpretations of single elements of an overall program.[2] This is not to say that comprehensive legislation programs are never enacted. The Economic Opportunity Act of 1965 (P.L. 67) and the National Industrial Recovery Act of 1933 are two examples of this. However, we find these to be rare; far more com-mon is the gradualism that we have described.

The significance of this fact for sociologists who wish to become involved in policy-relevant research is clear. We have seen how, in the past, sociologists have been inclined to begin policy-relevant research studies by stating the "big questions," in order to discover what is desirable and optimal in the best of all possible worlds and how present priorities must be changed to bring this to pass. Viewed from a policy perspective, this approach is unrealistic, except in the rare instances in which comprehensive changes are possible. Most of the time, the changes that are possible or feasible will be minor. If sociologists are to have a role to play in bringing them about they must begin to study the somewhat less daring, intellectually less interesting issues and questions that inevitably arise as legislative bodies plod along in stepwise incremental fashion when enacting legislative programs.

DEFINITION OF POLICY-RELEVANT CATEGORIES

What are examples of such issues and questions? Earlier we explained our objective in examining congressional policy enactments: to gain greater familiarity with the policy-making activities of government in order to identify some of the issues, or categories, that policy-making bodies commonly confront. When we first examined the materials we have compiled, our impression was of a process that is disjointed, impulsive and disorganized. Yet, as we delved into them further, we realized that this impression is inaccurate, as we found that all policy activities of Congress, which we studied, ultimately seemed to revolve around a few key policy issues, which seemingly required resolution before programs could operate properly. The issues themselves are not difficult to identify. They involve questions about such matters as *goals* (i.e., what shall be the objective of a program?), *coverage* (i.e., who shall benefit?), *financing* (i.e., how shall the program be funded, by whom and at what level of support?), *administration* (i.e., who shall be responsible for implementing the program and how shall it be put into effect?), *equity* (i.e., of those who are covered by the program, who shall receive what kinds of benefits?) and *time frame* (i.e., for what period of time shall the program last?).

No claim is made, of course, that these are the only issues that ever arise in policy deliberations; no doubt others will be added to the list as more exhaustive research on these and other policy areas is done. In the policy areas that we examined, these issues appeared in every instance and when they did, they immediately became of overriding concern until the Congress provided legislative guidelines to resolve them. We got the impression that unless guidelines existed for answering these questions, programs either functioned improperly or not at all. Thus, if enabling legislation failed to address some of these issues—at least in some way, so that no guidelines existed for them—problems cropped up, as programs floundered and lost direction. Pressures would then build up on the Congress to provide guidelines for those unresolved matters, ultimately resulting in legislative actions. This fact, when coupled with the knowledge that policies tend to evolve incrementally, can give the sociologist, doing applied research, some helpful clues for selecting topics and questions for research.

We say this for the following reason: one implication of the fact that policy evolves incrementally is that, with rare exception, most acts of legislation deal with only one (or at the most a few) of the issues that must be resolved before a program is able to function. The main pieces of legislation on housing that have been enacted in modern times illustrate this point. Typical of housing legislation is Public Resolution 22 which was passed in 1892 by the 52nd Congress. The bill dealt only with the issue of goals, appropriating money to support studies of slum conditions in certain American cities to clarify the extent and nature of the nation's housing problems. PL 302, passed in 1932, dealt only with the issue of financing. It authorized loans to corporations to provide housing for low-income families in their employment. Other housing bills passed between 1932 and 1939 dealt only with administration questions by creating Federal agencies through which programs relating to housing could be implemented. Housing laws passed during World War II dealt with issues of coverage and equity. One of these, P.L. 671, extended Federal housing relief to rural families and another, the Backland—Jones Act, dealt with the housing needs of war veterans. Indeed, with the exception of the 1949 Housing Act (mentioned earlier), every one of the pieces of housing legislation that Congress enacted in this century has dealt with one or a few, but not all, of the issues basic to policy implementation.

Precisely the same thing is true of legislation regulating communications and labor relations, for in both cases, the bulk of it deals with single issues. Legislation on Federal communication policy nicely illustrates the point. Aside from the unusually expansive Federal Communications Act of 1934, which established the Federal Communications Commission, most legislative enactments in this area have dealt with single-policy issues. Because the Federal Communications Commission is a regulatory agency, most early legislation dealt with the issue of jurisdiction. For example, Congress gave the

FCC authority to enforce laws relating to radio broadcasts presented by educational monitors. In 1948, it passed a law which brought mail-order businesses under FCC control; and in 1949 the FCC was given responsibility for monitoring and regulating radio frequencies used by the railroads. Over time, questions of finance that earlier legislation had ignored became urgent and, in 1948, a bill was passed outlining the methods and limits of public expenditures for enforcing Federal communication policies. This in turn raised questions about administration and equity, and in the years following other bills were passed that directed the FCC to reduce its monitoring and field operations and to invest the savings in measures that would reduce a growing administrative backlog.

Exceptions to this general pattern exist, of course. Examples of this, in addition to the Federal Communications Act of 1934, include the National Labor Relations Act of 1935, establishing the National Labor Relations Board; the National Industrial Recovery Act, P.L. 67, passed in 1932, which, among other things, authorized Federal funds to finance and build low-cost housing and provided the administrative structure and guidelines for doing this; and the Federal Housing Act of 1961, which contained President Kennedy's bold initiatives for dealing with national housing problems. In every case the laws enacted contained initial efforts by government to create programs to deal with national problems. As such, they were far more expansive than Congressional bills typically are. Yet, even here none of the bills address all of the policy issues we listed at the beginning of the discussion. The closest any of these came to doing this was the Communications Act of 1934 which tried to deal simultaneously with issues of goals, finances, coverage, equity and administration. Some of the issues received greater emphasis than others, but on the whole this particular bill stands out as exceptional for the scope and breadth of its coverage.

Clearly, most legislative enactment entails only modifications of single aspects of existing programs or, when no program exists, enactments that address only a few of the issues basic to policy-making. What significance does this observation have for sociologists wishing to do policy-relevant research? *This knowledge enables the sociologist to anticipate and study in advance issues and questions that eventually come up in policy deliberations.* Knowing that certain issues will eventually arise that must be resolved if programs are to operate properly and that most legislative enactments will deal with no more than a few of these at any one time, the sociologist can anticipate the kinds of questions that policy-making groups will eventually confront. By studying these in advance, using procedures that yield results that will be relevant and germane to the policy-making process when they are needed, the sociologist will be in a position to offer knowledge and information to policy-making bodies that are directly pertinent to their concerns. For example, the sociologist will know that a new policy initiative, which deals only with program goals and nothing else, means that subsequent deliberations by Congressional and other policy-making bodies will necessarily have to resolve questions involving finance, administration, coverage, equity and time; and when more than one issue has been dealt with by past legislation, the policy-making bodies will be able to determine which ones remain to be resolved. In either case, they have the dual advantage of knowing what kind of study is required to produce results that are relevant to policy concerns and the time to be able to execute it before these issues arise for deliberation. These regularities associated with policy-making in government are not difficult to discern and can be anticipated on the basis of a small amount of preliminary investigation into the past history of legislative enactments in any given area.

An example from the field of labor relations illustrates our point. We have said that the National Labor Relations Board (NLRB) was created by a 1935 law, the National Labor Relations Act. Although this bill covered a wide range of problems, the only real "teeth" in it dealt with the issues of goals and administration. The bill established a Federal board for the purpose of helping to eliminate strikes by forcing employers and labor leaders to engage in collective bargaining, and it dealt with administrative matters by creating the NLRB, including specification of its composition, and the procedures it should follow in collective bargaining sessions. However, the bill was notably lacking in jurisdictional guidelines, or in attention to issues of financing and time frame, and the subsequent history of labor-related legislation can be viewed as an attempt to come to terms with the problems this entailed. Initially, the main issues that arose centered around NLRB's life-span and the mechanism and procedures for funding it. Because enabling legislation never addressed these questions, NLRB officials had no way of knowing from one year to the next if the board would continue to operate or what level of funding it could expect to receive. This made it nearly impossible for them to function as a regulatory agency and so they were forced to ask the Congress to resolve these issues. This was done in 1939, when Congress enacted a bill that prolonged the life of the Board indefinitely, guaranteeing financial support. Soon jurisdictional issues arose and the attempts to resolve them are contained in the Labor Management

Relations Act of 1947 and in subsequent laws passed in 1954 and 1955, as well as in the Anti-Corruption Labor Bill of 1959. Other bills, such as ones passed in 1952 and 1954, dealt with problems of equity and coverage, further clarifying administrative procedures that govern the Board's operation.

An additional insight into the dynamics of the policy-making process in Congress can be gleaned from our analysis. We have said that this process tends to follow a predictable course, dictated by the fact that programs tend to flounder unless basic policy issues are resolved. But this factor only accounts for a part of the predictability of the policy-making process; other factors must be taken into account to understand it fully.

The issues that we have discussed—goals, coverage, equity, finance, administration and time frame—do not exist, isolated from one another. Instead we find that policy-making exemplifies the type of process in which there is a finite number of component parts that are interrelated in such a way whereby a change in one aspect ramifies throughout the others. That is, issues of finance are not unrelated to questions about goals—nor can administrative issues be resolved without carrying implications for coverage or equity. This carries important implications for understanding the course that policy-making activities commonly follow; simply because enabling legislation typically deals with one or a few issues that are basic to policy, we cannot assume that other issues that have been left unaddressed by an initial policy statement are themselves unaffected by the actions taken with respect to those that are addressed. That is, explicit decisions about costs and financing, for example, have implications for goals, administration, coverage, equity and time frames. Thus, even though enabling legislation may focus only on one or a few of the issues we have identified, ignoring the others, this does not mean that initial decisions about particular issues do not have ramifications for the other issues that the legislation does not address. They do, and this means that in many cases basic issues of social policy are resolved by default. Congress or the President, by proposing the creation of a given type of administrative structure to deal with a problem like poverty, is at the same time unwittingly making decisions about ways in which other core issues involving poverty will be resolved. This fact is seldom appreciated by those who are engaged in the process of making social policy. Their concerns are necessarily political and because they must act quickly in response to pressures in the immediate political environment, they often fail to comprehend the fact that decisions taken with one problem or issue in mind at the same time imply basic decisions about issues of which they may be unaware. This points to another way in which sociologists can make a special contribution to social policy-making. *It is to identify and study the implications and consequences for all issues basic to social policy of proposed decisions involving any one of them.* Such a task involves calling on the sociologist's conceptual skills as well as his ability to conduct social research. Once he or she understands the full range of issues that must be resolved that policy might be made, he or she can then begin to identify and study in advance the larger implications and consequences of particular courses of action so that those who are doing policy work can be made to understand more fully the wide range of implications of the programs they propose.

The systematic character of policy-making has another implication that bears on sociology's contribution to public affairs. Decisions that are taken on any given issue are seldom, if ever, final for all time. Thus, since changes in any one segment of the policy process ramify throughout it, it follows that any significant action taken today will have implications for issues previously resolved. This is evident in the case of legislation that governs Federal communications policy. Here the enabling legislation, the Communications Act of 1934, addressed most of the policy issues we have discussed in a rather straightforward way. The Bill specified the goals of the FCC, which were to regulate interstate and foreign commerce communications by wire and radio; it described in detail the FCC's jurisdiction and indicated areas in which it had none and questions of financing were dealt with as were those of administration and time. Here we have an example of policy initiative that explicitly tries to come to grips with most of the issues that are basic to social policy. Much of the subsequent history of legislation in this area involves modifications and extensions of original positions. What is interesting about this is that they follow a predictable pattern. Initially, questions about jurisdiction were raised. Laws were passed making it illegal to interfere with radio programs broadcast by educational monitors and getting the FCC authorities to see that this law was enforced. Another bill brought mail order insurance under the jurisdiction of the FCC and a third bill gave them authority to supervise and monitor radio frequencies for airlines and railways. Once this was accomplished, changes began to occur in all the other component parts of the original legislation. First, a set of administrative corrections were needed to deal with the new jurisdictional authorities. This in turn raised questions about financing, giving rise to a series of bills that addressed this issue. Congress became concerned about rising costs and so ordered the FCC to cut back in certain areas, to provide competent coverage in others without increasing overall basic costs. This, in turn, altered the organization's goals and so on.

The point is that the predictable dynamic that lies beyond policy-making derives in part from a self-correcting process in which changes in one part of the system ramify throughout the whole system, forcing changes in it. This insight adds new meaning to the idea that social policies change incrementally. One reason they do, of course, is political; however, the other is related to the fact that changes in one segment necessarily lead to changes in another; some part of the gradual stepwise incremental dynamic of the evolution of social policy is merely a reflection of this fact. The implication of this for the applied sociologist is fairly straightforward. *Armed with this insight about the policy process, he or she will now be in a position to know what directions policy activities are apt to move in—on the basis of knowledge about the past history of policy-making activity in a given area up to a given point.* It enables one to map out systematically the full range of issues that policy-making bodies will eventually confront and to begin to study questions related to them that will address these problems in highly meaningful and useful ways.

To be effective, applied sociology must begin and end with policy concerns. This requires a fundamental shift in the perspective sociologists now have toward applied work. It requires them to begin to study social policy as a process. Unless they know how it operates, they cannot know the kinds of questions to research to produce knowledge about them. Our discussion presents some ideas that we have developed from our study of social policy-making in Congress and the implications these carry for applied research. How tenable these ideas are we cannot presently say: this can only be determined by doing more careful exhaustive research on a wide range of policy areas. As the results of this research emerge, we suspect that the illustrations we have presented will undergo substantial modifications; yet, this fact in no way undermines the validity of our basic point.

RESEARCH PROCEDURES

We find that policy-making activities in Congress tend to follow a regular and predictable course. This knowledge gives the sociologist an advantage, for by having even a little knowledge about acts of enabling legislation, or by placing present debate within a processural framework tied down by enabling legislation, one can anticipate and study questions germane to subsequent policy deliberations. Knowing what these categories are, the sociologist can consult with those actually involved in the policy-making process to clarify key issues and questions. This implies added dimensions to procedures we normally employ in the conduct of research.

Basic to the process for doing policy-oriented research is the commitment to begin and to end with policy concerns. Before a sociologist can ever hope to make a contribution to the policy process he or she must study the natural development of the policy process to which one wishes to contribute. Most of the areas in which we become engaged are ones in which there is already evolving a series of legislative efforts. The sociologist's first task must be to study these immediate and past efforts to deal with social problems. That is, sociologists must in effect undertake to review the literature—but with a special aim in mind. Their goal is not to review social science literature, as this will come later. It is to review the history of legislative enactment to date to determine which policy issues have been addressed thus far and which ones have been ignored; whether proposed legislation represents a bold new initiative that will replace already existing policies with novel approaches to a problem of whether it is a piecemeal effort to resolve partial problems arising from the fact that previous legislation did not address certain issues basic to policy in this area; what issues remain unaddressed and unresolved; and so on. Once this is done, the sociologist is then in a position to make decisions about possible topics for study.

These decisions would have to deal with at least two questions. First, having already identified the kinds of issues that are apt to arise in immediate and subsequent policy deliberations in this area, the sociologist could then turn to experts who are members of a policy-making body to solicit their views about the sequence and form in which questions about these issues are apt to rise. Second, for each issue, the sociologist can learn from policy-makers what are the most likely policy options that will be considered or entertained as politically and practically feasible. With respect to both, it will be necessary to emphasize two sets of considerations—one political, the other sociological. The political issue involves a discernment of the range of options that are practically feasible, options that fall within politically defined areas of "policy space." The latter involves the impact of past targets of debate. What options are already foreclosed as a result of past actions and what options remain open? What implications do proposed options have for the manner in which issues already addressed have been resolved? And so on.

Once realistic options on issues are identified, the sociologist is then, and only then, in a position to discover if he or she has anything to contribute to illuminating policy problems. Are there questions that can be answered within a time frame in which results will be available when policy bodies begin to deliberate—which address aspects of the issues that arise? How important are these questions apt to be in these deliberations? Here too, the counsel of the appropriate policy-making body must be gained; they are in the best position to say just how useful research on various questions and topics may be.

Assuming that such questions do exist, the sociologist will then be able to turn to the discipline for guidance. He or she will want to undertake a review of sociological literature for the purpose of discovering if there exists any social science research bearing on the questions for study. Note that the purpose of this search for literature is not to discover what questions sociologists should study, as these will already have been decided before one turns to social science literature for help. It is to discern *if there exists* in the accumulated knowledge of the discipline empirical materials (information or data) or general theories that can be applied to the policy problems that he or she has decided to study.

Since most of the research that sociologists have done is guided by disciplinary concerns, it is unlikely that one would find existing sociological literature to be an unusually rich source of information for policy problems. In all likelihood, the sociologist will discover that he will have to handle his own research to answer the questions he has posed. In developing the design, it is essential that he do so with the knowledge that the findings he produces, to be useful in a policy context, will need to possess the kinds of features that are discussed in the appendix. That is, in designing research and selecting variables for study the sociologist must be aware of the fact that his theoretical model must be simple and robust; the variables for study malleable in the context of operational programs; and the findings dramatic enough to justify policy initiatives.

In addition to altering the order in which the literature is reviewed (disciplinary knowledge is reviewed last, not first) and to putting to test the utility of variables chosen for study, the sociologist must be aware that more than casual interaction with policy-makers will be useful during the conceptualization of the research. This means that applied, policy-relevant sociology must bring together two rather different perspectives: that of the action-oriented policy-maker and that of the synthesizing, reflective, empirically-oriented sociologist (Conway et al., 1976: 264—269). Even if the sociologist takes the steps we outlined above to bridge these perspectives, he still runs the risk that his formulations of problems may still seem foreign or distant to a legislator, policy-maker or program director. In the end, of course, the conceptualization chosen for research will differ somewhat from the everyday language of policy-makers. But the nuances to be gained by an *iterative* process of statement and restatement, presentation and discussion, will help assure relevance of the research·even as the sociologist, in the end, determines what the final research decisions will be. This approach differs from that sometimes employed by sociologists when they ask, at the end of a study, for the comments of the subjects being studied. Here a statement of the problem is brought into the discourse between researcher and policy-maker from the outset, with the sociologist determining, through successive interplay, just how much closer to action or to today's formulations he will venture, as opposed to studying issues more abstract or more immediately relevant to a body of theory.

Once the research is executed, the sociologist can then present a report to the appropriate policy-making body. The sociologist may have much detail to explain the significance of the problems he has addressed for the policy questions that confront the deliberative body; he may also take pains to indicate how his results may be usefully considered in the work that they are about to do, but here his influence ends, as he can be given no assurance that policy-makers will "listen" to what he has to say. They may simply ignore him. However, if these guidelines are followed, the sociologist will be assured that the questions he will have studied have dealt with issues that the policy-makers will have no choice but to confront, and perhaps that some of the results obtained will have features that render them amenable to direct application to the policy deliberations that will surely transpire.

MAJOR DIFFERENCES IN VARIABLES AND CONCLUSIONS IN POLICY-ORIENTED STUDIES AND CONVENTIONAL STUDIES

Our analysis in this chapter, though brief and general, illustrates what it means to say that sociologists engaged in work for application must begin and end their studies with policy concerns in mind. Our point is that if we begin to learn more about social policy—who makes it, how this is done and in what ways—we will then be in a position to know what kinds of questions and issues to address. We have said that one of the reasons sociologists who do policy research have so often missed the mark is not because they have not done enough research, but because they have not understood the appropriate kind of study. This will only become apparent as we begin to study social policy-making as a process in its own right and understand how it operates. Until now, sociologists interested in applying disciplinary knowledge and methods of research to policy problems have allowed disciplinary concerns to dictate the questions they ask. But if sociologists were to allow policy concerns to dictate their research, they would ask different kinds of questions. To illustrate what we mean we will describe briefly three specific research projects in which we ourselves have participated either singly or together, contrasting a disciplinary approach to the problem with the policy approach we are recommending.

Studies of housing. For several years Shore, the junior author, has been associated with Oscar Newman's Institute for Community Design as a consultant; with this experience he has had an opportunity to observe the contrast between disciplinary and policy studies of housing. Most disciplinary studies of housing can be characterized in this way: the emphasis is on understanding how an essential, such as housing, relates to social activities and how, in turn, these are related to a standard array of control variables including age, education, socioeconomic standing and so on. The variables for study include such things as racial discrimination in housing; tenant satisfaction; levels of racial tension; residents' lifestyles; patterns of neighboring associated with age, education, socioeconomic and geographical grouping; the development of neighborhoods and communities in new housing areas; the movement of populations into and out of housing areas and the effect that this has on the stability and stratification of neighborhoods; and so on. The form in which findings of such studies appear are also characteristic: for example, that neighborhood cohesiveness depends on the ethnic mix of its residents; or that households identify with neighborhoods through identification with major institutions; or that participation in voluntary associations varies with socioeconomic standing, which is directly related to education and ethnicity; and so on. Moreover, the focus on housing is not steadfast but is made part of the study of large collectivities, most especially the neighborhood or the community.

Policy-oriented studies of housing differ from this in basic ways. Such studies begin and sustain a focus on housing variables that can be manipulated by administrative actions and with a firm eye on the cost of making changes. Dependent variables are measures of behavior and independent variables are derived from direct policy concerns. Examples of policy-relevant variables that inform research in this Institute are type of housing, e.g., high rise, walkup, row; types of areas, e.g., halls, stairs, play areas, sitting areas; inexpensive modifications, e.g., curbing, lighting, fencing; management variables, e.g., proportion of occupancy by ethnicity, type of family, number of teenagers; and other variables, such as crime victimization rates, amount of vandalism, occupancy rates and so on. The kinds of findings that emerge from studies whose variables are directly policy-relevant include: small, inexpensive changes in already-existing housing can have large effects in defensive behavior (e.g., changes in lighting and curbing outside a walkup will affect where residents sit, where children play, who breaks up fights, and so on); or, controlling proportions of occupants by family type will reduce turnover rates and occupancy rates; and so forth. Or, at a grander level, sociologists might ask: What are the social implications of different mechanisms of financing housing programs? What are the social implications of housing specially targeted to a group or locale on the wider distribution oif social groups in geographic entities within it? What are the effects of different ways of organizing housing administrations on their ability to handle comprehensive social action programs? And so on.

Blindness studies. The senior author, Scott, was engaged for a number of years in studies of blindness and has published articles and books on the topic. On reflection, his work was more conventional than it was policy-oriented in the sense defined in this book, but his continued association with this field of research, coupled with his interest in policy-oriented studies, has led him to draw out some of the major variables and concerns of a policy-oriented study of blindness and to conjure up some possible general conclusions. His original studies were disciplinary in focus. They asked: How does blindness affect personality? How do stereotypes of blind vary from culture to culture? What consequences, if any, do these variations have on the ways in which people experience their disability? In what ways do agencies for the blind socialize their clients into blindness-related social roles? Which blind people get socialized by agencies and who do not—with what kinds of consequences for each? What determines a particular agency's approach to rehabilitation?

As this work has shifted away from a purely disciplinary concerns to more policy-oriented issues, questions of a different sort emerge. For example, we now ask: How large or how differentiated must a program of services for the blind be to be viable? What are the sociological consequences of different sized agencies—differiented in various ways? How should coverage be defined—by standard criteria such as the Snellen charts, by subjective criteria or by some combination of the two? And what are the sociological consequences of one or the other of these ways of defining coverage? Should programs be developed to return an individual to one's home or community or should the program aim to care for the individual in institutional surroundings? The questions suggested by disciplinary concerns point to the conclusion that the blind are made, not born, and that organizations play a major role in creating an individual's experience of blindness. More policy-oriented studies point to the conclusion that program administration depends in large part on numbers, and therefore, that the criteria used to assess blindness and the nature and variety of program activities are determined primarily by the economies of scale and policy. In turn, this conclusion helps to identify the social consequences of having programs of various sizes.

Welfare reforms studies of the negative income tax. Both authors worked for a number of years on the New Jersey—Pennsylvania Negative Income Tax experiment; one of the authors, Shore, was also involved in setting up the Seattle—Denver experiment. A conventional disciplinary approach to this problem was worked out by others working on the project, who compiled questions for study that was based upon a review of sociological literature. This review led them to ask questions: Do feelings of self-efficacy change as a result of receiving negative tax payments? Does participation in voluntary organizations vary with the generosity of plans? What is the impact of income maintenance on health? What impact does it have on religious participation? On quality of life? On political commitments and political participation? On one's views about American society?

The policy-oriented approach that we adopted focused upon problems in the administration of the problem and on major issues affecting the political acceptability of the problem, for example, the effect of negative tax payments on household stability. We asked: What are the effects of negative tax plans on household composition over time? What is the relation between rules and composition, where one can define the family as a unit (and therefore make payments to an individual only if he resides with the unit) or one can define the individual as a unit (and therefore make payments to the individual even if residing with a family unit)? How does one define income for program purposes, in light of the need for establishing horizontal and vertical equity, while at the same time attempting to keep administrative forms simple? What effect does knowledge of program rules have on behavior? For example, do individuals respond differently if programs are based on payments as such, or on their ability to anticipate changes in payments as a function of changes in earning, and so on?

CONCLUSION

Although the perspectives that we have proposed and the procedures that we have outlined are not completely different from ones commonly used by sociologists doing applied research today, nevertheless they are different in basic respects—different enough to raise fundamental questions about the discipline itself, especially the relationships that are possible between so-called "pure" and "applied" research. Procedures presently used in our field imply that these relationships are straightforward, if at times complicated. They assume that the most direct way to develop a genuinely policy-relevant social science is through the continued conduct of basic research into questions that reflect disciplinary concerns; and that the conduct of applied social science research differs in no significant way from the conduct of any other kind of research in our field. The procedures that we propose and the perspective from which they come are ones that call these assertions into question. In order to be relevant to social policy concerns, the questions for research must be dictated by social policy concerns, not disciplinary concerns. As we have seen, the kinds of issues that arise when this perspective is adopted are not those that are apt to excite the imagination of academically oriented sociologists. Academics are interested in such things as the social nature and consequences of poverty, not in what stage of progression poverty legislation is at the present time. If our analysis is correct, then, we would anticipate that there would develop a schism between sociologists doing routine disciplinary research and those engaged in research on policy questions. The divisions between the two will never be complete and, in fact, they may be much less severe than our anlaysis implies, but there will be a schism that poses problems for the discipline. It raises questions about graduate training for those sociologists who wish to undertake careers in applied research. It raises questions about the basis upon which sociologists have sought to justify support from the government for basic research, graduate education and, indeed, the establishment of academic departments of sociology in many public universities. Finally, it raises questions about sociology's purpose in society; if the type of knowledge that most titillates the sociologists' imagination does not provide an adequate basis for planned social action, then what is the ultimate justification for the discipline? We make no effort to answer these questions here, nor do we propose to discuss them further. Instead we end with the hope that there is room within the discipline for analyses that will help to clarify the questions that must be asked.

NOTES

1. The distinction between distributive and regulatory policies is suggested by Lowi. See Lowi (1964:689).
2. The exact same pattern is evident in two other sequences of policy initiatives involving housing, one spanning the years 1932–1939, the other 1961–1968. We also find this same pattern in Federal legislation on welfare, day care and poverty.

Appendix

We have seen that what sociologists have offered policy-makers is almost exclusively research carried out by using disciplinary procedures.

Knowledge for Understanding and Knowledge for Action

This fact raises a basic question: Does sociological knowledge gained from disciplinary research provide the type of knowledge that is appropriate for the purposes of doing policy? Are there nontrivial differences between the procedures one needs to adopt in order to develop disciplinary knowledge and those one would need to employ in order to acquire knowledge that is useful for policy? To answer these questions we need to be aware of some of the features of the two worlds of scholarship and of action that make them different from each other.[1] Since our readers will no doubt recognize the academic's world without prompting, our focus will be on the major ways in which the policy-maker's world differs from it.

Most basic is the difference in *goals*. The academic sociologist's main goal is to further understanding about society; the policy-maker's goal is to initiate programs of social action in order to change society. The *problems* that the academic sociologist studies originate inside the discipline; the policy-maker is concerned with immediate exigencies in the "real" social world. Even if the two choose the same problem, the *questions* they ask about the problem differ. The academic asks, "What do we *know*?"; the policy maker asks, "What do we *do*?" The academic can pursue answers in a *timeless* and *disinterested atmosphere,* but the policy-maker must operate in *"real time"* and in a politicized environment which involves conflict, control of scarce resources and the pursuit of self and group interests (Coleman, 1972: 3). The academic's task is to develop *powerful, parsimonious theories* to explain the events he observes; to formulate laws and generalizations about them; and to enhance his predictive power. The policy-maker wants to know *what to do*; for him prediction means anticipating how a given policy will affect the problem. The academic sociologist accepts the idea that *the more understanding one has about a phenomenon the better*; the policy-maker wants to know whether what is known indicates *what is to be done*. To the policy-maker, increased knowledge may actually confuse the issue. And the *end product* of an academic study is publication of a book or an article in a professional journal circulated to an audience of professional sociologists. The end product of the policy-maker's efforts is a social policy that helps resolve an immediate problem.

The principles around which the policy-maker's world is organized carry major implications for the type of study necessary for his or her purposes. Both *theories* and *research findings* will need certain qualities not necessarily important in disciplinary research. Consider first some of the characteristics of theory necessary for the policy-maker's work.

THEORY

Social problems in their "natural state" are unitary phenomena; to understand them requires a perspective that takes into account their totality. Scholarly disciplines, in contrast, have been developed for specialization; thus no single discipline alone can deal with most complicated social problems. To take into account the complexity of social problems, explanations or theories must draw on the perspectives of several disciplines. The policy-maker will be aided in his search for action by research that is informed by interdisciplinary theories and perspectives. Irving Louis Horowitz described the problem: "Policy problems do not come in neat discipline-defined packages, but rather require the simultaneous consideration of issues that traditionally have been regarded as the province of several social science disciplines" (Horowitz, 1971: 3). Similarly, David Easton, a political scientist, points out that "social sciences are analytic, while social problems are totalistic" (Easton, 1972: 88–89). And Klaus Lompe recognizes the same problem, although from a slightly different approach: "One of the problems of applying social science knowledge to social policy is the fact that there must be interdisciplinary teams to apply such knowledge" (Lompe, 1968: 172).

The difficulty is that most sociological theories are not interdisciplinary or holistic, nor can one see how they might be adapted to or meshed with theories of other social science disciplines to derive the kind of interdisciplinary perspective that programs of social action demand. As Easton points out, the problem is that "There are theoretical barriers to the integration of analytically derived social knowledge" (Easton, 1972: 88–89)—barriers so great that he believes we must first develop a "philosophy of science in terms of which we seek to validate the whole scientific enterprise" in the social sciences (Easton, 1972: 98). If this could be done, then he feels it might enable "a reinterpretation of social science that will permit us to transform our generalized knowledge more easily into an applied form . . . . If each of the social sciences used this as a base for its own more specialized explanations, the difficulty of conversion from general to applied knowledge would be reduced" (Easton, 1972: 98–99).

Easton and Lompe have thus both suggested possible solutions to the problem. But these solutions remain to be enacted. Until and unless they are, we must be prepared to acknowledge that most routine disciplinary research will fail to provide the kind of interdisciplinary knowledge that is required by policy-makers who must cope with social problems. As we saw in Chapter 2, this is a major source of concern to sociologists involved in work for application today.

The world of policy also places a high premium on "simple" explanations. For the policy-maker the word "simple" means "feasible." Policy-makers want explanations for problems that will help them to set policy. From this point of view, the less complex things are, the better. Policy implications *may* emerge from a study if one can reduce a complex question to its simplest forms and identify the minimal, feasible effort necessary to achieve maximally effective change. But, policy implications almost certainly will *not* emerge if the explanations offered are excessively complicated, sophisticated or intellectually elegant. Thus, to policy-makers, simple means straightforward, workable and feasible (Caplan, 1976: 232).

The academic sociologist also values a "simple" explanation, but he has a very different meaning in mind—one closer to the terms "intellectually elegant or parsimonious." As Coleman reminds us, the work connotes economy of information (Coleman, 1972: 3). The academic's objective is to make predictions possible in specific instances for which only partial information exists. That is, he tries to stretch a small amount of information a long way by using general laws and theories. The more simple, less complicated, less qualified these general laws and theories are, the more effectively the sociologist is able to predict events and outcomes associated with specific situations for which only limited information exists.

Although these meanings of a simple explanation are not necessarily incompatible, they are certainly not synonymous. This suggests that a sociologist doing policy research could develop an explanation for certain events that is a "simple" explanation from a disciplinary point of view, yet it is not simple, and definitely not satisfactory, to the policy-maker because it fails to provide an indication of what a workable, feasible solution might be. For example, in the disciplinary sense, one of the simplest explanations for the existence of slums is a lack of community structure or community identification. This explanation is simple, and some feel that it goes to the heart of the problem. Yet in policy-maker's terms, this is a hopelessly complex explanation: it does not point clearly to the means of alleviating slums. It would appear to require the creation of an alternative kind of social structure, a task which few, if any, social scientists claim to have mastered.[2] In this respect, then, there are grounds for supposing that the standards and procedures for disciplinary research may not be entirely appropriate for research that is policy-oriented.

The policy-maker also requires a theory that offers *causes* for the situation or condition. If a single factor or set of factors can be isolated and said to "cause" or make a problematic event occur, then effective intervention becomes a possibility. The model that is used is borrowed from clinical medicine, as is the conception of how to proceed. Explanations must be "causal" so that policy-makers can intervene for change.

Although disciplinary research also seeks to develop causal explanations, the meaning of the term "causal" is somewhat different for the social scientist. In fact, few terms are used with greater caution in scholarly research. By its very nature, scientific inquiry forces the investigator to appreciate the complexity of whatever he studies. Even though his task is to arrive at explanations that are simple in the sense of intellectually elegant, he can do so only if he has an appreciation for the complexity of the phenomenon he studies. Thus, scientists who use the term "causal" carelessly may be scorned by their colleagues. Its meaning is both subtle and sophisticated, illustrated by the work of Blalock and others on the difficult problems of causal modeling (Blalock: 1971). To formulate scientifically meaningful statements about causal relationships between sets of variables is difficult; therefore, causal explanations are rare.

Since research carried out in accordance with disciplinary standards is unlikely to result in causal explanations, it is also likely to frustrate the policy-maker. However, social science research that adopts a policy perspective can lead to explanations, simple and causal in the policy-maker's sense, but not necessarily simple and causal in scientific terms. Such explanations do not necessarily constitute an advance in disciplinary theory. Of course, one cannot rule out the possibility that applied research can make important contributions to disciplinary work and vice versa, but it seems evident that such contributions are neither certain nor common.

By its nature then, policy-making calls for the development of interdisciplinary, simple, causal theories of events. To be serviceable, such theories must be "robust." By analogy with the meaning of the term when used to describe a quality of statistical tests, we use "robust" to mean a theory or explanation that can be applied with some success even in situations in which assumptions are only partially met. The world of action, the policy-maker's world, is an open system constantly buffeted by fluctuation and change. Theoretical models can be successfully applied in such circumstances only if the models are robust enough to hold up in these difficult, changing, real-world situations. Coleman explains it:

> Applied research necessarily involves the use of research design and research procedures that give good results with a high probability rather than more sophisticated techniques that give excellent results if they are correct, but may be very inaccurate if some of the assumptions are not met, if there is measurement error, if there is sampling bias, if some variables have been overlooked and left out, or if other of the frequent sources of defective data exist (Coleman, 1972: 5).

In contrast, the sociologist doing disciplinary research has a distinct advantage, since he is dealing with a closed system in which variables can be held constant and controlled in order to isolate, study and specify the relationships of special interest. His theories need not have the same degree of robustness since he has greater control over the assumptions and variables. Whether the theories and conceptual models that guide most sociological disciplinary research can be applied to real-world situations is an unanswered question, deserving serious study. It surely seems premature to assume, as many sociologists doing applied social science apparently have, that most disciplinary theory and conceptual models are *ipso facto* applicable to policy-relevant, real-world studies.

In this regard it is interesting to think about other fields, such as economics, that have had a greater impact on public policy than sociology. While there are many reasons for its important role in the world of public affairs, surely one of them has been the economists' handling of this problem of robustness. As a rule, sociologists have simply tried to apply sociological theories to the real world as it exists. In contrast, economists have sought to persuade politicians to enact programs and laws that modify the real world so that it begins to assume the characteristics necessary to make possible predictions based on economic theories. That is, some proportion of what is called "economic policy" involves the creation of restraints on the national economy so that over time this unit will begin to acquire artificially features that will then make intervention, control and prediction possible. Economists *have recognized* that problems raised by the robustness of a theoretical model can be handled in one of three ways: by changing the model, by modifying the situations to which one applies it or by some combination of the two. Almost without exception, sociologists who have thought about this problem at all have considered only the first of these three options.

Thus, it becomes clear that applying theories and conceptual models developed for the purpose of advancing disciplinary knowledge about the social world to real-life situations is a process fraught with complexities and problems. Policy-making as a practical activity calls for theories and conceptual models that are holistic, simple, causal and robust—qualities that disciplinary theories do not necessarily possess.

The special needs and goals of the policy-maker have at least one further implication for the kind of theory used in research. We have said that the policy-maker values "causal" explanations, in the broad sense of the term, because such explanations offer him options for intervention. Again because of the policy-maker's goal of intervention to change the situation is viewed as problematic, he also highly regards theories and explanations that are based upon independent variables—susceptible to *control or manipulation*. In disciplinary research, the sole consideration in selecting variables for study is the extent to which they are likely to help explain the variants associated with one dependent variable. In policy research, however, it is not enough to show that one variable is correlated with another. To be useful for policy purposes, the study must involve independent causal variables that are malleable—susceptible to manipulation and control in the context of an operational program.[3] Many sociologists seem to understand the theoretical advantage of malleable variables in a policy study. However, few understand the difficulty of actually designing a research study based upon use of malleable variables.

As we have pointed out elsewhere, most policy-relevant research is actually only disciplinary research done on problems of public concern. This means that the procedures used for selecting independent variables in these studies are the same as for any disciplinary study. Consequently, variables are selected primarily for their high predictive power; presumably, the sociologist assumes that some of these variables will be tractable as well. This procedure poses a serious problem for policy research because on close examination it appears that in sociology there is a paucity of independent variables that are both predictively powerful and amenable to control and manipulation in the context of operational social programs.[4] Henry Riecken explains the problem: "A great many 'theories of the middle range' in sociology are built around variables over which perhaps no one has much control, such as early childhood experience, the structure of the nuclear family, father's occupation, age and sex, ordinal position in the family, and similar fixed characteristics" (Riecken, 1969: 110). Given the procedures usually followed in policy research, it should not surprise us to discover that policy-related sociological research frequently produces findings that are statistically significant and extremely interesting but are utterly useless to policy-makers because they do not allow for control or manipulation. As we saw in Chapter 1, this point about the usefulness of the findings of sociological policy research is a central one in discussions about the problems of applied sociology in practice today.

There is a further point to be mentioned here. It is that sociological studies may be not only useless for policy purposes, but deleterious as well. Riecken states the problem succinctly:

> The sociological explanation somehow arrives at the conclusion that things could not be otherwise than the way they are; the nature of the explanation is such that we do not arrive at a vision of the future as different from that of the past. By fixing attention upon variables about which no action can be taken, most sociologists provide theoretical and explanatory statements that have neither interest nor promise for the social problem solver because he cannot use them as handles or levers" (Riecken, 1969:110).

It would seem logical to solve this problem by working out alternate procedures for policy-relevant research studies that would emphasize the selection of malleable independent variables. After all, as Howard Freeman has explained, "There is considerable difference between selecting variables for study on the basis of a theoretical notion of causality and on the basis that they can be manipulated to evoke change in the phenomenon that is regarded as the dependent variable" (Freeman, 1963: 152). Elsewhere we have outlined such a procedure for conducting sociological policy research to maximize the possibility that the results obtained will include "actionable" variables (Scott and Shore, 1974). The procedure is designed to select in advance, for special consideration, those independent variables that past research and theory suggest ought to be correlated with or affect the policy problem, and which are apt to be malleable in an applied context. Such a procedure focuses the study upon empirical relationships between outcome variables of high policy salience and variables that are manipulable in the context of an operational program. Variables that are, so to speak, "intractable", are not ignored entirely, since knowledge about them can be put to use in qualifying findings and therefore in the administrative planning of social action programs. But primary consideration is given to variables that are tractable.

Such a procedure helps to guarantee production of findings involving independent variables that are genuinely policy-relevant. In our own efforts to apply it, however, we discovered that it greatly narrowed the range of primary variables for study. We found that many of the standard variables that probably would have been included in the strictly disciplinary study of the problem we were studying were of secondary interest because even if we found a strong relationship between them and the dependent variable, the finding could carry no discernible policy implication.

One way out of this problem would be to follow the lead of economics and develop a Keynesian-like sociological theory of society (Feuer, 1954: 683–684). We say this because in the field of economics prior to Keynes the situation that confronted the field was similar to the one that now faces sociology. There were a variety of different economic theories, all academically worthwhile but none particularly useful from the point of view of government decision-makers trying to decide national economic policy. This problem was resolved by Keynes who provided an economic theory, the independent variables of which were at least in principle amenable to manipulation and control. In an essay on the topic, Feuer writes: "Keynesian ideas . . . have . . . provided a set of causal laws whose independent variables are accessible to control in the immediate present" (Feuer, 1954: 603–604). Charles Lindblom adds:

> The greatest significance of Keynes is that he provided a set of concepts and a theoretical model that were operational in the specific sense that policy makers could manipulate the variables of his model. For the first time, man had a set of concepts and a theoretical model that could immediately and directly guide policy. Keynesian analysis, taken together with national income accounting, made possible a kind of rational or scientific policy making new to the world (Lindblom, 1972: 3–4).

The example of Keynesian economics suggests that sociology might become an effective applied science if it were to develop self-consciously a theory of society consisting of independent variables that are in principle accessible to direct and simple control.

We must realize, however, that the development of such a theory of society may not constitute a disciplinary breakthrough. We cannot assume that by creating such a theory of society, we will necessarily enhance our understanding of it. The experience of economics in this regard should make us somewhat wary of the idea that a single theory can serve both purposes. Feuer, in his otherwise exuberant essay on the virtues of Keynesian theory, points emphatically at the problem: "Keynesian ideas have been accepted, not because they explain more than others, but because they produce a set of causal laws whose independent variables are accessible to action in the immediate present" (Feuer, 1954: 683–684). We are not especially trained in economics. And we do not feel competent to judge whether Feuer's explanation is accurate. Others who are knowledgeable about this discipline have suggested that when the field of economics embraced Keynes' theories, it accepted a theory for action that did not further the economists' understanding of core intellectual questions of that discipline. But, it did provide a way of thinking about the economy in terms that lead directly to its manipulation and control. Jerome Ravetz is one of the most ardent proponents of this view. He argues that the dominance of Keynesian theory has brought with it disadvantages for the discipline of economics. While it is the case that Keynes made economics an enormously useful science for purposes of policy, Ravetz believes that when economists embraced this model, they also abandoned scholarly research into many of the great intellectual issues of that field (Ravetz, 1971: 377–402). To Ravetz, policy relevance was achieved at a very high price to the discipline. It strikes us that Ravetz's argument should be carefully considered for its relevance to sociology. The development of a theory of society consisting of independent variables accessible to control would appear to be an obvious solution to the present difficulty of lack of policy relevance, but such a development might prove a mixed blessing, introducing new problems for the discipline of sociology.

RESEARCH FINDINGS

There are also important differences with respect to the kinds of findings that suit the purposes of the academic sociologist and those of the policy-maker. We shall mention a few briefly to illustrate this basic fact.

To prove usable for social policy, the findings of a research study must be *specific*. This means that the variables studied must be defined narrowly and precisely and the empirical relationships among them specified clearly if the results of such research are to serve as effective guides for action. The need for specific findings poses a problem because few sociological theories are refined enough to yield such precise results. Much of sociological theory consists of variables that are too large or undifferentiated to be of any practical use. "The role of the physician," "need achievement," "the sick role" or "the social context" are examples. Henry Riecken describes the difficulty with conceptual "globs" of this kind: "Such concepts presumably point to consequential phenomena, but they do not tell us enough specifically about them to be usable in an action frame of reference" (Riecken, 1969:10).

Moreover, whereas in disciplinary research the investigator's interest is focused upon the question of whether or not statistically significant differences exist between the groups that are compared on any given item, in policy research the findings must be not only statistically different, but *dramatically* different. As Freeman notes, findings must be dramatic enough to lead to policy outcomes that can justify the investment of manpower and money in them (Freeman, 1963:149). For example, it has been shown that rates of recidivism among civil offenders are lower for those who receive job training and other support services during the period of their incarceration when compared with those who do not (Martinson, 1973). But the magnitude of the difference between the two groups, though statistically significant, is not so dramatic as to justify wide-scale adoption of this costly alternative in the criminal justice system.

In addition to being specific and dramatic, research findings for policy purposes must also emphasize dependent variables that measure *behavior* directly as opposed to variables that relate to behavior obliquely or not at all. This is because policy-makers must have demonstrable evidence that consequential differences exist in order to justify adoption of a particular policy. As a rule this means evidence pertaining to differences in behavior. As Freeman sees it: "One reasonably safe assumption is that the policy system is least concerned with attitudinal phenomena and most concerned with behavioral ones; consequently, the latter have greater action potential" (Freeman, 1963:150). For example, in a study of neighborhood safety, the policy-maker would prefer a dependent variable showing actual declines or increases in precinct crime rates rather than one showing changes in residents' feelings of safety. Ideally, he would want both kinds of information, but if forced to choose, he would prefer actual crime statistics. Thus, Freeman explains, "Social policy research virtually always requires a selection of dependent variables that are measures of behavior rather than of attitudes and motives" (Freeman, 1963:150–151). Some problems for the sociologist following ordinary disciplinary research procedures arise from this requirement, for a great deal of sociological research deals with attitudes. Since the relationship between attitudes and behavior is not understood (Deutscher, 1973), it may not be possible to determine the policy implications of studies that are based primarily on attitudinal data until this complex issue is clarified; and the specific policy relevance of research findings based on attitudes will remain undetermined.

The requirements for specific, dramatic and behaviorally-measured findings will limit the usefulness of much research carried out with the use of normal disciplinary procedures. The obstacles to producing findings with these characteristics require us to recognize that disciplinary findings cannot be automatically and easily adapted to policy problems. Far more significant, however, are the problems raised by the special kinds of theory needed for policy purposes. If anything, our discussion about the kinds of theory needed for policy purposes and the kinds needed for disciplinary purposes would suggest that disciplinary theory is often an inappropriate basis for conducting research that is supposed to be related to social policy, a fact that raises fundamental questions about the validity of some of the proposals that have been made for enhancing sociology's relevance to policy through strengthening theory and research procedures for discipline.

Consequences for the Discipline of Sociology

The primary purpose of this discussion has been to consider whether policy-makers are apt to receive the kind of knowledge they need for planning social policy from research based upon the theory and method of academic sociology. The conclusions we have reached about this subject have important implications for the discipline of sociology. The financial consequence is certainly one of the most serious. If it is unlikely that disciplinary sociological research will be routinely relevant for policy purposes, then one of the main justifications for public financial support for academic sociology is seriously undermined. Traditionally, academic leaders in our discipline have argued that investing public monies in basic research and graduate education in the field of sociology will ultimately pay off in the form of knowledge that will serve as a basis for developing effective social programs to ameliorate society's problems (House of Representatives, *The Use of Social Research in Federal Domestic Programs*, 1967). We have no wish to see the withdrawal of support for basic scientific research in sociology, but we are acutely uneasy about the prospects that sociology may be called into account for this promise. If there is truth to the argument we have developed in this chapter, then sociologists in the future must avoid making careless promises about relevance that probably cannot be fulfilled by pursuing research in accordance with disciplinary procedures alone. Perhaps a safer, more honest course would be to premise such requests for public support on two principles instead of one. We would continue to use the earlier justification for public support, after carefully modifying it so as to avoid making promises we cannot hope to fulfill.

A second argument for support would be the traditional premise on which all respected academic fields have been developed, namely, that the pursuit of knowledge for its own sake is an inherent good that no fully civilized society can afford not to undertake. In this sense, the purpose of supporting academic departments of sociology would be to further understanding of society for its own sake. No social science discipline can be secure if it is based on just one or the other of these principles. But surely many of the tensions we have identified would be reduced if academic sociologists were freed from the often oppressive pretense of searching for concrete answers to social problems, and if policy-oriented sociologists did not have to define the latent theoretical significance of their work to retain status and respect in the eyes of their more academically oriented colleagues.

If we are correct in our conclusion that disciplinary research does not often result in knowledge useful for the formulation of social policy, then the old argument to justify public support for sociological research is not only misleading, it is also dangerous to the development of the discipline. This is because policy relevance, having been promised, will in turn be encouraged by patterns of government funding. As Philip Green points out, "Involvement of social science with government poses a serious threat to the independence of social science. In order that social science may be useful to government officials, it must meet their criteria of reality and practicality" (Green, 1971:17).[5] Herbert Kelman explains the danger in greater detail:

> If the major criterion for what is considered acceptable in legitimate social science research is going to be determined by what research is supported, encouraged, or even permitted, then the whole basis of the scientific process will be threatened . . . . If we are to adopt a short range criterion of relevance, some of the most important work—important even from the perspective of those seeking to bring about social change—will be excluded. When we make judgments of this kind we are

really involved in making political decisions about what should and should not be studied. To promote a state of affairs in which decisions about what social science research should and what it should not investigate are based on political criteria is to abandon what I regard as the fundamental role of social science—its role as a source of independent perspective on society, on social institutions, and on social life (Kelman, 1972:196).

These same sentiments are voiced by David Truman, who reminds us that:

One measure of a developing discipline is that it sets its own agenda in terms of those things that its members as scientists regard as important, that at least a temporary withdrawal from the area of public policy is to be expected as the social sciences mature. If the preoccupations that in large part define a discipline are being set by the problems of public policy, then in some measure they are not being set by the problems that confront the discipline itself as an intellectual enterprise (Truman, 1968a:509).

The strictest warning is issued by Jerome Ravetz (Ravetz, 1971:380–400). Ravetz depicts the social sciences as disciplines that are often unable to establish facts within their own closed world of controlled experience (Ravetz, 1971:383). He warns that such disciplines are even less capable of drawing conclusions about the problems of a raw and unstable reality (Ravetz, 1971:383). Yet, the temptation for practitioners in the "soft" sciences to become involved in the realm of policy is great, and good justification for doing so can always be found, i.e., the belief "that a large scale research program is necessary before adequate decisions can be taken on an urgent practical or technical problem . . . the natural desire to expand, the illusion that a field has reached the point of maturity required by the problem or that engagement of the problem will bring it over the top . . ." (Ravetz, 1971:383–384). He adds, "Even if the leaders of the field have private doubts about its effectiveness in this respect, they can legitimately reassure themselves that in the absence of its intervention ignorance and self interest will dominate among any decisions to be taken" (Ravetz, 1971:384).

The danger posed to the discipline that accepts these arguments and yields to the temptation is disciplinary "hypertrophy," a situation in which the rate of growth is so rapid that the "existing social mechanisms of quality control cannot perform their customary functions" (Ravetz, 1971:384). In response to urgent calls for helpful research, Ravetz fears that possibilities exist for clever mediocrity to build an empire and attain power and prestige at the expense of those with more scruples. In the absence of efforts to control from within the discipline he believes that the worst excesses of "shadowy science" can occur, and that programs of graduate study can become a travesty in which "all the contradictions inherent in the teaching of immature science are made much more acute, as the small core of successful craft techniques and aphoristic wisdom is imbedded in a doctrine imitating a matured science, theoretical and applied" (Ravetz, 1971:385). This is stern warning; although we believe that Ravetz has exaggerated the danger, our discipline can ill afford to ignore his predictions about the fate that may befall the scientific discipline of sociology if it places too great an immediate emphasis on policy relevance.[6]

A further implication of our conclusion that disciplinary research and policy research are different in purpose and procedure is that they perhaps need not be done in the same place. In fact, some claim that policy research is better pursued outside of the university setting. James Coleman explains one of the reasons for excluding policy research from university settings: "At universities both the departmental structure and its centers and institutes have one property that makes them inappropriate for certain types of policy research. This is its dedication to open publication of research results. Universities are not appropriate places in which to do policy research" (Coleman, 1972:19–20). Alvin Gouldner provides another: " . . . the applied social scientist must sometimes forego sources of knowledge, however rich they may be, if he fears their use will impede the intended change" (Gouldner, 1957:96). Clearly, this stance would be unthinkable to an academic sociologist. Herbert Gans and Amitai Etzioni have also commented on the unsuitability of academic social science departments for policy research (Gans, 1971:19; Etzioni, 1971:9). An alternative setting is suggested by Coleman, who believes that policy research is best done by organizational units that specialize in research—units that are close to the policy-maker but at the same time sufficiently independent to allow independent development (Coleman, 1972:19–22).[7]

Their argument makes sense, but it has serious implications for the support of academic sociology that are not always clarified. In an environment where public bodies, which have traditionally supported research and development of the discipline, are calling for immediate and concrete answers to questions that they insist on formulating, we should expect that what little public money may exist for the social sciences will go to policy-related research done in independent research firms. Since many sociology departments are heavily dependent on such research money for support of basic programs of graduate training, the physical and organizational separation of policy research and disciplinary research could lead to very serious reductions in disciplinary research.

CONCLUSIONS

To summarize, we have seen that sociological knowledge and procedures developed for the purpose of advancing our understanding of society are not necessarily an adequate basis upon which to attempt to change society; and we have noted some potential dangers to the development of sociology as a discipline in continuing to assume that knowledge for understanding and knowledge for action are exactly comparable. This does not mean that sociologists should disregard proposals for strengthening the discipline. Instead, it means that the criteria that are used when doing this must be carefully tailored to the problem of action and of policy if they are to enhance the relevance of the discipline for public affairs.

NOTES

1. Kathleen Archibald has identified three basic approaches to applied policy-relevant social science research. These are the academic, the clinical and the strategic. For a discussion of these styles and various subtypes of each, see Archibald (1970).
2. The failure of this approach has, in fact, been documented. See, for example, Moynihan (1969) and Levitan (1969).
3. A number of sociologists have recognized this fact. Amitai Etzioni, for example, states: "There is a distinction as vital to the policy researcher and policy maker as it is irrelevant to the basic researcher, namely, the degree to which a variable is 'malleable,' that is, the degree to which it is characterized as moveable" (Etzioni, 1971:1). Howard Freeman points out that "independent variables need to have a high influence potential; they not only need to be correlated with the dependent one but also be open to manipulation by members of the operating system" (Freeman, 1963:152). James Coleman reminds us that it is necessary to treat differently "policy variables subject to policy manipulation and situational variables which are not" (Coleman, 1972:5). Finally, in his groundbreaking essay on applied social science, Alvin Gouldner emphasizes that "the applied social scientist is ultimately concerned with identifying those independent variables which can not only account for but . . . remedy . . . social problems" (Gouldner, 1957:93). That is, "The applied social scientist's knowledge must have certain characteristics . . . for one he inspects his independent variables to determine the extent to which they are accessible to control . . . . The applied social scientist is concerned not only with identifying predictively potent independent variables, but also with discovering some that are accessible to control" (Gouldner, 1957:96–97). For additional discussions of this point, see Bauer and Gergen (1968:107).
4. Our impression is shared and substantiated by Gross and Fishman (1967), Glock and Nicosia (1967), Coleman (1972), Riecken (1969) and others.

5. Irving Louis Horowitz makes a similar point in *The Use and Abuse of Social Science* (Horowitz, 1971), and Eliot Friedson concentrates on the possible effects on sociology of its relationship with the field of medicine in *The Profession of Medicine* (Friedson, 1972).
6. Ravetz holds up the field of economics as a prime example of what he believes could happen to other social science disciplines, describing it somewhat contemptously as a "cliche science" (Ravetz, 1971:385).
7. For other statements in support of this position see Pye (1968:260) and Lindblom (1968).

Adams, Stuart. 1975. *Evaluation Research in Corrections: A Practical Guide*. Washington, D.C.: United States Department of Justice, LEAA, National Institute of Law Enforcement and Criminal Justice.

Bibliography

Advisory Committee on Government Programs in the Behavioral Sciences, National Research Council. 1968. *The Behavioral Sciences and the Federal Government*. Washington, D.C.: National Academy of Science.

Alexander, Thomas. 1972. "The Social Engineers Under Fire," *Fortune* (October), pp. 132–148.

Alpert, Harry. 1958. "Congressmen, Social Scientists, and Attitudes Toward Federal Support of Social Science Research," *American Sociological Review* (December), pp. 682–686.

———— 1959. "The Growth of Social Research in the United States," in Daniel Lerner, ed., *The Human Meaning of the Social Sciences*. New York: Meridan Books.

———— 1967. "The Government's Growing Recognition of Social Science," in House of Representatives, *The Use of Social Research in Federal Democratic Programs*. (A staff study for the Research and Technical Programs Subcommittee of the Committee on Government Operation. Part I—Federally Financed Social Research—Expenditures, Status, and Objectives. 90th Congress, First Session.) Washington, DC: U.S. Government Printing Office; and "The Government's Growing Recognition of Social Science," *Annals*, AAPSS (June, 1960), pp. 64–67.

Anderson, Patrick. 1968. *The President's Men*. New York: Doubleday.

Archibald, Kathleen. 1967. "Federal Interest and Investment in Social Science," in House of Representatives, *The Use of Social Research in Federal Domestic Programs*. (A staff study for the Research and Technical Programs Subcommittee of the Committee on Government Operation. Part I—Federally Financed Social Research—Expenditures, Status, and Objectives. 90th Congress, First Session.) Washington, DC: U.S. Government Printing Office.

———— 1970. "Alternative Orientation to Social Science Utilization," *Social Science Information* 9 (April), 7–34.

Arrow, Kenneth. 1951. *Social Change and Individual Values*. New York: Wiley.

Arrow, Kenneth et al. 1970. *Urban Processes as Viewed by the Social Sciences*. National Academy of Science Symposium organized by the Urban Institute, moderated by William Gorman. Washington, DC: The Urban Institute.

Banfield, Edward. 1968. *The Unheavenly City*. Boston: Little Brown.

Baritz, Loren. 1960. *The Servants of Power: A History of the Use of Social Science in American Industry*. Middletown, CT: Wesleyan University Press.

Bauer, Raymond A. 1966. *Social Indicators*. Cambridge, MA: MIT Press.

―――― 1968. "The Study of Policy Formation: An Introduction," in Bauer and Gergen, eds. *The Study of Policy Formation*. New York: Free Press.

Bauer, Raymond A. and Kenneth Gergen, eds. 1968. *The Study of Policy Formation*. New York: Free Press.

Baumol, William J. 1952. *Welfare Economics and the Theory of the State*. Cambridge, MA: Harvard University Press.

Beard, Charles A. 1908. *Politics*. New York: Columbia University Press.

―――― 1913. *An Economic Interpretation of the Constitution of the United States*. New York: Macmillan.

―――― 1914. *Contemporary American History*. New York: Macmillan.

Beckman, Norman. 1971. "Congressional Information Processes for National Policy," *Social Science and the Federal Government*, Annals, AAPSS (March), pp. 84–99.

Behavioral and Social Sciences Survey. 1969. *The Behavioral and Social Sciences Outlook and Needs*. Washington, DC: National Academy of Science and the Social Science Research Council.

Bell, Daniel. 1966. "Government by Commissions," *Public Interest* (Spring).

―――― 1973. *The Coming of Post-Industrial Society*, New York: Basic Books.

Berelson, Bernard, Paul Lazarsfeld and William McPhee. 1954. *Voting: A Study of Opinion Formation in a Presidential Campaign*. Chicago: University of Chicago Press.

Bernard, Luther and Jessie Bernard. 1943. *Origins of American Sociology*, New York: Crowell.

Biderman, Albert D. and Elizabeth Crawford. 1968. *The Political Economics of Social Research: The Case of Sociology*. Washington, DC: Bureau of Social Science Research.

Blalock, Herbert. 1971. *Causal Models in the Social Sciences*. Chicago: Aldine.

Blau, Peter and W. Richard Scott. 1962. *Formal Organizations*. San Francisco: Chandler.

Bogart, Leo. 1969. *Social Research and the Desegregation of the United States Army*. Chicago: Markham Publ. Co.

Bordua, David J. and Albert J. Reiss, Jr. 1967. "Law Enforcement," in Lazarsfeld et al., eds. *The Uses of Sociology*. New York: Basic Books, Chapter 10, pp. 275–303.

Bowers, Patricia F. 1974. *Private Choice and Public Welfare: The Economics of Public Goods*. Hinsdale, IL: The Dryden Press.

Bowers, Raymond V. 1967. "The Military Establishment," in Lazarsfeld et al., eds., *The Uses of Sociology*. New York: Basic Books, Chapter 9, 234–274.

Braybrooke, David and Charles Lindblom. 1963. *A Strategy of Decision*. New York: Free Press.

Bremner, Robert H. 1956. *From the Depths: The Discovery of Poverty in the United States*. New York: New York University Press.

Buchanan, James M. 1968. *The Demand and Supply of Public Goods*. Chicago: Rand McNally.

Burns, Eveline M. 1944. "Social Insurance in Evolution," *American Economic Review* 34 (March, Supplement, Part 2), 199.

Cahn, Edmund. 1955. "Jurisprudence," *New York University Law Review* XXX, 150.

Caldwell, Catherine. 1970. "Social Science as Ammunition," *Psychology Today* (September), pp. 38–41, 72–73.

Campbell, Donald T. 1969. "Reforms as Experiments," *American Psychologist* 24(4), 409–429.

———— 1972. "Methods for the Experimenting Society," *American Psychologist* 27(2), 164.

Caplan, Nathan. 1976. "Factors Associated with Knowledge Use Among Federal Executives," *Policy Studies Journal* 4(3), 229–234.

Caplan, Nathan and Eugenia Barton. 1976. *Social Indicators 1973: A Study of the Relationship Between the Power of Information and Utilization by Federal Executives*. Ann Arbor: Institute for Social Research.

Caplan, Nathan, Andrea Morrison and Russell J. Stambaugh. 1975. *The Use of Social Science Knowledge in Policy Decisions at the National Level*. Ann Arbor: Institute for Social Research. University of Michigan.

Chalmers, W. Sherwin and Raymond S. Isenson. 1967. "Project Hindsight," *Science* 156 (June 23), 1571–1577.

Chambers, Clarke A. 1967. *Seedtime of Reform: American Social Science and Social Action, 1918–1933*. Ann Arbor: University of Michigan Press.

Charlesworth, James C., ed. 1972. *Integration of the Social Sciences Through Policy Analysis*. AAPSS Monograph 14. Philadelphia: AAPSS.

Cherns, Albert, 1970. "Relations Between Research Institutes and Users of Research." *International Social Science Journal* 22, 227–242.

Church, R. L. 1974. "Economists as Experts: The Rise of an Academic Profession," in Lawrence Stone, ed., *The University in Society*, Vol. II. Princeton, NJ: Princeton University Press.

Churchman, C. West. 1967. *The Use of Science in Public Affairs*. AAPSS Monograph 7. Philadelphia: AAPSS, pp. 29–48.

Civil Service Commission. 1975. *Current Federal Workforce. Washington, DC: U.S. Government Printing Office*.

Clark, Ian D. 1974. "Expert Advice in the Controversy About Supersonic Transport in the United States," *Minerva* XII (October).

Clark, Kenneth B. 1960. "The Desegregation Cases: Criticism of the Social Scientist's Role," *Villanova Law Review* V, p. 224.

Cloward, Richard A. and Lloyd E. Ohlin. 1960. *Delinquency and Opportunity.* New York: Free Press.

Coleman, James. 1966. "The Possibility of the Social Welfare Function," *American Economic Review* LVI (December) 1105–1122.

—— 1972. *Policy Research in the Social Sciences.* Morristown, NJ: The General Learning Press.

—— 1973. "Ten Principles Governing Policy Research," *Footnotes,* Number 1 (March), p. 1.

—— 1974. *Youth: Transition to Adulthood.* Report of the panel on youth for the President's Science Advisory Committee. Chicago: University of Chicago Press.

—— 1975. "The Emergence of Sociology as a Policy Science," presented at the American Sociological Association Convention, San Francisco.

Commager, Henry Steele. 1950. *The American Mind: An Interpretation of American Thought and Character Since the 1880's.* New Haven: Yale University Press.

Commons, John. 1913. "Constructive Investigation in the Industrial Commission of Wisconsin," *The Survey* 29(4), 440–448.

Congressional Quarterly Almanac. 1945–1974. Vol. 1–30, Washington, DC: U.S. Government Printing Office.

Congressional Research Service. 1971. *Annual Report:* Congressional Research Service, Library of Congress, Fiscal Year, 1971. Washington, DC: U.S. Government Printing Office.

Conway, Richard et al. 1976. "Promoting Knowledge Utilization Through Clinically Oriented Research: The Benchmark Program," *Policy Studies Journal* 4(3), 264–269.

Cook, Thomas D. et al. 1975. *Sesame Street Revisited: A Case Study in Evaluation Research.* New York: Russell Sage Foundation.

Crawford, Elizabeth. 1971. "The Sociology of the Social Sciences," *Current Sociology* 19(2), 7–10.

Croly, Herbert. 1909. *The Promise of American Life.* New York: Macmillan.

—— 1915. *Progressive Democracy.* New York: Macmillan.

Cronin, Thomas E. 1971. "Everybody Believes in Democracy Until He Gets to the White House . . . An Examination of White House Departmental Relations," in *Papers on the Institutionalized Presidency.* New York: Harper and Row.

Cronin, Thomas E. and Sanford Greenberg. 1969. *The Presidential Advisory System.* New York: Harper and Row.

Curti, Merle. 1956. *The American Paradox: The Conflict of Thought and Action.* New Brunswick: Rutgers University Press.

Davison, W. Phillips. 1967. "Foreign Policy," in Lazarsfeld et al., eds., *The Uses of Sociology*. New York: Basic Books.

Demerath, N.S., III, Otto Larsen, and Karl Schuessler, eds. 1975. *Social Policy and Sociology*. New York: Academic Press.

Deutsch, Morton. 1976. "On Making Social Psychology More Useful," *Items, SSRC* 30(1), 1–6.

Deutscher, Irwin. 1973. *What We Say/What We Do*. Glenview, IL: Scott, Foresman.

Dewey, John. 1887. *Psychology*. New York: Harper.

————— 1888. *The Ethics of Democracy*. University of Michigan Philosophical Papers. Second Series, Number 1. Ann Arbor: University of Michigan Press.

————— 1891. *Outlines of a Critical Theory of Ethics*. Ann Arbor: Register Publ. Co.

————— 1899. *The School and Society*. New York: McClure, Phillips.

————— 1902. "The Evolutionary Method as Applied to Morality," *Philosophical Review* XI, 111–122.

————— 1917. *Creative Intelligence: Essays in the Pragmatic Attitude*. New York: Holt.

————— 1927. *The Public and Its Problems*. New York: Holt.

Dewey, John and James H. Tufts. 1908. *Ethics*. New York: Holt.

Dolbeore, Kenneth M. 1975. *Public Policy Evaluation*. Vol. 2. Sage Yearbooks in Politics and Public Policy, Beverly Hills, CA: Sage Publ. Co.

Dreyfuss, Daniel A. 1976. "The Limitations of Policy Research in Congressional Decision Making," *Policy Studies Journal* 4(3), 269–274.

Dror, Yehezkel. 1971a. "Applied Social Science and Systems Analysis," in Irving Louis Horowitz, ed., *The Use and Abuse of Social Science*. New Brunswick, NJ: Transaction Books, pp. 109–132.

————— 1971b. *Ventures in Policy Sciences: Concepts in Application*. New York: American Elsevier Publ. Co.

Dunk, W. 1961. "The Role of the Public Servant in Policy Formation," *Public Administration* 20 (June), 99–104.

Dupree, A. Hunter. 1957. *Science in the Federal Government: A History of Policies and Activities to 1940*. Cambridge, MA: The Belknap Press of Harvard University Press.

Easton, David. 1972. "Comment on Robert Lane's Political Science and Policy Analysis," in Charlesworth, James C., ed., *Integration of the Social Sciences Through Policy Analysis*. AAPSS Monograph 14. Philadelphia: AAPSS, pp. 88–89.

Edelman, J. 1960. "Symbols and Political Quiescience," *APSR* 54 (September), 695–704.

Ellis, William et al. 1964. *The Federal Government in Behavioral Science: Fields,*

Methods and Funds. Washington, DC: American Enterprise Institute for Public Policy Research.

Ely, Richard. 1917. *The Foundations of National Prosperity.* New York: Macmillan.

—— 1918. *Outline of Economics.* New York: Macmillan.

—— 1938. *Ground Under Our Feet.* New York: Macmillan.

Etzioni, Amitai. 1964. *Modern Organizations.* Englewood Cliffs, NJ: Prentice-Hall.

—— 1968. *The Active Society.* New York: Free Press.

—— 1971. "Policy Research," *The American Sociologist,* 6 (Supplementary Issue: June, entitled "Sociological Research and Public Policy") 8–12.

Ezekiel, Mordekai. 1939. "Jobs for All Through Industrial Expansion," in *$2500 A Year: From Scarcity to Abundance.* New York: DaCapo Press.

Felt, Jeremy P. 1969. *Hostages of Fortune: Child Labor Reform in New York State.* Syracuse: Syracuse University Press.

Feuer, Lewis S. 1954. "Causality in Social Sciences," *Journal of Philosophy* 51 (November), 681–695.

Fox, Daniel. 1967. *The Discovery of Abundance: Simon N. Patten and The Transformation of Social Theory.* Ithaca, NY: Cornell University Press.

Fraser, Donald M. 1970. "Congress and the Psychologist," *American Psychologist* (April), pp. 323–327.

Freeman, Howard E. 1963. "The Strategy of Social Policy Research," *Social Welfare Forum.* New York: Columbia University Press for the National Conference on Social Welfare.

Friedson, Eliot. 1972. *The Profession of Medicine.* New York: Dodd, Mead, and Company.

Froman, Lewis A., Jr. 1967. "An Analysis of Public Policies in Cities," *Journal of Politics* 29 (February), 94–108.

—— 1968. "The Categorization of Policy Contents," in Ranney, ed., *Political Science and Public Policy.* Chicago: Markham Publ. Co.

Furner, Mary O. 1975. *Advocacy and Objectivity: A Crises in the Professionalization of American Social Science: 1865–1905.* Lexington, KY: University of Kentucky Press.

Gans, Herbert J. 1967. "Urban Poverty and Social Policy," in Lazarsfeld et al., eds., *The Uses of Sociology.* New York: Basic Books, Chapter 16, pp. 437–476.

—— 1971. "Social Science for Social Policy," in Horowitz, *The Use and Abuse of Social Science.* New Brunswick, NJ: Transaction Books, pp. 13–33.

Geis, Gilbert and Robert E. Meier. 1977. *White Collar Crime.* Rev. ed. New York: Free Press.

Gergen, Kenneth J. 1968. "Assessing the Leverage Points in the Process of Policy Formation," in Bauer and Gergen, eds., *The Study of Policy Formation.* New York: Free Press, pp. 181–203.

Gil, David G. 1970. "A Systematic Approach to Social Policy Analysis," *Social Service Review* 44(4), 411–426.

Glazer, Barney G. and Anselm L. Strauss. 1967. *The Discovery of Grounded Theory*. Chicago: Aldine.

Glazer, Nathan. 1967. "The Ideological Uses of Sociology," in Lazarsfeld et al., eds., *The Uses of Sociology*. New York: Basic Books, Chapter 3, pp. 63–80.

Glock, Charles Y. 1961. *Case Studies in Bringing Behavioral Science into Use*. Stanford, CA: Institute for Communication Research, Stanford University.

Glock, Charles Y. and F. M. Nicosia. 1967. "The Consumer" in Lazarsfeld et al., eds., *The Uses of Sociology*. New York: Basic Books, Chapter 12, pp. 359–390.

Goodwin, Leonard. 1973. *Can Social Science Help Resolve National Problems? Welfare, A Case in Point*. Washington, DC: (mimeo).

Gouldner, Alvin W. 1957. "Theoretical Requirements of the Applied Social Sciences, *American Sociological Review* 22 (February), 92–102.

——— 1970. *The Coming Crises of Western Sociology*. New York: Basic Books.

Gouldner, Alvin W. and S. M. Miller. 1965. *Applied Sociology: Opportunities and Problems*. Glencoe, IL: Free Press.

Graham, Elinor. 1965. "The Politics of Poverty," in B. Seligman, ed., *Poverty as a Public Issue*. New York: Free Press, pp. 234–250.

Graham, Otis. 1976. *Toward a Planned Society*. New York: Oxford University Press.

Grantham, Dewey W., Jr. 1964. "The Progressive Era and the Reform Tradition," *Mid-America* 46(4), 227–251.

Green, Philip, 1971. "Knowledge, Power and Democratic Theory," *Social Science in the Federal Government, Annals, AAPSS* (March), pp. 13–27.

Gregor, A. J. 1963. "The Law, Social Science, and School Segregation: An Assessment," *Western Reserve Law Review* XIV, 612–636.

Gross, Bertram M. 1967. "Social Goals and Indicators for American Society," *Annals, AAPSS* (May), p. 371.

Gross, Neal and Joshua A. Fishman. 1967. "The Management of Educational Establishments," in Lazarsfeld, et al., eds., *The Uses of Sociology*. New York: Basic Books, Chapter 11, pp. 304–358.

Grossman, David. 1973. Professors and Public Service, *1885–1925: A Chapter in the Professionalization of the Social Sciences*. Ph.D. Thesis: Washington University, St. Louis.

Guettkow, Harold. 1959. "Conversion Barriers in Using the Social Sciences," *Administrative Science Quarterly* 4 (June), 68–81.

Gusfield, Joseph. 1975a. "The (f) Utility of Knowledge?: The Relation of Social Science to Public Policy Toward Drugs," *Annals, AAPSS* (January), pp. 1–15.

———— 1975b. "Categories of Ownership and Responsibility in Social Issues: Alchohol Abuse and Automobile Use," *Journal of Drug Issues* 5 (Fall), 285–303.

Habermas, Jurgen. 1970. *Toward A Rational Society.* Boston, Beacon Press.

———— 1973. *Theory and Practice.* Boston, Beacon Press.

Hamby, Alonzo. 1973. *Beyond the New Deal: Harry Truman and American Liberalism.* New York: Columbia University Press.

Hanset, Elizabeth. 1975. *Perfection and Progress: Two Models of Utopian Thought.* Cambridge, MA: MIT Press.

Harrington, Michael. 1963. *The Other America.* Baltimore: Penguin Books.

Hauser, Philip. 1949. "Social Science and Social Engineering," *Journal of Philosophy of Science* 16(3), 209–218.

Hays, Samuel P. 1959. *Conservation and the Gospel of Efficiency: The Progressive Conservation Movement, 1890–1920.* Cambridge, MA: Harvard University Press.

Heaton, Herbert. 1952. *A Scholar in Action.* Cambridge, MA: Harvard University Press.

Heller, Walter. 1964. Hearings Before the Subcommittee on the War on Poverty Program, Committee on Education and Labor, U.S. House of Representatives, 88th Congress, 2nd Session, on H. R. 10440.

Hofstadter, Richard, ed. 1955. *The Age of Reform.* New York: Knopf.

———— 1963a. *The Progressive Movement: 1900–1915.* Englewood Cliffs, NJ: Prentice-Hall.

———— 1963b. *Anti-Intellectualism in American Life.* New York: Knopf.

Holmes, Oliver W., Jr. 1881. *The Common Law.* Boston: Little Brown.

———— 1897. "The Path of the Law,"in Holmes, Oliver W., Jr., *Collected Legal Papers.* New York: Harcourt Brace, pp. 167–202.

———— 1920. *Collected Legal Papers.* New York: Harcourt Brace.

Horowitz, Irving Louis, ed. 1971. *The Use and Abuse of Social Science.* New Brunswick, NJ: Transaction Books.

Horowitz, Irving Louis and James Everett Katz. 1975. *Social Science and Public Policy in the United States.* New York: Praeger.

House of Representatives. 1967. *The Use of Social Research in Federal Democratic Programs.* (A staff study for the Research and Technical Programs Subcommittee of the Committee on Government Operation. Part I—Federally Financed Social Research—Expenditures, Status, and Objectives. 90th Congress, First Session.) Washington, DC: U.S. Government Printing Office.

Huitt, Ralph K. 1968. "Political Feasibility," in Ranney, ed., *Political Science and Public Policy.* Chicago: Markham Publ. Co.

Hunter, Robert. 1904. *Poverty.* New York: Grosset and Dunlap.

Huntington, Samuel P. 1961. *The Common Defense*. New York: Columbia University Press.

Hyman, Martin D. 1967. "Medicine," in Lazarsfeld et al., eds., *The Uses of Sociology*. New York: Basic Books, Chapter 6, pp. 119—115.

Janowitz, Morris. 1972. *Sociological Models and Social Policy*. Morristown NJ: The General Learning Press.

Jayson, Lester S. 1974. Statement Before Joint Committee on Congressional Operations Regarding the Congressional Research Service, May 16, 1974 (mimeo).

Johnson, Donald B. 1956. *National Party Platforms, 1840—1956*. Urbana: University of Illinois Press.

Jones, Charles O. 1970. *An Introduction to the Study of Public Policy*. Belmost, CA: Duxbury Press.

Jones, Charles O. and Robert D. Thomas. 1976. *Public Policy-Making in a Federal System*. Beverly Hills, CA: Sage Publications.

Jordan, David Starr. 1916. "Governmental Obstacles to Insurance," *Scientific Monthly* 2 (January), 28.

Karl, Barry. 1969. "Presidential Planning and Social Science Research: Mr. Hoover's Experts," *Perspectives in American History*. Cambridge, MA: Charles Warren Center for Studies in American History, Vol. III, pp. 347—409.

Keefe, William J. 1972. *Parties, Politics, and Public Policy in America*. New York: Holt, Rinehart and Winston.

Kelman, Herbert C. 1972. "Roles of the Behavioral Scientist in Policy Oriented Research," in George Coelko and Elia Rubinstein (eds.) with the assistance of Elinor Stillman, *Social Change and Human Behavior: Mental Health Challenges of the Seventies*. Rockville, MD: NIMH.

Kirkendall, Richard. 1966. *Social Scientists and Farm Politics in the Age of Roosevelt*. Columbia, MO: University of Missouri Press.

Kluger, Richard. 1976. *Simple Justice*. New York: Knopf.

Knight, Frank H. 1957. "Intelligence and Social Policy," *Ethics*, 67 (April), 155—168.

Komarovsky, Mirra. 1975. *Sociology and Public Policy*. New York: American Elsevier Publ. Co.

Lane, Robert. 1972. "Political Science and Policy Analysis," in Charlesworth, ed., *Integration of the Social Sciences Through Policy Analysis*. Philadelphia: AAPSS, pp. 71—78.

Larsen, Otto. 1975. "The Commission on Obscenity and Pornography: Form, Function and Failure" in Komarovsky, ed., *Sociology and Public Policy*. New York: American Elsevier Publ. Co., Chapter 1, pp. 9—42.

Lasswell, Harold. 1971. *A Preview of Policy Science*. New York: American Elsevier Publ. Co.

Lazarsfeld, Paul F., with Jeffrey G. Reitz and the assistance of Ann K.

Pasanella. 1975. *An Introduction to Applied Sociology*. New York: Elsevier Scientific Publ. Co.

Lazarsfeld, Paul F., William H. Sewell and Harold Wilensky, eds. 1967. *The Uses of Sociology*. New York: Basic Books.

Lecuyer, Bernard-Pierre. 1970. "Contribution of the Social Sciences to the Guidance of National Policy," *International Social Science Journal* 22(2), 264–300.

Lerner, Daniel. 1959. *The Human Meaning of the Social Sciences*. New York: Meridan Books.

Lerner, Daniel and Harold Lasswell, eds. 1951. *The Policy Sciences: Recent Developments in Scope and Method*. Stanford, CA: Stanford University Press.

Leuchtenburg, William E. 1969. *Franklin D. Roosevelt and the New Deal*. New York: Harper and Row.

Leverett, Lynn et al. 1935. *The National Recovery Administration*. Washington, DC: Brookings Institution.

Levitan, Sol A. 1969. *The Great Society's Poor Law*. Baltimore: Johns Hopkins University Press.

Lindblom, Charles E. 1965. *The Intelligence of Democracy: Decision-Making Through Mutual Adjustment*. New York: Macmillan.

—— 1968. *The Policy-Making Process*. Englewood Cliffs, NJ: Prentice-Hall.

—— 1972. "Integration of Economics and Other Social Sciences Through Policy Analysis," in Charlesworth, ed., *Integration of the Social Sciences Through Policy Analysis*. Philadelphia: AAPSS.

Light, John M. 1975. *Norm Formation Processes in "Prisoner's Dilemma" Situations*. Ph.D. Thesis: Department of Sociology, UCLA.

Link, Arthur. 1954. *Woodrow Wilson and the Progressive Era: 1910–1917*. New York: Harper.

—— 1959. "What Happened to the Progressive Movement in the 1920's?" *American Historical Review* LXIV(4), 833–851.

Lippmann, Walter. 1914. *Drift and Mastery: An Attempt to Diagnose the Current Unrest*. New York: Mitchell Kennerly.

—— 1937. *The Good Society*. Boston: Little.

Lompe, Klaus. 1968. "The Role of the Social Scientist in the Process of Policy-Making," *Social Science Information* 7 (December), 1959, 176.

Los, Maria. 1973. "Social Science Expertise," Warsaw: Polish Academy of Science (mimeo).

Lowi, Theodore J. 1964. "American Business, Public Policy, Case Studies and Political Theory." *World Politics* 16 (July), 677–715.

Lubove, Roy. 1962. *The Progressives and the Slums*. Pittsburgh: University of Pittsburgh Press.

—— 1968. *The Struggle for Social Security 1900–1935*. Cambridge, MA: Harvard University Press.

Luce, Duncan R. and Howard Raiffa. 1967. *Games and Decisions: Introduction and Critical Survey*. New York: Wiley.

Lundberg, George A. 1961. *Can Science Save Us?* Longman, Green and Co.

Lyons, Gene M. 1969. *The Uneasy Partnership*. New York: Russell Sage Foundation.

———— 1971. "The Social Science Study Groups," in Horowitz, ed., *The Use and Abuse of Social Science*. New Brunswick, NJ: Transaction Books.

McCord, William. 1972. "Comment by William M. McCord," in Charlesworth, ed., *Integration of the Social Sciences Through Policy Analysis*. Philadelphia: AAPSS.

McGee, William J. 1909. "Water as a Resource," in *Conservation in Natural Resources, Annals, AAPSS* (May), pp. 33, 37–50.

McGowan, Eleanor Farrar. 1976. "Management by Evaluation," *Policy Studies Journal* 4(3), 243–248.

MacMahen, Arthur W., John D. Millet and Gladys Ogden. 1941. *The Administration of Federal Work Relief*. Published for the Committee on Public Administration of the Social Science Research Council. Chicago: Public Service Administration.

Macrae, Duncan. 1970. "Social Science and the Sources of Policy: 1951–1970," 60th Annual Meeting, APSA. Los Angeles.

———— 1971. "A Dilemma of Sociology: Science Versus Policy," *American Sociologist* 6 (Supplementary Issue), 2–7.

———— 1973a. "Science and the Formation of Policy in a Democracy," *Minerva* XI(2), 228–242.

———— 1973b. "Sociology in Policy Analysis," in *Policy Studies Journal* 2(1), 4–8.

———— 1974. "Policy Analysis as an Applied Social Science Discipline," 1974 ASA Meeting, Montreal.

March, James G. and Herbert A. Simon. 1958. *Organizations*. New York: Wiley.

Martinson, Robert. 1973. "What Works?" *Public Interest* (Spring).

Matthew, Frederick H. 1973. "Robert E. Park and the Development of American Sociology," Ph.D. Thesis: Department of Social Relations, Harvard University.

Maxwell, Robert S. 1956. *LaFollette and the Rise of the Progressives in Wisconsin*. Madison: The State Historical Society of Wisconsin.

Meade, James. 1949. Planning and the Price Mechanism. London: Allen and Unwin.

Merton, Robert K. 1964. "Practical Problems and the Uses of Social Science," *Transaction* 1 (July), 18–21.

———— 1973a. "Technical and Moral Dimensions of Policy Research," in R. K. Merton, *Sociology of Science*, Chicago: University of Chicago Press.

———— 1973b. *The Sociology of Science*. University of Chicago Press.

Merton, Robert K. and Edward Devereux. 1949. "The Role of Applied Social Science in the Formation of Policy," *Journal of Philosophy of Science* 16(3), 161−181.

Merton, Robert K. and Daniel Lerner. 1951. "Social Scientists and Research Policy," in Lerner and Lasswell, eds., *The Policy Sciences: Recent Developments in Scope and Method*. Stanford, CA: Stanford University Press.

———— 1957. *Social Theory and Social Structure*. Glencoe, IL: Free Press.

Michel, Don. 1973a. "Technology and the Management of Change from the Perspective of a Cultural Context," *Technological Forecasting and Social Change*, 5(3), 219−232.

———— 1973b. *On Learning to Plan . . . and Planning to Learn*. San Francisco: Jossey-Bass.

Miller, Samuel M. and Frank Reissman. 1968. *Social Class and Social Policy*. New York: Basic Books.

———— 1974. "Policy and Science," *Journal of Social Policy* 3(1), 53−58.

Miller, Samuel M. and Martin Rein. 1965. "The War on Poverty: Perspectives and Prospects," in Seligman, ed., *Poverty as a Public Issue*. New York: Free Press, pp. 272−320.

Mowry, George. 1958. *The Era of Theodore Roosevelt*. New York: Harper and Brothers.

Moynihan, Daniel P. 1969. *Maximum Feasible Misunderstanding*. New York: Free Press.

Myers, Frank E. 1974. "Applying Political Science to the Estimation of Political Feasibility: The Case of Costal Zone Management," Annual Meeting, APSA.

Myrdal, Gunnar. 1968. "The Social Sciences and Their Impact on Society," in Herman B. Stein, ed., *Social Theory and Social Invention*. Cleveland: Case Western Reserve University Press, pp. 145−163.

Nagel, Stuart S. 1975. *Policy Studies and the Social Sciences*. Lexington, MA: Lexington Books, D. C. Heath and Co.

National Commission on the Causes and Prevention of Violence. 1969. "To Establish Justice, to Insure Domestic Tranquility." Final report.

National Research Council. 1978. *Knowledge and Policy: The Uncertain Connection*. Washington, DC: National Academy of Sciences.

National Science Foundation. 1967−1974. "Federal Funds for Research Development and Other Scientific Activities. Fiscal Years 1967−1974," Vol. 17−24, *Surveys of Science Resources Series*. Washington, DC: U.S. Government Printing Office.

———— 1969. *Knowledge into Action: Improving the Nation's Use of the Social Sciences*. Washington, DC: U.S. Government Printing Office.

New York Times. 1975. "U. D. C.'s Eligibility Rules Keep Apartments," Sunday, May 11, Section 8, pp. 1 and 10.

——— 1978. "How Urban Policy Gets Made—Very Carefully," *The Week in Review*, Sunday, April 2, Section 4, p. 1.

Noble, David F. 1977. *America by Design*. New York: Knopf.

Oberschall, Anthony. 1972. *The Establishment of Empirical Sociology: Studies in Continuity, Discontinuity and Institutions*. New York: Harper and Row.

Office of Management and Budget. 1974. *Social Indicators*. Washington, DC: U. S. Government Printing Office.

Office of Science and Technology. 1967. "The Situation of the Social Sciences in the United States: Part I," in House of Representatives, *The Use of Social Research in Federal Domestic Programs*. (A staff study for the Research and Technical Programs, Subcommittee of the Committee on Government Operation. Part I—Federally Financed Social Research—Expenditures, Status, and Objectives. 90th Congress, First Session.) Washington, DC: U. S. Government Printing Office.

Ohlin, Lloyd E. 1975. "The President's Commission on Law Enforcement and Administration of Justice" in Komarovsky, ed., *Sociology and Public Policy*. New York: American Elsevier Publ. Co., Chapter 4, pp. 93–116.

Olson, Mancur. 1965. *The Logic of Collective Action*. Cambridge, MA: Harvard University Press.

Orlans, Harold. 1968. "Making Social Research More Useful to Government," *Social Science Information* 7 (December), 151–158.

——— 1971. "Social Science Research Policies in the United States," *Minerva* 9 (January), 7–31.

——— 1974. "Neutrality and Advocacy in Policy Research," APSA Annual Meeting, Chicago, August 31.

Patten, Simon. 1902. *The Theory of Prosperity*. New York: Macmillan.

——— 1907. *The New Basis of Civilization*. New York: Macmillan.

Palumbo, Dennis. 1975. "Should We Try to Be Rational in Public Policy Decisions?" APSA Annual Meeting, San Francisco, CA.

Polsby, Nelson W. 1971. *Congress and the Presidency*. Englewood Cliffs, NJ: Prentice-Hall.

Polsby, Nelson W. and Aaron Wildavsky. 1971. *Presidential Elections*, New York: Scribners.

Popper, Karl. 1963. "The Poverty of Social Science," in *Conjectures and Refutations*. New York: Basic Books.

Pressman, Jeffrey and Aaron Wildavsky. 1973. *Implementation*. Berkeley: University of California Press.

Price, Donald K. 1965. *The Scientific Estate*. Cambridge, MA: Harvard University Press.

Purcell, Edward A. 1973. *The Crises of Democratic Theory*. Lexington, KY: University of Kentucky Press.

Pye, Lucian. 1968. "Description, Analysis and Sensitivity to Change," in

Ranney, ed., *Political Science and Public Policy*. Chicago: Markham Publ. Co., 237–272.

Quinney, Richard. 1972. "From Repression to Liberation: Social Theory in A Radical Age," in Scott and Douglas, eds., *Theoretical Perspectives on Deviance*. New York: Basic Books, 317–341.

Ranney, Austin. 1968. *Political Science and Public Policy*. Chicago: Markham Publ. Co.

Rauschenbusch, Walter. 1907. *Christianity and the Social Crises*. New York: Macmillan.

Ravetz, Jerome R. 1971. *Scientific Knowledge and Its Social Problems*. New York: Oxford University Press.

Recent Trends in the United States. 1933. New York: MacGraw-Hill.

Rein, Martin. 1970. *Social Policy: Issues of Choice and Change*. New York: Random House.

Reiss, Albert J., Jr. 1970. "Putting Sociology into Policy," *Social Problems* 17 (Winter), 289–294.

Reitz, Jeffrey G. 1973. "Social Interaction Between Policy Makers and Social Scientists." New York: BASR, Columbia University Press.

Resek, Carl. 1967. *The Progressives*. Indianapolis: The Bobbs-Merrill Co.

Report of the Commission on Obscenity and Pornography. 1970. Washington, DC: Government Printing Office. Also published by Bantam Books.

Report of the National Commission on Law Enforcement and the Administration of Justice. 1968. Washington, DC: U. S. Government Printing Office.

Riecken, Henry. 1969. "Social Science and Social Problems," *Social Science Information* (February), pp. 101–109.

———— 1971. "The Federal Government and Social Science Policy," in *Social Science and the Federal Government*, Annals, AAPSS, pp. 173–190.

Riis, Jacob. 1971. *How the Other Half Lives*. New York: Dover. (Preface by Charles A. Madison. Unabridged Republication of 1901 edition.)

Rivlin, Alice. 1971. *Systematic Thinking of Social Action*. Washington, DC: Brookings Institute.

Robinson, James Harvey and Charles Beard. 1907. *The Development of Modern Europe*. New York: Ginn, 2 volumes.

———— 1908. *History*. New York: Columbia University Press.

———— 1921. *The Mind in the Making*. New York: Harper.

Roosevelt, Theodore. 1910. "The New Nationalism." New York: Spectrum Classics in History Series.

Rose, Arnold M. 1967. "The Social Scientist as an Expert Witness in Court Cases," in Lazarsfeld et al., eds., *The Uses of Sociology*. New York: Basic Books, Chapter 5, pp. 100–118.

Rose, Richard. 1976. *The Dynamics of Public Policy: A Comparative Analysis*. Beverly Hills, CA: Sage Publ. Co.

Ross, Dorothy. 1975. "The Development of the Social Sciences in America: 1865–1920." A paper prepared for the American Academy of Arts and Sciences.

Ross, Edward A. 1901. *Social Control: A Survey of the Foundations of Order.* New York: Macmillan.

Rossi, Richard H. and Katherine Lyall. 1976. *Reforming Public Welfare: A Critique of the Negative Income Tax Experiment.* New York: Russell Sage Foundation.

Rule, James B. 1978. *Insight and Social Betterment: A Preface to Applied Social Science.* New York: Oxford University Press.

Schlesinger, Arthur. 1957. *The Age of Roosevelt.* Boston: Houghton, Mifflin.

Schoettle, Enid Curtis Bok. 1968. "The State of the Art in Policy Studies," in Bauer and Gergen, eds., *The Study of Policy Formation.* New York: Free Press, pp. 149–179.

Schorr, Alvin L. 1968. *Explorations in Social Policy.* New York: Basic Books.

Scioli, Frank T. and Thomas J. Cook. 1975. *Methodologies for Analyzing Public Policies.* Lexington, MA: D. C. Heath and Company.

Scott, Robert A. 1967. "The Factory as a Social Service Organization: Goal Displacement in Workshops for the Blind," *Social Problems* 15 (2), 160–175.

——— 1969. *The Making of Blind Men.* New York: Russell Sage Foundation.

Scott, Robert A. and Jack Douglas, eds. 1972. *Theoretical Perspectives on Deviance.* New York: Basic Books.

Scott, Robert A. and Arnold Shore. 1974. "Sociology and Policy Analysis," *The American Sociologist* 9 (May), 51–59.

Seligman, Benjamin B. 1965. *Poverty as a Public Issue.* New York: Free Press.

Shapley, Willis H. 1976. *Research and Development in the Federal Budget: FY 1977.* Washington, DC: American Association for the Advancement of Science.

Sharkansky, Ira. 1970. *Policy Analysis in Political Science.* Chicago: Markham Publ. Co.

Short, James. 1975. "The National Commission on the Causes and Prevention of Violence: The Contributions of Sociology and Sociologists," in Komarovsky, ed., *Sociology and Public Policy.* New York: American Elsevier Publ. Co. Chapter 3, pp. 61–92.

Shostak, Arthur B. 1966. *Sociology in Action.* Homewood, IL: Dorsey Press.

Small, Albion. 1895. "The Era of Sociology," *American Journal of Sociology* 1 (July), 1–15.

——— 1905. *General Sociology.* Chicago: University of Chicago Press.

Somit, Albert and Joseph Tenenhaus. 1967. *The Development of American Political Science: From Burgess to Behaviorism.* Boston: Allyn and Bacon.

Special Commission on the Social Sciences. 1969. *Knowledge into Action.* Washington, DC: The National Science Board.

Spencer, Herbert. 1877. *First Principles.* New York: Appleton and Co.

Spengler, Joseph H. 1969. "Is Social Science Ready?", *Social Science Quarterly* 50 (December), 449–468.

Stein, Herman. 1968. *Social Theory and Social Invention.* Cleveland: Case Western Reserve University Press.

Sternsher, Bertrand. 1964. *Rexford Tugwell and the New Deal.* New Brunswick, NJ: Rutgers University Press.

Subcommittee on Children and Youth. 1973. *Examination of the Influence That Government Policies Have on American Families.* Committee on Labor and Public Welfare, U. S. Senate, 93rd Congress, 1st Session. Washington, DC: U. S. Government Printing Office.

Suchman, Edward A. 1967. "Public Health," in Lazarsfeld et al., eds. *The Uses of Sociology.* New York: Basic Books. Chapter 21, pp. 567–611.

Sumner, William G. 1963. *Social Darwinism: Selected Essays.* Englewood Cliffs, NJ: Prentice-Hall.

Taylor, D. 1971. "Interpretation and the Science of Man," *Review of Metaphysics* (September).

Taylor, Frederick. 1911. *The Principles of Scientific Management.* New York: Harper.

The Commission on Population Control and the American Future. 1972. Washington, DC: U. S. Government Printing Office.

Thelen, David. 1972. *The New Citizenship: Origins of Progressivism in Wisconsin, 1885–1900.* Columbia, MO: University of Missouri Press.

Tribe, L. 1972. "Policy Science: Analysis or Ideology?" *Philosophy and Public Affairs* 2 (1), 66–110.

Trilling, Lionel. 1950. *The Liberal Imagination.* New York: Viking Press.

Truman, David B. 1968a. "The Social Sciences and Public Policies," *Science* 160 (May 3), 508–512.

———— 1968b. "The Social Scientist: Maturity, Relevance and the Problem of Training," in Ranney, ed., *Political Science and Public Policy.* Chicago: Markham Publ. Co., Chapter 12.

Tugwell, Rexford. 1932. "The Principle of Planning and the Institution of Laissez-Faire," *American Economic Review* XXII (1, Supplement).

Tugwell, Rexford and Thomas Cronin. 1974. *The Presidency Reappraised.* New York: Praeger.

Uliassi, Pio D. 1976. "Research and Foreign Policy; A View from Foggy Bottom," *Policy Studies Journal* 4(3), 239–243.

United States National Goals Research Staff. 1970. *Towards Balanced Growth: Quantity with Quality.* Washington, DC: U. S. Government Printing Office.

VandenHaag, Ernest. 1960. "Social Science Testimony in the Desegregation Cases: A Reply to Professor Kenneth Clark," *Villanova Law Review* IV, 69.

256

van de Vall, Mark. 1973. "A Theoretical Framework for Applied Social Research," *International Journal of Mental Health,* No. 2, pp. 6–25.

Veblen, Thorsten. 1898. "Why Is Economics Not an Evolutionary Science?" *Quarterly Journal of Economics* XII (July), 373–397.

—— 1899. *The Theory of the Leisure Class.* New York: Macmillan.

—— 1921. *The Engineers and the Price System.* New York: Heubsch.

Veysey, Lawrence. 1970. *The Emergence of the American University.* Chicago: University of Chicago Press.

Ward, Lester. 1883. *Dynamic Sociology or Applied Social Science, as Based upon Statical Sociology and the Less Complex Sciences.* New York: Appleton and Co.

Watts, Harold. 1969. "Graduated Work Incentive: An Experiment in Negative Taxation," *American Economic Review* 58, 463–472.

Weber, Max. 1949. *On the Methodology of the Social Sciences.* Glencoe, IL: Free Press of Glencoe.

Weinstein, James. 1968. *The Corporate Ideals in the Liberal State: 1900–1918.* Boston: Beacon Press.

Weiss, Carol H. 1972. *Evaluation Research.* Englewood Cliffs, NJ: Prentice-Hall.

—— 1976a. "Introduction by the Symposium Editor," *Policy Studies Journal* 4(3), 221–224.

—— 1976b. "Policy Research in the University: Practical Aid or Academic Exercise?" *Policy Studies Journal* 4(3), 224–229.

Weiss, Janet A. 1976. "Using Social Science for Social Policy," *Policy Studies Journal* 4(3), 234–238.

Weiss, Nancy J. 1974. *The National Urban League: 1910–1914.* New York: Oxford University Press.

Westoff, Charles. 1973. "The Commission on Population Growth and the American Future: Its Origins, Operations and Aftermath" *Population Index* 39 (4), 491–507.

—— 1975. "The Commission on Population Growth and the American Future: Origins, Operations, and Aftermath," in Komarovsky, ed., *Sociology and Public Policy.* New York: American Elsevier Publ. Co. Chapter 2, pp. 43–60.

Wiebe, Robert H. 1967. *The Search for Order: 1877–1920.* New York: Hill and Wang.

White, Morton G. 1949. *Social Thought in America: The Revolt Against Formalism.* New York: Viking Press.

Wildavsky, Aaron. 1964. *The Politics of the Budgetary Process.* Boston: Little Brown.

—— 1971. *Revolt Against the Masses.* New York: Basic Books.

Wilensky, Harold. 1967. *Organizational Intelligence.* New York: Basic Books.

Williams, Walter. 1971. *Social Policy Research and Analysis.* New York: American Elsevier Publ. Co.

Wilson, Woodrow. 1913. *The New Freedom.* New York: Spectrum Classics in History Series.

Yarmolinsky, Adam. 1971. ''The Policy Researcher: His Habitat, Care and Feeding,'' in Horowitz, ed., *The Use and Abuse of Social Science.* New Brunswick, NJ: Transaction Books, pp. 196–211.

Young, Pauline. 1939. *Scientific Social Surveys and Research.* Englewood Cliffs, NJ: Prentice-Hall.

Zeisel, Hans. 1967. ''The Law,'' in Lazarsfeld et al., eds., *The Uses of Sociology.* New York: Basic Books, Chapter 4, pp. 81–99.

Zetterberg, Hans L. 1962. *Social Theory and Social Practice.* New York: Bedminster Press.

Index

A

Abstract analysis, 46
Activism, 89−98
Adams, Henry Carter, 103, 106, 111, 112
Adler, Felix, 118
Advisory Committee on Government
    Programs in the Behavioral Sciences of
    the National Academy of Sciences, 31
Advocacy and Objectivity (Furner), 110
Age of Roosevelt (Schlesinger), 168
Agricultural Adjustment Act, 126
Agricultural Extension Services, 125
Agriculture Adjustment Administration
    (AAA), 124, 174, 183
Alpert, Harry, 12
American Association for Labor Legislation
    (AALL), 115−116
American Historical Review, The, 108
American Journal of Sociology, The, 7, 108
American Mind, The (Commager), 90−91
American Social Science Association (ASSA),
    110
American Sociological Society, 15, 128
Anderson, Patrick, 173
*Annals of the American Academy of Political
    and Social Science, The,* 108
Anti-Corruption Labor Bill (1959), 213
Applied sociology, present-day, 9−12
Archibald, Kathleen, 49−50
Ash, Roy, 181

B

Backland−Jones Act, 210
Bacon, Francis, 84
Baker, Ray Stannard, 99
Baumol, William J., 157
Beard, Charles A., 82−88, 91, 92, 96, 103
*Behavioral Sciences and the Federal
    Government, The,* 31
*Behavioral and Social Sciences, The: Outlook
    and Needs,* 32
Behaviorism, 84
Bemis, Edward, 113
Berle, Adolph, 171, 174
Beveridge, Albert J., 193
Biderman, Albert, 11
Blacks, 118−119

Blalock, Herbert, 227
Blind, the, services for, 136−140, 152−154,
    220−221
Bowers, Patricia F., 156
Brain Trust, 173−174
Bronfenbrenner, Urie, 194
Brooks, Harvey, 32
Brown University, 9
Buchanan, James M., 157
Bureau of Agricultural Economics, 127

C

Calvinism, 82
Caplan, Nathan, 19−20, 43, 72, 152,
    186−188
Caplan study, 72
Center for Social Reform, 123
Chicago, University of, 9, 113, 119, 122
Child Development Act (1971), 194
Christgau, Victor, 125
Christgau Bill, 125, 126
City College of New York, 118
Civil rights, 167
Clark, Ian D., 195
Clark, John, 106
Cloward, Richard A., 24
Coleman, James, 5 n, 26, 42, 45, 59, 134,
    161, 226, 237
Columbia University, 9, 83, 115, 118, 119,
    126, 127
Commager, Henry Steele, 90−91
Commission on the Causes and Prevention of
    Violence (1969), 15, 16, 21, 28−29,
    143, 171
Commission on Civil Disorder, 137, 143
Commission on Law Enforcement and the
    Administration of Justice (1968), 15,
    22, 30−31, 143, 171
Commission on Obscenity and Pornography
    (1970), 15, 17, 21, 27, 30, 143, 171,
    176

Commission on Population Growth and the American Future (1972), 15, 17—19, 21, 27, 31, 143, 144, 151, 171, 173
Committee on Government Operations of the 90th Congress, 23, 54
Committee on Urban Conditions, 119
Common Law, The (Holmes), 83, 86
Commons, John, 9, 103, 106, 107, 109, 111, 113, 115, 124
Comte, August, 8
Confidence, 96—97
Congressional Quarterly Almanac, The, 207
Congressional Record, The, 207
Congressional Research Service (CRS), 163, 196—197
Congressional Subcommittee on Research and Technical Operations, 54
Conservation, 116—118
Cooley, Charles Horton, 7, 103, 105, 111
Cornell University, 113, 115, 126, 194
Cost—benefit analysis, 66
Cottell, 120
Council of Foreign Relations, 120
Crawford, Elizabeth, 11, 38, 40, 42
Croly, Herbert, 79—81, 96, 97, 99, 105

D

Daddario, Emilio, 194
Darwin, Charles, 81, 82
Delphi, 66
Depression, the, 13, 153, 174
Determinism, 81—84, 104
  economic, 84
Devereux, Edward, 38
Development of Modern Europe, The (Robinson and Beard), 86, 88, 91
Developmentalism, 85—87
Devine, Edward T., 107, 118
Dewey, John, 13, 82—92, 95, 96, 103, 104, 109, 122
Dickson, 120
Disciplinary policy perspective, 35—62
  increasing usefulness of sociology for policy, 53—59
    communicating with policy-makers, 58—59
    strengthening the discipline, 54—58
  policy-relevant research, 48—53
  sociology for policy, 36—48
    to contribute substantive ideas, 39—42
    to enlighten, 37—39
    to evaluate, 43—45
    to study policy, 45—48
    to supply information, 42—43
Division of Program Surveys (1939), 127

Domestic Council, 181
Dreyfuss, Daniel A., 191, 192
Drift and Mastery (Lippmann), 79
Dror, Yehezkel, 28—30, 38, 43, 46, 65, 160, 161
DuBois, W. E. B., 118
Durkheim, Émile, 81
Dynamic programming, 66
Dynamic Sociology, or Applied Social Science, as Based upon Statical Sociology and the Less Complex Sciences (Ward), 8, 103

E

Easton, David, 29, 55, 225, 226
Economic determinism, 84
Economic Interpretation of the Constitution of the United States, An (Beard), 88
Economic Opportunity Act, 195, 196, 208
Educational opportunity, equal, 26
Ehrlichman, John, 181
Eisenhower, Dwight D., 166—172, 175—180, 198, 208
Ely, Richard, 9, 103, 106, 109, 111—112, 115, 117, 125
Engineer and the Price System, The (Veblen), 91
Ethics (Dewey and Tufts), 87, 89, 124
Etzioni, Amitai, 38—39, 65, 69, 148, 237
Ezekiel, Mordekai, 148

F

Farm policy, 124—126
Farm Security Act (1937), 126
Farnan, Henry, 115
Federal Communications Act (1934), 210, 211
Federal Communications Commission, 210—211, 214
Federal domestic policy, sociology's impact on, 13—32
Federal Home Loan Board, 207
Federal Housing Act (1961), 211
Federal Housing Administration (FHA), 207
Federal housing policy, 207—208
Feuer, Lewis S., 231, 232
Fisk University, 119
Fiske, John, 99
Ford, Gerald, 165—168, 177, 178
Foreign Broadcast Intelligence Service, 189
Foreign policy, 26
Formalism, 81—84, 104
Franklin, Benjamin, 84
Freeman, Howard E., 43, 51, 160, 230, 233—234

Froman, Lewis, 46
Furner, Mary, 109−114

G

Gans, Herbert, 38, 40, 45, 64, 66, 160, 237
Garfield, James R., 116−117
Gay, Edwin, 120, 123
General Sociology (Small), 8−9, 105−106
Glazer, Nathan, 37
Glock, Charles, 43
Goals for America, 175
Goldschmidt, Walter, 127
Gouldner, Alvin W., 47, 51, 114, 237
Government receptiveness to planning in politics, 162−200
  in Congress, 190−197
  in executive branch, 165−177
  executive−legislative cooperation, 197−198
  in federal bureaucracy, 177−185
  in federal institutions, 164
  in legislative branch, 190−196
  in permanent government, 185−190
  in presidency, 166−185
  technical use of social science by Congress, 196−197
  See also names of presidents
Graham, Otis, 144, 150−151, 158, 166−167, 170, 177
Gray, Lewis C., 125−126
Great Society program, 171, 173, 192
Green, Philip, 235

H

Hadley, Arthur, 106
Handler, Philip, 32
Harrington, Michael, 24
Harrison, Shelby, 9, 122, 149
Harvard Business School, 120
Harvey, George, 120
Haynes, Edward, 119
Hays, Samuel P., 116, 118
Hegel, Georg Wilhelm, 81, 82
Heller, Walter, 195
Hill, 120
Historicism, 87
History (Robinson), 83
Hofstadter, Richard, 93−95
Holmes, Oliver W., Jr., 82−86, 91, 92, 95, 96, 101, 103
Hoover, Herbert, 106, 114, 117, 149, 159
  receptiveness to planning in politics, 175, 176, 179, 180

research committee on social trends, 121−123, 129, 149, 159, 175
  social science in rational planning and, 121−123, 129
Hopkins, Harry, 184
Horowitz, Irving Louis, 11, 12, 69, 225
Housing Act (1947), 208
Housing Act (1949), 210
Housing reform studies, 13, 118, 124, 219−220
Houston, Emanuel, 119
How the Other Half Lives (Riis), 118
Huitt, Ralph K., 191
Humphrey, Hubert, 193
Hunt, Edward E., 122−123
Hunter, Robert, 118

I

Industrial Commission of Wisconsin, 107, 115
Inland Waterways Commission, 117
Institutionalism, 84
Instrumentalism, 84

J

Jackson, Henry, 193
James, Edmund, 111
James, William, 7, 13, 82, 84, 91, 96
Janowitz, Morris, 38, 41
Jefferson, Thomas, 84
Jinks, J. W., 115
Johnson, Charles S., 119, 126
Johnson, Lyndon B., 102, 144
  receptiveness to planning in politics, 166−184, 192, 198
Journal of Political Economy, The, 108
Judd, Charles, 123

K

Karl, Barry, 122, 159
Katz, James Everett, 11, 12, 69
Keller, Frances, 118
Kelman, Herbert C., 38, 40, 43, 47, 235−236
Kennedy, Edward, 193−194
Kennedy, John F., 102, 151
  receptiveness to planning in politics, 166−171, 177, 179, 211
Keynes, John Maynard, 231−232
Kirkendall, Richard, 126, 128
Klineberg, Otto, 23
Knowledge into Action, 31, 32, 54
Knowledge and Policy: The Uncertain Connection, 32 n
Kroeber, A. L., 127

L

Labor Management Relations Act (1947),
      212–213
LaFollette, Robert M., 107, 193
Land use, 124
Lane, Robert, 38, 65, 160, 161
Larsen, Otto, 27, 30, 55, 59
Lasswell, Harold, 46, 65–69, 76, 204
Laughlin, J. Lawrence, 106
Law enforcement, 26
Lazarsfeld, Paul F., 26, 59
Legal realism, 84
Light, John M., 155–156, 193
Likert, Rensis, 127, 189
Lindblom, Charles E., 65, 137, 145–147,
      149, 207, 231
Lindsay, Samuel McCune, 115
Lindzey, Gardner, 32
Linear programming, 66
Lippman, Walter, 79–81, 92, 95–99, 105,
      109
Lodge, Henry Cabot, 193
Lompe, Klaus, 38, 43, 65, 225, 226
Lubove, Roy, 115
Lynd, Robert, 123

M

McCord, William, 161–162
McDougal, 120
McGee, W. J., 117
McNamara, Robert, 182
Magnunson, Senator, 195
Management by Objectives (MBO), 181–182
Manpower, 167
Marxism, 82
Maximum Feasible Misunderstanding
      (Moynihan), 40–41
Mayor, 120
Mead, Margaret, 194
Medicine, 26
Merriam, Charles, 9, 120, 122
Merton, Robert K., 38, 55, 59
Michel, Don, 150
Michigan, University of, 9
Military, the, 26
Miller, Samuel M., 40
Mind in the Making, The (Robinson), 91
Mitchell, Wesley, 9, 122, 123, 149
Moley, Raymond, 171, 174
Mondale, Walter, 193–195
Morris, G. S., 82
Mowry, George, 82
Moyers, Bill, 173

Moynihan, Daniel P., 40–41, 43, 150, 162,
      167, 171
Myers, William, 126
Myrdal, Gunnar, 31, 47

N

National Academy of Science, 32
National Bureau of Economic Research
      (NBER), 120
National Family Policy, 194
National Fertility Studies (1965 and 1970), 19,
      21
National Goals Research Staff, 150
National Growth Policy, 150, 170, 171
National Industrial Recovery Act (1933), 183,
      208, 211
National Institute of Mental Health, 189
National Labor Relations Act (1935), 211, 212
National Labor Relations Board, 211, 212
National Recovery Administration (NRA),
      124, 148, 169, 174, 183
National Research Council, 31, 32 *n.*, 121
National Research Institutes, 54
National Science Board, 32
National Science Foundation, 11, 12, 54, 189
National Urban League, 119
Naturalism, 85, 87–89
Negative income tax studies, 24, 44, 221–222
New Basis of Civilization, The (Patten), 107
New Deal, 11, 13, 96, 127–128, 167, 173,
      177, 181, 192
New Frontier program, 171
New Jersey–Pennsylvania Negative Income
      Tax Experiment, 24, 44, 221–222
New Rationalism, 100–102
New Republic, The, 99
New York State Child Labor Committee, 118
Newcomb, Simon, 111
Newton, Sir Isaac, 82
Nixon, Richard M., 102, 150, 151, 157
   receptiveness to planning in politics,
      166–171, 177–182, 194, 198
North Carolina, University of, 122

O

O'Connor, D. Basil, 174
Odum, Harold, 9, 122, 126, 149
Office of Economic Opportunity (OEO), 184,
      189
Office of Education, 189
Office of Management and Budget, 181
Office of Naval Research, 189
Office of Science and Technology (OST), 151

Office of War Information, 189
Ogburn, William, 9, 122, 127, 149
Ohlin, Lloyd E., 15−16, 22, 24, 30−31
Olson, Mancur, 157
Operations research, 66
Opportunity: Journal of Negro Life, 119
Optimism, 96−97
Organizational change, 26
Orlans, Harold, 28, 29, 30, 43, 55, 59, 66, 161
Oscar Newman's Institute for Community Design, 219
Other America, The (Harrington), 24
Otis, 120

P

Park, Robert, 9, 105, 111
Parrington, Vernon Louis, 103
Pasanella, Ann K., 26
Patten, Simon, 9, 103, 106−107, 126
Percy, Charles, 195
Perkins, Francis, 107
Phillips, David Graham, 99
Pierce, Charles, 82
Pinchot, Gifford, 117
Planning in politics, 133−202
  limitations of planning, 133−162
    deficiencies of planning model, 135−136
    rationality and stability, 147−159
    self-sufficiency and reliance on orderly procedure, 136−147
  receptiveness of government to planning, 162−200
    in Congress, 190−197
    in executive branch, 165−177
    executive−legislative cooperation, 197−198
    in federal bureaucracy, 177−185
    in federal institutions, 164
    in legislative branch, 190−196
    in permanent government, 185−190
    in presidency, 166−185
    technical use of social science by Congress, 196−197
  See also names of presidents
Planning-Programming-Budgeting System (PPBS), 66, 68−69, 144, 145, 148, 182, 183
Policy, sociology and, 7−34
  applied sociology, 9−12
  enacted policy, 23−27
  in federal domestic policy, 13−32
  in government work, 10−12
Policy conceptions, scientific planning and, 63−75

procedures for, 69−73
Policy-relevant research, 48−53
Policy-relevant sociology, 9
Politics, planning and, 133−202
  limitations of planning, 133−162
    deficiencies of planning model, 135−136
    rationality and stability, 147−159
    self-sufficiency and reliance on orderly procedure, 136−147
  receptiveness of government to planning, 162−200
    in Congress, 190−197
    in the executive branch, 165−177
    executive−legislative cooperation, 197−198
    in federal bureaucracy, 177−185
    in federal institutions, 164
    in legislative branch, 190−196
    in permanent government, 185−190
    in presidency, 166−185
    technical use of social science by Congress, 196−197
  See also names of presidents
Political corruption, 13
Political Science Quarterly, The, 108
Politics (Beard), 87
Popper, Karl, 65
Population, 124, 167
Populism, 101
Poverty, 13, 124, 167
Poverty (Hunter), 118
Pragmatism, 84, 89, 91, 92
Price, Donald K., 38, 66
"Principle of Planning and the Institution of Laissez-faire, The" (Tugwell), 158
"Private Decisions and Public Goods" (Buchanan), 157
Progressive Democracy (Croly), 80
Progressivism, 81, 96−102, 108−114, 117−118
Project Clear, 24
Promise of American Life, The (Croly), 79−80, 97
Public health, 26
Public and Its Problems, The (Dewey), 122
Pye, Lucien, 31, 55

Q

Quarterly Journal of Economics, The, 108
Quinney, Richard, 114

R

Ranney, Austin, 146
Rational planning, 76−132

Rational planning [cont.]
  origins of, 79–114
    activism in America, 92–98
    development of progressive ideas,
      98–102
    impact of social science, 102–108
    intellectual origins, 81–92
    outlines of new social philosophy, 92
  social science in (1900–1940), 115–128
    Hoover's research committee and,
      121–123, 129
    Roosevelt (Franklin D.) and, 123–128
Ravetz, Jerome R., 232, 236–237
Reconstruction Finance Corporation (RFC),
  151–152
Reid, Ira, 119
Reiss, Albert J., Jr., 55, 59
Reissman, Frank, 40
Reitz, Jeffrey G., 26
Relevant sociology, 203–223
  blindness studies, 220–221
  categories in policy deliberation, 206–207
  conventional studies, 218–222
  housing studies, 219–220
  nature of policy change, 207–209
  negative income tax studies, 221–222
  policy-oriented studies, 218–222
  policy-relevant categories, 209–215
  research procedures, 215–218
  for social policy, 204–206
Renaissance, 84
Report on National Growth, 150
Research, policy-relevant, 48–53
Riecken, Henry, 230, 233
Riis, Jacob, 118, 119
Rivlin, Alice, 66, 144–145
Robinson, James Harvey, 82–88, 91, 92, 103
Rockefeller Foundation, 123
Roethlisberger, 120
Roosevelt, Franklin D., 102, 107, 114, 148,
  149, 151, 158
  applied social science in rational planning
    under, 123–128
  receptiveness to planning in politics,
    165–184, 192, 198
Roosevelt, Theodore, 100, 116–117, 121,
  122
Roseman, Samuel, 174
Ross, E. A., 7, 8, 10, 13, 103, 105, 111, 112
Rural Sociological Society, 128
Russell Sage Foundation, 44, 122

S

Schlessinger, Arthur, 168, 179
Schorr, Alvin, 30

Scientific planning, 63–132
  described, 64–65
  origins of, 79–114
    activism in America, 92–98
    development of progressive ideas,
      98–102
    impact of social science, 102–108
    intellectual origins, 81–92
    outlines of new social philosophy, 92
  policy conceptions and, 63–75
    procedures for, 69–73
  social science in (1900–1940), 115–128
    Hoover's research committee and,
      121–123, 129
    Roosevelt (Franklin D.) and, 123–128
Seager, Henry, 115
Services for the blind, 136–140, 152–154,
  220–221
Sesame Street (TV show), 44
Shapley, Willis H., 12
Sheltered workshops, 152–153
Short, James, 16–17, 28–29, 137
Sinclair, Upton, 99
Small, Albion, 7–9, 10, 13, 103, 105–106,
  111
Smith, J. Allen, 9, 103
Snellen charts, 140, 221
Snow, C. P., 31
Social Control (Ross), 8
Social Darwinism, 7–9, 85
Social Indicators, 42
Social Policy Research and Analysis
  (Williams), 59
Social Problems Research Institutes, 54
Social Science Research Council, 32, 120
Society for Ethical Culture, 118
Special Commission on the Social Sciences of
  the National Science Board, 23, 31–32
Spellman, Willis J., 124
Spencer, Herbert, 7, 8, 81, 103, 104
Spengler, Joseph, 55
SST controversy, 195
Stanford Leland, 113
Stanford University, 9, 113, 121
Steffens, Lincoln, 99
Stein, Herman, 55, 161
Sumner, William Graham, 7–8, 103
Sutherland, Edwin, 9, 123
Systematic Thinking for Social Action (Rivlin),
  144–145
Systems analysis, 66

T

Talent Search, 24
Tarbell, Ida, 99

Taussig, Frank, 103, 111
Taylor, Carl L, 127–128
Taylor, E. B., 82
Taylor, Frederick, 120
Taylor, Henry, 126
Taylor, Paul, 127, 160
Teleology, 8
Tennessee Valley Authority (TVA), 124
Terman, 120
Theory of Prosperity, The (Patten), 107
Thomas, W. I., 9
Tolley, Howard R., 124–126
Truman, David, 29, 33, 55, 236
Truman, Harry, 166–170, 177, 179, 180
Tufts, James H., 82, 84, 87, 103, 124
Tugwell, Rexford, 107, 126, 158, 171, 174, 178
Turner, Frederick Jackson, 82, 103

U

Uliassi, Pio D., 70
U.S. Bureau of Labor Statistics, 189
U.S. Census Bureau, 189
U.S. Department of Agriculture, 124–126, 158, 187
　Special Committee on Farm Tenancy, 126
U.S. Department of Commerce, 117, 121, 187, 189
U.S. Department of Defense, 20, 182, 187
U.S. Department of Health, Education and Welfare, 30, 187
U.S. Department of Housing and Urban Development, 187, 189
U.S. Department of the Interior, 20, 123, 187, 189
U.S. Department of Justice, 187
U.S. Department of Labor, 187, 189
U.S. Department of State, 187
U.S. Department of Transportation, 187
U.S. War Department, 121
University of Chicago Press, 7
Upward Bound, 24
Urban Development Corporation of the State of New York, 154–155
Urban planning, 26, 118
Urban renewal, 118
Urban unrest, 167

V

Veblen, Thorsten, 7, 82–86, 88, 91, 92, 95, 96, 103, 109

Vera Institute of New York, 26
Vietnam war, 170
Violence, 167
Vista, 24

W

Wagner O'Day Act, 153
Wallace, Henry, 126, 127
War on Poverty, 24
War Production Board, 189
Ward, Lester, 7, 8, 10, 13, 84, 103–105, 109, 111, 204
Warner, 120
Warren, George F., 126
Watergate affair, 191
Weiss, Carol H., 32, 39, 41–42, 49, 69–70, 194
Weiss, Janet A., 57
Welfare, 124
Welfare Economics and the Theory of the State (Baumol), 157
Westoff, Charles, 17–19, 27, 31
Weyle, Walter, 99
White, Leonard, 123
White, Morton G., 82, 83, 85, 88, 90–92
Whitaker, John, 157–158
Wiebe, Robert H., 71, 93, 98
Wilbur, Ray L., 123
Wildavsky, Aaron, 145, 148
Williams, Walter, 28–30, 59
Wilson, Milburn L., 124–126
Wilson, Woodrow, 100, 101, 120, 121
Wirth, Louis, 9
Wisconsin, University of, 9, 107, 111, 115
Works Projects Administration (WPA), 183, 184
World War I, 120, 169
World War II, 13, 77, 78, 153, 169, 189, 210

Y

Yale University, 115, 194
Yarmolinsky, Adam, 160
Yerkes, 120

Z

Zeisel, Hans, 25–26
Zero population growth, 18
Zigler, Dr. Edward, 194